Education Savings Accounts

Education Savings Accounts

The New Frontier in School Choice

Edited by
Nat Malkus, Adam Peshek,
and
Gerard Robinson

ROWMAN & LITTLEFIELD
Lanham • Boulder • New York • London

Published by Rowman & Littlefield
A wholly owned subsidiary of The Rowman & Littlefield Publishing Group, Inc.
4501 Forbes Boulevard, Suite 200, Lanham, Maryland 20706
www.rowman.com

Unit A, Whitacre Mews, 26-34 Stannary Street, London SE11 4AB

British Library Cataloguing in Publication Information Available

Library of Congress Cataloging-in-Publication Data Available

ISBN: 978-1-4758-3022-4 (cloth : alk. paper)
ISBN: 978-1-4758-3023-1 (pbk. : alk. paper)
ISBN: 978-1-4758-3024-8 (electronic)

♾™ The paper used in this publication meets the minimum requirements of American National Standard for Information Sciences—Permanence of Paper for Printed Library Materials, ANSI/NISO Z39.48-1992.

Printed in the United States of America

Contents

v

Foreword

Frederick M. Hess & Elizabeth English

Since the first voucher and charter school laws of the early 1990s, school choice has been central to American education policy debates. For years, charter schools, voucher programs, and tax-credit scholarships made up the bulk of these debates.

Those more familiar forms of choice were joined by another in 2011, when Arizona enacted the nation's first education savings account (ESA) program. Created for students with special needs, the program allowed families to decide when and how to spend public funds to educate their child. In doing so, the bill provided a dramatic extension of the school choice intuition— which previously had allowed families to choose a new school, but not to control decisions beyond that. While Arizona's ESA program promised to dramatically extend the choice conversation, only a small group of advocates, legislators, and analysts initially understood the implications.

In 2015, ESAs were thrust into the national spotlight when Nevada established the first state-wide, near-universal ESA program. Mississippi and Tennessee also created ESA programs in 2015, but it was Nevada's ambitious program that put ESAs on the national map. Almost overnight, ESAs took their place in the broader school choice debate. This posed something of a challenge, as newcomers to the topic had trouble finding comprehensive discussions of how ESAs work or what they could mean for K–12 education.

The book you hold in your hands seeks to offer just that. A joint project between the American Enterprise Institute (AEI) and the Foundation for Excellence in Education (ExcelinEd), it features contributions from the nation's leading school choice scholars, legal experts, and advocates. In May 2016, AEI and ExcelinEd hosted a research conference in Washington, D.C. to explore ESAs at length. The goal was to develop a resource for those unfamiliar with the nation's newest form of educational choice and to help clarify what it would take for ESAs to deliver on their promise. This volume is the fruit of those efforts.

In recent years, ESAs have made rapid headway in state legislatures, with dozens of states considering and proposing new laws. The appeal is self-evident. ESAs not only extend school choice, but also extend the logic of choice beyond schools in ways that alter how K–12 education is delivered to students. They mean that families are no longer limited to choosing between school A and school B, instead giving parents unprecedented control over the public funds allocated for their child's education. ESAs allow parents to customize their child's educational experience using different providers, including therapists, online providers, and traditional schools. They open up opportunities to expand virtual education and develop new approaches to tutoring, homeschooling, and special education services.

As is true of any new form of school choice, ESAs have proven controversial. Notably, they have also proven to be legally resilient. To reach their potential, ESA legislation must do more than fend off inevitable constitutional challenges, as it did most recently in the Supreme Court of Nevada. ESAs also require sustainable funding sources, an issue that forced Nevada's high court to put the state's constitutionally viable ESA program on hold in the near term.

Passing viable ESA laws is only a first step, however. It will take careful planning and attentive management for ESAs to pass the implementation tests that will come once programs are in place. Serious regulatory questions surrounding what services are eligible, how to regulate against frauds, and how to manage quality control will have to be negotiated. There are also administrative questions about which students should be eligible for ESAs, how funds should be distributed, and what uncertainties ESAs introduce for those operating schools and systems. Looming questions about accountability, equity and funding amounts will have to be addressed and reassessed as programs develop. There is a lot to get right—and enacting legislation is only the first of many steps in ensuring that ESA programs actually deliver for kids. It is vital that those who support ESAs, with their promise to empower families and educators and to introduce immense flexibility into educational provision, be thinking from the start about these questions and how to address them.

This volume is so valuable in large part because of the savvy, acclaimed experts who conceived it and edited it. Nat Malkus, research fellow at AEI and K–12 education policy specialist, has written extensively on school choice and school finance. Adam Peshek, director of educational choice at the Foundation for Excellence in Education, has played a significant role in developing many of the ESA programs discussed in the volume. Gerard Robinson, resident fellow at AEI, and an expert on state regulations and procedures, is the former secretary of education in Virginia and commissioner of education in Florida. Together, the editors offer insights and accounts that help readers flesh out the details of these nascent policies and examine the challenges and opportunities ahead.

ESAs represent a promising new frontier in American education. We trust you will find this volume as helpful as we have in understanding how ESAs work, what it will take for them to deliver on their potential, and how policymakers and parents should think about the expansive new landscape of educational options that ESAs make possible.

Acknowledgments

We are indebted to all of those who have been involved in this project and pushed our thinking on these questions. We especially thank the following discussants for their outstanding and concentrated feedback during our May 2016 conference: Max Eden of the Manhattan Institute, Kevin Chavous of the American Federation for Children, Nevada senator Scott Hammond, U.S. Representative Luke Messer (R-IN), and U.S. Department of Education Secretary Betsy DeVos. We also owe our appreciation to AEI and ExcelinEd for generously providing financial support for this project, and we are deeply grateful for their involvement and encouragement throughout the process.

We are indebted to AEI for its steadfast support, and its president, Arthur Brooks. We are also thankful to Rick Hess, Director of Education Policy at AEI, for his assistance shaping this volume and the conference that led to it. We'd also like to thank the terrific staff at AEI, especially Elizabeth English for her work managing and overseeing this project and coordinating the conference; Meg Cahill for efforts in promoting the scholarly contributions; and Ian Lindquist, Sarah DuPre, Jenn Hatfield, Kelsey Hamilton, Rooney Columbus, and Paige Willey for their vital assistance. We are also grateful for the staff at ExcelinEd for their work promoting the conference and scholarly contributions presented in this volume. We would especially like to thank ExcelinEd CEO, Patricia Levesque, and Jaryn Emhof, Barbara Ross, and Jennifer Diaz on the ExcelinEd communications team. Finally, we express our gratitude to Rowman and Littlefield, particularly our editor, Tom Koerner, who offered skillful and timely guidance throughout the course of this project.

Introduction

Adam Peshek and Gerard Robinson

School choice has been central to the American education policy debate for a quarter-century. From the initial voucher and charter school policies in the early 1990s to the current landscape dotted with seven thousand charter schools and fifty private choice programs, school choice has been lauded, reviled, researched, and debated. Yet, for more than two decades, school choice had been just that—*school* choice. In a potentially profound development, ESAs focus on *educational* choice and upend many assumptions that have framed education policy issues. Instead of limiting parents' educational choices to schools, ESAs give families almost unfettered control over the public funds allocated for their child's education.

With an ESA, parents are able to customize their child's education by combining traditional schools, homeschooling, and different education providers, including tutors, therapists, online and blended models. The ability to direct education funds to the schools and services of parents' choice gives them an unprecedented amount of discretion over their child's education. This freedom of choice has the potential to catalyze the creation or expansion of new, innovative school models, such as micro schools and tech-focused, competency-based schools.

Yet, with this freedom comes new responsibilities—for parents, government agencies, schools, and education service providers. There may come a time when ESAs are used by millions of parents across dozens of states, but not until important steps are taken to ensure quality, equity, scalability, financial accountability, and many other issues surrounding ESAs that remain unsolved. This volume seeks to make sense of this new frontier of educational choice with the first comprehensive review of ESAs. In the pages that follow, contributors detail the intent, history, and implementation of ESAs, provide a review of existing policy challenges, and offer a fair-minded assessment of what is needed for ESAs to fulfill the goal of creating a dynamic, market-based, and student-centered system of educational choice.

THE UNBUNDLING OF HIGHER EDUCATION, HEALTH CARE, AND TRANSPORTATION

In an increasingly unbundled world, ESAs hold great promise for the American education system. Entrepreneurs and university leaders have learned that times are changing, and sticking with the same, rigid style of whole-school universities does not reflect the demands of the students they serve or the times in which they live. Instead of remaining complacent, these leaders are giving more attention to certifying competencies that employers seek and unbundling courses and programs from the traditional model, which often values seat time and number of courses. An entire sector—massive open online courses (MOOCs)—has been developed by industry leaders like edX, Coursera, and Udacity to provide individual courses, programs, and certifications by partnering with colleges and educators to create university-level material that students can access for free or for a nominal fee no matter where they live.

The demand for such unbundling is clear. In 2015, more than thirty-five million students signed up for at least one MOOC—more than double the amount from the prior year.[1] In the fall of 2011, professors from Stanford University created what is widely considered to be the first MOOC when they posted their artificial intelligence courses online, for free, and for anyone to participate. A staggering 160,000 students from 190 countries signed up to participate. In fact, the program was so popular internationally that the small Baltic country of Lithuania enrolled more students in the online course than the entirety of Stanford University's enrollment.[2]

In every state in the United States, the two largest government expenditures are health care and education. With increases in life expectancy and Baby Boomers coming into retirement, the tensions between funding health and education will only continue (see chapter 1 by Matthew Ladner for more on this). Yet, in terms of innovation, health care is doing far more experimentation than K–12 education. Consumer-directed options like health savings accounts (HSAs) and flexible spending accounts (FSAs) have been created to empower consumers with ownership over their health care funds, encouraging them to be cost-conscious, and providing incentives and rewards for savings. According to a 2016 report, more than $30 billion is estimated to be held in 16.7 million HSA accounts across the country.[3]

The transportation sector is also seeing dramatic changes. Passengers unsatisfied with the service of traditional taxicabs now have alternatives such as Uber and Lyft. In the past, if a passenger needed a taxi and they were unable to hail one from the street, they had to call a central dispatch and wait ten, twenty, thirty minutes, or more for a taxi to show up. Instead, Uber uses a smartphone app to process all requests and connect drivers and riders in real time, showing exactly where each party is and how long until the driver will arrive. And instead of requiring massive capital investments in the form of purchasing and maintaining a fleet of Yellow Cabs, ridesharing services rely on existing capital—the drivers' own cars.

None of these innovations were created to reform an existing system— they were new systems created to run parallel to existing options. MOOCs were not created to upend the higher education system or to entice people to one university over another—they started as a completely organic experiment in disseminating quality, college-level material beyond the confines of geographic location. Yet, today they are seen as one of the largest disruptors to a centuries-old American higher education sector. Uber was not created to reform a dysfunctional taxicab commission—it was created to replace it. It is a clear example of how providing new choices empowers the consumer over the provider. Finally, unlike traditional health plans, consumer-directed health plans like HSAs remove the middle-man from health care and give consumers more ownership. Instead of a gatekeeper telling the insured which services are allowed, an HSA provides the consumer with more discretion and responsibility over where their health care dollars are directed.

K–12 IS A RELATIVELY UNDISRUPTED SECTOR

Yet, the American K–12 education system clings to a century-old system of take-it-or-leave-it, one-size-fits-all education. In 2016, the United States had approximately 13,000 public school districts. Although this figure is demonstrably smaller than the 119,000 districts in operation in 1938, much about the bureaucratic model for the delivery of teaching and learning inside a classroom remains relatively the same.[4] The same is true for school attendance zones. This delivery model assumes that one geographically assigned school can meet the learning styles, cultural preferences, and various other school characteristics for a diverse set of students with differing needs.

Our existing model for funding K–12 public education remains unchanged as well. Most states continue to rely on property taxes to fund schools, which creates disparities in funding based on the property values within each district. Too often, this funding is not tailored to students' needs, let alone the outcomes that states desire. According to the National Association of State Budget Officers, state governments spent $344.6 billion on elementary and secondary education in 2014. Although Medicaid was the largest state expenditure at $445 billion, of which the federal government paid 58.2 percent, elementary and secondary education remains the largest recipient of general funds in the states. When it comes to the source of spending, state governments provide 45.6 percent, local governments 45.3 percent, and the federal government 9.1 percent.

This one-size-fits-all approach is failing too many students, both academically and in the ability to match students' preferences to the learning environment that best suits them. According to the U.S. Department of Education, half of the public schools in the country do not offer calculus and one-third do not offer physics. The picture is even worse for students of color. Among schools that serve large percentages of African American and Latino students, one-in-three do not offer chemistry and one-in-four do not offer Algebra II—a sad reality since many states have included these courses as graduation requirements.[5] Most students do not have the opportunity to leave schools that fail to provide them the learning opportunities that prepare them for college and career. The status quo approach to education does not work well for all students.

THE GROWTH OF SCHOOL CHOICE

Fortunately, a student-focused reform renaissance beginning in the 1990s slowly but steadily began to unbundle a monolithic system by providing school alternatives for parents. Between 1990 and 2015, lawmakers in more than forty states and the District of Columbia enacted a range of public charter and private school choice laws. The largest and most well-known school reform movement in the United States is charter schools. In 2016, 2.9 million students in forty-three states and the District of Columbia attend 6,723 charter schools, which accounts for 6 percent of public school enrollment.[6] Additionally, an estimated one million student names are on charter school waiting lists across the country, with numbers as high as 40,000 students in New York City and Boston.

Reformers have also looked to programs like vouchers and tax credits to offer eligible students scholarships to pay for private school tuition. Unlike charter schools, a voucher is a publicly funded scholarship a parent uses to pay for a private school education. In 2014–2015, more than 165,000 students in fourteen states and the District of Columbia benefited from twenty-five voucher laws. Wisconsin enacted the Milwaukee Parental Choice Program (MPCP) in 1990, which began the modern American school choice movement.[7] It provides a voucher worth $7,214 (grades K–8) and $7,860 (grades 9–12) to parents with a household income up to 300 percent of the federal poverty level, which is $73,401 for a family of four. As of September 2015, MPCP had 27,619 students enrolled in 117 schools, with the majority of them being religious.[8]

Unlike a voucher, a tax-credit scholarship gives a full or partial tax credit to individuals or corporations that donate money to a nonprofit organization that provides scholarships to students to attend a K–12 private school. Tax credits are among the fastest growing private school choice programs. In 2015, sixteen states benefited from twenty tax-credit scholarships, although three million scholarship opportunities are available under current law.[9]

ESAs: MOVING FROM SCHOOL CHOICE TO A NEW FRONTIER OF EDUCATIONAL CHOICE

While charters, vouchers, and tax-credit programs expand opportunity beyond the zip code-based attendance zones utilized by public schools, they still operate within a twentieth century context of whole-school education. With a few exceptions, charter schools and private choice programs still function as traditional schools. Indeed, existing choice programs fail to empower parents with money to customize the education of their child.

ESAs may create a new frontier in educational choice by altering two fundamental aspects of school choice as we know it: moving choice beyond schools to a wider array of education service providers and giving parents funding so they can combine services for a custom education program based on price and quality. ESAs abandon the expectation that parents should choose this school or that school and instead give them total control over the dollars allocated for their child's education. With an ESA, parents can choose to send their child to a private school; use some of the funding to purchase curriculum or an online program to facilitate homeschooling, pay for private tutoring, therapies for students with disabilities, or costs associated with obtaining an industry certification or take an Advanced Placement or college entrance exam. ESAs also abandon the idea that education is a "use it or lose it" scenario. With an ESA, parents can spend all of their child's annual education funds in that year, or they can economize and save for future K–12 or higher education expenses.

This new vision of broad, customizable choice was realized when Arizona became the first state to adopt an ESA program in 2011. Just a few short years later, four more states—Florida, Mississippi, Tennessee, and Nevada—had enacted ESAs and an additional 16 had proposed legislation to create their own ESA programs. With the interest they have garnered and the large-scale changes they promise, ESAs may prove to be the most significant shift in education choice of the early twenty-first century. Yet, for all their potential import, the future of ESAs still hangs on the outcomes of judicial and political battles over them.

The Nevada ESA story deserves special mention because it vividly illustrates the potential ESAs pose and the judicial and political struggles they face. Nevada's is far and away the most ambitious of the five existing ESA programs, because it opens eligibility to every public school student in the state.

Under the Nevada program, any family with students in public schools could elect to exit the public school system and receive more than $5,100 a year to customize their child's education beginning in the 2016–2017 school year. Families with special needs students would have qualified for $5,700 a year. Nevada's open eligibility stood in stark contrast to other state ESA programs, which limited eligibility to a portion of students, typically those with special education needs. But in September 2016, the promise of the Nevada program stalled for approximately 8,000 families who had applied to it.[10]

Predictably, opponents challenged the constitutionality of Nevada's ESA program, and two lawsuits were consolidated into a single expedited case heard by the state supreme court. ESAs have proven remarkably resilient to constitutional challenges, suffering no defeats in court to date. On September 29, 2016, the Nevada Supreme Court in a 4–2 decision ruled that the ESA program did not violate the state constitution, but the judicial victory was bitter sweet. In the same ruling that explicitly cleared the constitutionality of the program, the court also found that the legislature-approved funding source was only designated for public schools. Since the legislature did not fund ESAs through a separate appropriation, the court issued a permanent injunction against the program.

The court's ruling gave another constitutional victory to ESAs, but the decision on funding cast the contest over the Nevada program back to the political realm. As of this writing, the families who had enrolled in the program will now wait for the legislature to determine a new funding source before the ESA accounts are operational.

What happens next will alter the landscape of education in Nevada for years to come, but the political popularity of the ESA concept, its potential to work at a large scale, and the constitutional validation it has received point to a fertile landscape for this new form of choice. Of course, the political and judicial challenges are just the first step in creating a new form of educational choice that actually delivers on its promises. Evaluating and understanding the next steps in that journey is the purpose of this volume.

THE BOOK FROM HERE

ESAs are designed to change the way education is delivered and to expand opportunities for parents to select the educational programs that best meet the needs of their child. Yet, they also create a variety of challenges that must be dealt with if these programs are to work as intended. ESAs introduce serious regulatory questions regarding what services should be eligible and how to regulate against charlatans. There are administrative questions about what students should be eligible for ESAs, how to distribute ESA funds, and what uncertainties ESA models introduce for those operating schools and school systems. There are also legal questions about how ESAs fit with the education provisions of state constitutions and what they mean for state accountability and funding systems.

In chapter 1, Matthew Ladner, senior advisor of policy and research for the Foundation for Excellence in Education, lays out the vision for ESAs as the next step in the evolution of educational choice policies. His chapter describes the origins of the program in Arizona and how it created the impetus for many in the choice community to see ESAs as a paradigm shift from school choice to education choice. Ladner argues that ESA policies represent an important experiment in liberty and parental self-determination, and that the experiment represents the beginning of an evolutionary process in K–12 education.

In chapter 2, Tim Keller, managing attorney with the Institute for Justice, makes the constitutional case for ESAs. The concept of parental-controlled ESAs was born out of an Arizona Supreme Court decision that struck down two publicly funded voucher programs. Yet, the design of the ESA program proved to be quite robust and survived judicial scrutiny under the same constitutional provision that had been used to strike down the voucher programs. ESAs in Arizona proved to be a popular policy design, quickly garnering the interest of legislators around the nation. As ESA programs have spread across the country, lawsuits aimed at shutting them down have followed. In his chapter, Keller addresses these various arguments and compares the constitutionality of ESA programs with traditional school choice measures, such as vouchers and tax-credit programs.

In chapter 3, Adam Peshek, director of educational choice at the Foundation for Excellence in Education, examines the existing five ESA programs and key differences in how they function. He also investigates how ESA administrators are building a new sector by adapting tools and practices from industries as varying as healthcare, banking, and charter schools. One example is how states are operationalizing these accounts—traditionally with debits cards or reimbursement systems—each with their advantages and disadvantages. Peshek closes the chapter with examples of how states can expand existing programs and offers recommendations for innovative administrative reforms that have the potential to improve parent satisfaction while simultaneously lowering the risk of financial fraud.

In chapter 4, Robert Enlow, president and CEO of EdChoice,[11] and Michael Chartier, Director of State Programs and Government Relations at EdChoice, discuss the politics of ESAs through partisanship and public opinion polls. ESAs have become law because of overwhelming Republican support, though rural Republicans have been least enthusiastic about them because of the potential impact on public school jobs and the lack of private schools in rural areas to make them beneficial. However, no Democrat voted for an ESA in three states. Enlow and Chartier share the motivations of lawmakers in these states, with an emphasis on lawmakers' hopes for both expanding educational options in new ways and for systemic education reform that cannot be achieved from other school choice options.

In chapter 5, John Bailey, former vice president of policy for the Foundation for Excellence in Education, argues that ESAs demand a new generation of quality controls that must not only monitor student progress and ensure that funds are being spent properly, but must also require new market tools and systems to help parents navigate and select choice based on a number of qualities. For ESAs to operate as intended, Bailey recommends that program administrators create quality controls that will help cultivate effective markets, not just regulate them. His chapter reflects on lessons learned from past accountability efforts and examines best practices from other sectors to lay out a vision for effective quality controls over ESA programs.

In chapter 6, Gerard Robinson, resident fellow in education policy studies at AEI, addresses some of the institutional dynamics that will shape the delivery of ESAs to families and children. Although ESA laws vary depending on state constitutions, codes, and funding formulas, one thing is constant across all programs: it will be the program administrators that shape much of the regulatory landscape in which parents and vendors will operate. Robinson provides a number of different regulatory models that states can pursue, addresses how administrators can approach the challenges that will surely arise, how they can design smart regulations that enhance—not hinder—innovation, and how policymakers can help make the programs viable once they exist.

In chapter 7, Allysia Finley, editorial writer for the *Wall Street Journal*, explains how ESAs play out in the "real world." She highlights the trials and triumphs of families using ESAs in Arizona, Florida, and Mississippi. Finley addresses the benefits ESAs have brought to these families, as well as some of the drawbacks of the programs, such as limited options in some locales. To gain insight into the supply side of ESA programs, Finley also features interviews with education service providers in Arizona, Florida, and

Mississippi that serve ESA holders to explore whether ESAs are encouraging the proliferation of high-quality educational options or not.

In chapter 8, Michael Q. McShane, director of education policy at the Show-Me Institute, looks to the aviation sector for a frame of reference. Half a century ago, a world without highly regulated air travel might have seemed unlikely. Few could have predicted the rise of low-cost airlines, our complicated web of travel routes, or technology developed to maximize every consumer and airline dollar. Yet, in the 1970s, the country experienced radical air travel deregulation that turned the traditional system on its head. This radical transformation has many parallels to what could happen under an educational system transformed by ESAs. McShane details the changes in the airline sector and how we can apply those lessons learned to a new and innovative system of ESAs.

In the last chapter, Nat Malkus, research fellow in education policy studies at the AEI, plays the role of critical friend. Although he believes the passage of an ESA law in five states is a major advancement of parent choice, it will not be a "game changer" if it becomes another small-scale choice option that benefits a few families and students. To address this quandary, Malkus identifies significant challenges that might derail ESAs' potential to produce functioning markets for educational services. ESA eligibility is one challenge. For instance, four states limit student enrollment to special populations, which includes students with an Individualized Education Program (IEP) or children of military families. Funding is another challenge Malkus identifies. Malkus closes the chapter with a reminder that the risks posed to ESA programs are fixable and, with the right mix of optimism and philanthropic market support, ESAs might reach their promised potential.

ESAs could very well be the next frontier in education. Not only by offering educational choice, but also as a mechanism to fund individual students—not a system of government-operated schools. ESAs have the potential to encourage entrepreneurship and dynamism in a sector that is lacking both, and provide a mechanism for parents to take a commanding role in their child's education. But to realize this promise, much more work needs to be done. This volume intends to investigate if we can get there and, if so, how.

NOTES

1. Dhawal Shah, "MOOCs in 2015: Breaking Down the Numbers," *EdSurge*, December 28, 2015, https://www.edsurge.com/news/2015-12-28-moocs-in-2015-breaking-down-the-numbers.

2. Daniel K. Lautzenheiser, "What Does the Future Hold for MOOCs," *AEIdeas*, June 12, 2014, https://www.aei.org/publication/what-does-the-future-hold-for-moocs/print/.

3. Devenir Research, "2015 Year-End Devenir HSA Research Report," February 17, 2016, http://www.devenir.com/research/2015-year-end-devenir-hsa-research-report/.

4. National Center for Education Statistics, "120 Years of American Education: A Statistical Portrait," January 1993, http://nces.ed.gov/pubs93/93442.pdf.

5. U.S. Department of Education Office for Civil Rights, "Data Snapshot: College and Career Readiness," Issue Brief No. 3, March 2014, http://www2.ed.gov/about/offices/list/ocr/docs/crdc-college-and-career-readiness-snapshot.pdf.

6. Sara Mead, Ashley LiBetti Mitchel, & Andrew J. Rotherham, *The State of the Charter School Movement* (Bellwether Education Partners, September 10, 2015), http://bellwethereducation.org/publication/state-charter-school-movement. Seven states do not have a charter school law as of February 2016: Kentucky, Montana, Nebraska, North Dakota, South Dakota, Vermont, and West Virginia. Washington state's charter law was ruled unconstitutional by the state supreme court on September 4, 2015. The process in Washington is ongoing. National Alliance for Public Charter Schools, "A Closer Look at the Charter School Movement: Schools, Students and Management Organizations, 2015–16," February 3, 2016, http://www.publiccharters.org/publications/charter-school-movement-2015-16/.

7. Wisconsin Department of Education, "Private School Choice Programs," http://dpi.wi.gov/sms/choice-programs.

8. Milwaukee Parental Choice Program (MPCP), "Facts and Figures for 2015–2016 as of November 2015," http://dpi.wi.gov/sites/default/files/imce/sms/pdf/MPCP%20Sept%20Facts%20and%20Figures%202015-16.pdf; and MPCP, "Milwaukee Parental Choice Program Headcount and FTE—2015–16 School Year," http://dpi.wi.gov/sites/default/files/imce/sms/pdf/MPCP%202015-16%20Sept%20Numbers%20by%20School%20with%20all%20Pupils.pdf.

9. Friedman Foundation for Educational Choice, "The ABCs of School Choice: The Comprehensive Guide to Every Private School Choice Program in America," January 25, 2016, http://www.edchoice.org/wp-content/uploads/2016/01/2016-ABCs-WEB.pdf. Five states do not have a publicly funded private school choice law: Kentucky, Nebraska, North Dakota, South Dakota, and West Virginia.

10. Nat Malkus & Gerard Robinson, *AEI Ideas*, September 30, 2016, "ESAs in the Wild, Wild West," https://www.aei.org/publication/esas-in-the-wild-wild-west/.

11. On July 29, 2016, the Friedman Foundation for Educational Choice announced its name would be changing to EdChoice. Reports cited by the organization prior to July 29, 2016 are under the name "Friedman Foundation for Educational Choice."

Chapter One

You Say You Want an Evolution? The History, Promise, and Challenges of Education Savings Accounts

Matthew Ladner

If we are indeed doomed to a generation of slow growth, it's a lapse in our collective imagination, not in technological innovation, that is holding us back.

—Adam Davidson

A GREEN REVOLUTION IN AMERICAN EDUCATION?

Improved agricultural practices saved an estimated one billion people from starvation in the late twentieth century, but it did not happen easily, or without criticism. Norman Borlaug, an Iowa biologist known as the "Father of the Green Revolution" won both a Nobel Peace Prize and a Congressional Medal of Honor, but only by overcoming innumerable technical, cultural, and political obstacles. Borlaug developed a new type of wheat and improved agricultural practices that allowed Mexico to become self-sufficient in its food production during the 1940s. This proved a prelude for revolutionizing agriculture across the globe.

Borlaug faced a variety of obstacles in his attempt to improve agricultural productivity. The biggest and most common obstacle across multiple nations proved to be resistance among subsistence farmers, who were reluctant to change their centuries' old practices. Even the prospect of widespread famine failed to motivate many farmers to adopt new plants and techniques.

The pragmatic Borlaug overcame rustic skepticism with demonstration projects, writing that if a farmer saw an agricultural demonstration on his own farm or his neighbor's farm, he became "the most effective extension agent in the whole countryside."[1] After decades of hard struggle, Borlaug and his fellow Green Revolutionaries dramatically increased crop yields and reduced

1

world hunger. Despite his undeniable success, Borlaug was still subjected to consistent criticism. Borlaug fought back against these critics, however, noting that many of them had never stepped foot in the Third World, much less witness a famine. Borlaug dismissed Western critics as "fat bellied philosophers," noting that they were unwilling to trade places with people in developing countries where the life span was at least a third shorter and half of the children died before reaching age ten. "It is far better for mankind to be struggling with new problems caused by abundance rather than with the old problems of famine," Borlaug opined.[2]

Today, Americans are in the middle of a long-term struggle to improve academic achievement in the stagnant field of education. At the time of this writing, it remains far from clear that there will eventually be a Borlaug level of improvement in American education, or anything close to it. Americans should, however, hunger for a more effective and just system, as international comparisons show American schools to be high spending but low performing.

There have also been a great many attempts to improve K–12 education in America. One of these steps has been to inject competition into elementary and secondary schooling. The British coined the phrase "quasi-market mechanisms" to describe public policies that attempt to improve outcomes by utilizing elements of market exchange. The term captures the goal behind both charter schools and tuition vouchers nicely, where the hope is to harness the power of market exchange in order to improve education outcomes.

Our present purpose lies in suggesting a more powerful quasi-market mechanism for interjecting competition into K–12 schooling—education savings accounts (ESAs). ESAs build upon two and a half decades of experience with quasi-market K–12 mechanisms and take crucial steps to spur further improvement in K–12 outcomes. American education, for reasons discussed below, has gone into a prolonged stagnation in outcomes despite a large increase in per-student funding. Efforts to reverse these trends through quasi-market mechanisms such as vouchers and charters have, to date, only been embraced tentatively by state lawmakers. Forty-three states have embraced charter schools and roughly half of the states have private choice programs. Various forms of caps and/or funding limitations have, however, kept the vast majority of these policies as purely incremental contributors to overall state K–12 systems.[3]

Reformers' desire for more robust policy options will continue to grow for both moral and practical reasons. For proponents of the status quo, more taxpayer funding for education is the answer to any policy challenge. In a different time, Americans might be willing to continue the practice of showering ever-increasing levels of funding on district schools indefinitely.

However, the ongoing retirement of the Baby Boomer generation (the first of whom drew federal retirement benefits in 2008) continues to increase demands for public health care spending and constrains economic and thus state revenue growth. The United States will average 10,000 Baby Boomers reaching the age of sixty-five per day until 2030, at which point all surviving members will have reached retirement age. Meanwhile, a number of states also face large projected increases in the size of their K–12 populations to go along with profound aging.[4] In essence, we have ample reason to believe that the next fifty years of American public education will be profoundly different from the last fifty years—out of necessity if not wisdom.

While the first generation choice mechanisms demonstrated tangible academic benefits, especially in improving bang for the education buck, they lack key features of market exchange that limit their utility. It's time to put more emphasis on the "market" in our quasi-market mechanism.

WHAT EXACTLY IS A K–12 ESA?

ESAs represent a new practice in the effort to expand educational choice, enabled in large part by advances in modern technology. The use of the term "ESA" can be confusing, as there are preexisting mechanisms for parents to save for future higher education expenses that utilize the same term. K–12 ESAs, however, are something entirely different. In this volume, the term "ESA" refers to an account-based form of parental choice whereby public officials deposit a student's educational funds into a use-restricted account that can be used to pay for a wide range of services, such as tuition, tutoring, and testing.

The concept behind an ESA is to provide parents with a state monitored account, which they can actively manage in order to provide a customized K–12 education for their child. The existing five ESA statutes in Arizona, Florida, Mississippi, Nevada, and Tennessee each have multiple allowable uses for account funds spelled out in statute. Parents are free to utilize multiple public and/or private education service providers in the education of their child.

Existing programs vary in a variety of ways, but for purposes of illustration, we will focus on the first program, passed in Arizona in 2011. Arizona's Empowerment Scholarship Account statute specifies that parents can use account funds for private school tuition and fees, individual public school courses, certified tutors, testing expenses, online education programs, curriculum, and contributions to a federal Coverdell Savings Account, among other allowable uses (discussed at greater length later in this chapter). Through both this last provision and the capacity to roll over funds from year to year, parents have the ability and the incentive to budget their funds over a long period of time—thus putting the "savings" in ESAs. Once a participating student reaches a certain age, funds remaining in the Empowerment Scholarship

Account can be used within a certain period of time on higher education and training, but eventually revert to the state treasury if unused.

The pages to follow discuss the brief history of ESAs, and why, if perfected, they could prove to be a highly beneficial new practice. The pages of this book offer an in-depth exploration of the legal and practical challenges needed to maximize the potential value of the ESA approach. Whether ESAs prove to be like Borlaug's new strain of wheat, an intermediate step toward some unimagined practice, or a political dead-end will remain to be seen in the years ahead. Advocates have the audacity to hope that they will prove highly beneficial, for reasons explained later in this chapter, but even under the best-case scenario, advocates face a long and difficult struggle in order to modernize educational practices. Whether ESAs prove to be a big part of the solution to our education problems or not, the need for improvement in American K–12 will remain acute.

AMERICAN EDUCATION STICKS OUT LIKE A SORE THUMB RATHER THAN A GREEN THUMB

Agriculture is far from unique—a great many products and processes have become better and cheaper over time. Unfortunately, this is far from the case in American K–12.

In the American education system, spending and staffing levels have grown at a much faster pace than student learning gains, as depicted in figure 1.1. Some gloomy-minded people might think this is due to a general decline in the quality of American life. But such a narrative is false in many other aspects of American life. In fact, the opposite is true—unlike education,

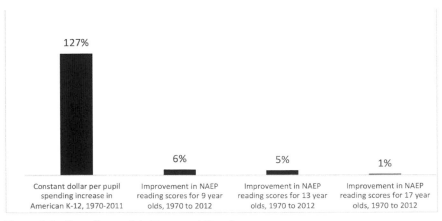

Figure 1.1   Spending and Achievement Trends.

which shows large cost increases for modest quality improvements, many other goods and services have become more effective and less costly to the consumer.

American Enterprise Institute economist Mark J. Perry delightfully documents the nonstop process of human material progress on his *Carpe Diem* weblog. In a 2014 post, Perry used a 1964 Sears catalog as a tangible example. A page out of the catalog pictured three antiquated furniture style television sets varying in price between $749 and $799. The higher priced television noted that it was a color (!) television. Adjusting for inflation, the modern price of this antiquated television would be between $5,700 and $6,100 in 2014.

Driving this point home, Perry listed the electronics that can be purchased today for $5,700. Using current store catalogs, he found that today's consumer can purchase five home appliances (including a washer and dryer, stove, and refrigerator), a laptop computer, professional camera, flat screen television, and half-a-dozen other products all for the equivalent price of a 21-inch color television in 1964.[5]

This can also be described by the number of hours of work needed to earn various products. In 1959, a color television cost $267 and the average wage was $2.09 per hour. It therefore took 127.8 hours for someone earning the average wage to buy a color television set. In 2013, you could buy a color television for $400, and the average hourly wage was $19.30, meaning that the average wage earner needed to work 20.7 hours to earn enough money to buy a color television. The fact that the 2013 television would have been of far higher quality than the 1959 product makes for a very nice bonus.[6]

Not to be outdone, economist Don Boudreaux posed the question as to whether a middle-income American in 2016 would wish to trade places with a billionaire in 1916. It might sound superficially appealing to be the richest person in the world, but the appeal of being the richest person in the world in 1916 quickly evaporates in Boudreaux's account:

> Your wi-fi connection was painfully slow—oh, wait, right: it didn't exist. No matter, because you had neither computer nor access to the Internet . . . Even the best medical care back then was horrid by today's standards: it was much more painful and much less effective . . . You (if you are a woman) or (if you are a man) your wife and, in either case, your daughter and your sister had a much higher chance of dying as a result of giving birth than is the case today. The child herself or himself was much less likely to survive infancy than is the typical American newborn today.[7]

A casual consideration of the quality, cost, and availability of various products and services a hundred years ago quickly leads to the conclusion that the average American would not trade places with John D. Rockefeller, still less with a Napoleon Bonaparte, Julius Caesar, or whatever other wealthy person you care to name from the past. This material progress, while sometimes gradual and at other times rapid, continually accumulates over time.

Most are unaware of the technological breakthroughs necessary to bring new products and services to market. Amazing new developments, including recent video streaming, online commerce with speedy home delivery and cheaper fuel due to innovative drilling techniques continue to appear. We quickly come to view them as normal, even unremarkable. All else being equal, we should expect products and services to become better and less expensive over time—it's entirely *normal*.

Education, however, remains a labor-intensive service—a sector generally resistant to productivity gains. Note, however, that several other services—including air travel, ride-sharing and even growing and distributing the food you buy at your grocery store—have, in fact, become more efficient over time. The key lies in the successful increase in competition and/or the adoption of technology to increase productivity. School systems run by boards elected in low-turnout/low-information elections do not alas constitute the primordial soup for continuous productivity gains.[8] Some thought on how to update what remains a system largely caught in its nineteenth century design seems appropriate.

EVOLVING OUT OF VOUCHERS: THE ORIGINS OF ESAs

Matthew Ridley's book, *The Evolution of Everything*, lays out the case for decentralized free exchange serving as a driving force behind material progress and well-being. As humans interact in a decentralized fashion, things change and frequently improve. Language, for instance, evolves over time through the innovation of speakers rather than the preferences of dictionary writers. Dictionary writers may imagine themselves as the dons of language, but in reality, they simply follow behind changes that have already been made. Whether the Oxford Dictionary recognizes "google" as a verb or not, people will still use it. Voluntary exchange spurs a decentralized process of experimentation and social learning over time that produces innovations irregularly.

Ridley notes that many patents granted to celebrated inventors came only slightly before other individuals or teams filed for a patent of their own for a similar technology. We celebrate inventors like Steve Jobs as if they brought fully formed new products and services to life in an amazing act of individual creation. The reality, however, is that innovations occur through a process of gradual improvement with teams of people grinding on problems.[9] Rather than emerging Athena-like and fully formed, clothed, and armed for battle from the mind of Zeus, innovations tend to emerge when they are ripe for development.[10] This usually occurs after a long process of experimentation and learning. ESAs evolved out of just such a process.

Milton Friedman launched the parental choice movement in the 1950s with an academic publication that suggested that monopolistic supply was a central problem in American K–12 schooling. While a rich academic literature sprang up on the subject, the central proposition can be summarized succinctly: American schools underperform because, unlike most firms, they don't suffer much in the way of consequences for failure. Friedman's plan proposed school vouchers that students could redeem at a school of their parent's choice as the first quasi-market K–12 mechanism.

But long before a school voucher program ever passed, University of California at Berkley law professors Jack Coons and Stephen Sugarman proposed a system remarkably similar to an ESA program of today in their 1978 book, *Education by Choice*. Coons and Sugarman, champions of the civil rights movement, envisioned a process of disintermediation whereby parents could directly secure services from educators. They described their vision:

> To us, a more attractive idea is matching up a child and a series of individual instructors who operate independently from one another. Studying reading in the morning at Ms. Kay's house, spending two afternoons a week learning a foreign language in Mr. Buxbaum's electronic laboratory, and going on nature walks and playing tennis the other afternoons under the direction of Mr. Phillips could be a rich package for a ten-year-old. Aside from the educational broker or clearing house which, for a small fee (payable out of the grant to the family), would link these teachers and children, Kay, Buxbaum, and Phillips need have no organizational ties with one another. Nor would all children studying with Kay need to spend time with Buxbaum and Phillips; instead some would do math with Mr. Feller or animal care with Mr. Vetter.[11]

Coons and Sugarman were far ahead of their time—at the time of their book's publication, the only school choice available to parents involved making liberal use of their wallets—either in the form of private school tuition or suburban school districts. The concept of a customized education system where parents choose among multiple providers was still far off, but steps began with the development of choice programs that allowed parents to choose between schools.

The first modern school choice law was passed in Wisconsin in 1990 with the goal of helping a small number of low-income children attending the Milwaukee Public School District. Since 1990, Wisconsin lawmakers have expanded the Milwaukee Parental Choice Program and extended eligibility outside of Milwaukee. Other states followed suit in creating voucher programs as well as scholarship tax credits, which debuted in Arizona in 1997.

Under a scholarship tax-credit program, states grant a tax credit for donations to nonprofits providing tuition scholarships for students to attend private schools.

In the early years of the new millennium, the father of the modern school voucher movement, Milton Friedman, proposed a path to move beyond vouchers. Like Coons and Sugarman proposed decades earlier, Friedman suggested a path in the direction of ESAs in a 2003 interview:

> Why is it sensible for a child to get all his or her schooling in one brick building? Why not add partial vouchers? Why not let them spend part of a voucher for math in one place and English or science somewhere else? Why should schooling have to be in one building? Why can't a student take some lessons at home, especially now, with the availability of the Internet? Right now, as a matter of fact, one of the biggest growth areas has been home schooling. There are more children being home schooled than there are in all of the voucher programs combined. [12]

It would take another eight years and special circumstances to operationalize the notion that thinkers such as Coons, Sugarman, and Friedman had speculated. All the while, charter schools raced ahead of private choice programs to become the largest form of publicly funded parental choice. Minnesota lawmakers passed the first charter school law in 1991, and today forty-three states have charter laws.

In 2016, three million students attended charter schools, almost ten times the number of students in private choice programs.[13] Many private choice programs remain in their proverbial diapers, having only been recently established, but we have every reason to expect that charter students will continue to outnumber private choice students for the foreseeable future.

The main systemic impact of the private choice movement to date may have been indirect in making the world safe for other reforms such as charter schools—public schools funded on a per-student basis, without attendance boundaries (other than state lines), and typically independent of district administration. Charter schools have been expanding much faster than private choice programs, and are especially popular in high population states that serve hundreds of thousands of students who have to date eschewed private choice programs, like California, Texas, and New York. The National Center for Education Statistics projects that these three states will educate 29 percent of the nation's schoolchildren in 2020. Each of these mega-states has an active charter school movement, but no private choice program.

Both school vouchers and charter schools, however, lack a crucial feature of true market exchange—the incentive to seek the highest possible value for funds. Parents simply enroll children in charter schools and the state directly funds the charter school on a per-student basis. This means that while the charter school has an incentive to seek enrollment, the parent has no incentive to inquire as to whether the charter school is making optimal use of funds. They either enroll their child, or they don't.

Likewise, school vouchers represent a single use, take it or leave it proposition. The original school voucher program demonstrates a problem that caps the possible utility of vouchers—every school in the system has an incentive to tie their cost structure to the maximum voucher amount. Failing to do so would entail leaving money on the table.

For instance, the Milwaukee Parental Choice Program provides participating schools either $7,214 per student *or* the cost of the school's private tuition, whichever is less. The program's designers structured the payment in this fashion to avoid a constitutionally impermissible subsidy to religious schools (in other words, so the state would avoid paying religious schools more than the cost of educating the child in the private school).

Under these incentives, it can be expected that schools will build their cost structures around the maximum voucher amount. But what if an innovator develops a high-quality school model that could deliver great results for less, say, $5,000 per child? Under the Milwaukee Parental Choice Program incentives, such a school seems unlikely to materialize. This would-be innovator might prefer to open schools as a for-profit charter operator, but even then, the company would reap the full benefit of the innovation as profit without sharing the benefit with the parent. The parent still lacks a basic element of market exchange—an incentive to seek maximum value from funds.

States arrive at a spending per pupil figure for charter and district schools annually through a complicated political process. If the number is $10,000 per child, the schools will spend something close to that amount, mostly on staff costs. No one should fault them for doing so. Don't, however, hold your breath waiting for the Steve Jobs of education to produce a high quality school model that delivers results at $6,000 per child. Realistically, there is no incentive to do so.

In other words, if we would like to see a continual rate of improvement in the cost-effectiveness of education spending, we need to do things differently. The most cost-effective system would encourage parents to treat publicly provided education spending as carefully as their own money in a system providing multiple options. The multiple allowable uses within an ESA program—including the ability to save for future higher education expenses—uniquely create this crucial incentive.

Arizona lawmakers created the first ESA program in 2011 through a circuitous route. In 2006, they passed into law two small voucher programs, which choice opponents filed suit against in the Arizona court system. That same year, Heritage Foundation Senior Analyst Dan Lips proposed the concept of a multiple-use education account in a white paper for the Phoenix-based Goldwater Institute.[14]

The justification for the lawsuits are rooted in so called "Blaine Amendments," which were adopted by a majority of states during a wave of late nineteenth and early twentieth century anti-Catholic hysteria. Public schools were pervasively religious at the time, but with a Protestant, "nonsectarian" (read: not Catholic) emphasis. Anti-Catholic nativist groups such as the Know-Nothings and the Ku Klux Klan supported efforts to deny Catholic schools public funding, including the creation of thinly veiled anti-Catholic provisions in state constitutions. Arizona's Blaine Amendment—Article 9 Section 10—reads, "No tax shall be laid or appropriation of public money made in aid of any church, or private or sectarian school, or any public service corporation."

Choice opponents claimed that school vouchers violated this clause. The Arizona Supreme Court agreed and struck down the school voucher programs in the 2009 decision *Cain vs. Horne*. Arizona choice advocates, however, took note of the Arizona Supreme Court's preoccupation with the fact that those voucher funds could only be used at private schools. In particular, they noted in the conclusion of the decision:

> The voucher programs appear to be a well-intentioned effort to assist two distinct student populations with special needs. But we are bound by our constitution. *There may well be ways of providing aid to these student populations without violating the constitution.* But, absent a constitutional amendment, because the Aid Clause does not permit appropriations of public money to private and sectarian schools, the voucher programs violate Article 9, Section 10 of the Arizona Constitution (emphasis added).[15]

Arizona choice advocates detected an opening in the Arizona Supreme Court's decision for a new type of choice program based upon a multiple use account. Even more gradually, it occurred to them that such a program had the potential to be superior to the traditional voucher model in many respects.

In 2011, Arizona lawmakers created the Arizona Empowerment Scholarship Accounts (ESA) program. Originally, ESA eligibility was only granted to students with disabilities. In 2012, Arizona lawmakers expanded eligibility to include students attending public schools and school districts that received a grade of "D" or "F." In that same year, ESA eligibility expanded to children within the foster care system, and the children of active duty military members. In 2015, Arizona lawmakers made children living on Arizona's Native American reservations eligible to participate in the program. Collectively, this eligibility pool represents more than 20 percent of Arizona's public school student population.[16]

Participating parents sign an agreement with the state to provide an education for their student that includes reading, grammar, mathematics, social studies, and science. The parent agrees not to enroll their child in a district or charter school for the following year as a full time student and also releases the school district from any obligation to educate the child.

In return, the state of Arizona deposits 90 percent of the funding that would have otherwise gone to the child's public school into an account controlled by the child's parent or guardian. Parents access those funds with a debit card, and the statute specifies the allowable use of the accounts. In Arizona, parents may use ESA funds for the following purposes:

- tuition or fees at a private school;
- textbooks;
- educational therapies or services from a licensed or accredited practitioner;
- curriculum;
- tuition or fees for a nonpublic online learning program;
- fees for a standardized norm-referenced achievement exam;
- fees for an Advanced Placement examination;
- fees for a college or university admission exam;
- tuition or fees at an eligible postsecondary institution;
- contributions to a qualified Coverdell college tuition savings program; and
- management fees from financial institutions selected by the Arizona Department of Education to oversee the accounts.

The state makes quarterly payments into ESA accounts, and parents have the ability to withdraw from the program. They are free within the limits of the law to design an education that best fits the needs of their student—whether from a single school or multiple providers outside of a traditional school setting. Students also have the ability to withdraw from the program and return to district or charter schools, but cannot be simultaneously enrolled.

Institute for Justice Attorney Tim Keller, who helped to successfully defend the Arizona ESA program, provides an in-depth review of constitutional issues and ESAs in his chapter. For now, simply note that the Arizona Empowerment Scholarship Accounts program withstood a legal challenge in the same court system that found vouchers unconstitutional.

The Arizona program provides parents with two methods to save funds for future use. First, parents can roll over funds from year to year within the account itself. Accounts can be used for higher education expenses and students may retain the accounts past the age of eligibility for the K–12 system (although state payments into the accounts end once the student is no longer eligible to attend a K–12 school). Funds remaining in an Empowerment

Scholarship Account will eventually revert to the state if not used for higher education expenses within limits established in statute.[17]

Parents can also save for future higher education expenses by making deposits directly into a Coverdell Savings Account, which is an allowable expense in most ESA programs. The federal government established Coverdell Accounts for the purpose of allowing tax-free savings for K–12 and higher education expenses. Coverdell funds earn interest and operate under a regulatory framework established and maintained by the federal government.

Empowerment Scholarship Accounts remain a relatively small-scale program in terms of the overall Arizona public school enrollment. Consistent with previous private choice programs, a mad rush for the exits of public schools did not materialize. In 2014, Florida lawmakers created the nation's second ESA program for children with severe disabilities. In 2015, Mississippi and Tennessee lawmakers also passed account-based programs for special needs students. Nevada lawmakers, however, made history in 2015 when they passed an ESA broadly available to all public school students as a part of a broad strategy to improve Nevada education results.

NEVADA LAWMAKERS MAKE HISTORY WITH NEAR-UNIVERSAL ESA PROGRAM

Nevada has long been the state with the fastest rate of population growth, which has led to chronic overcrowding in its public schools. In 2014, the *New York Times* ran a piece on the Clark County School District, which encompasses the greater Las Vegas area and educates nearly 74 percent of the state's children. The *Times* piece noted that the district had the equivalent of forty elementary schools of students housed in portable buildings. "I could build twenty-three new schools and they would open full and overcrowded," Clark County Superintendent of Schools Pat Skorkowsky reported.[18]

Due in large part to its growing student population, the Nevada public school system has also been unable to keep up with either physical or human capital needs. Chronic teacher shortages, which include the extensive use of substitute teachers, prompted the state government to create state-funded $5,000 sign on bonuses in 2015 for qualified instructors to teach in disadvantaged, low-income areas.

Bursting at the seams with enrollment growth and suffering from below average academic achievement, Nevada lawmakers continue to face both gigantic capacity and substantial quality problems. In 2015, Nevada Governor Brian Sandoval and the state legislature took dramatic action to address these problems. That year, a large number of K–12 reform bills were enacted with the goal of improving traditional public schools and increasing the supply of new charter and private schools. Most notably, lawmakers took action to improve early literacy, increase charter school offerings, and increase the supply of private educational options by creating an ESA program open to all public school students.

In creating the ESA program, supporters did not compare the potential of ESAs to some sort of idealized version of public education à la the little red schoolhouse. Rather, reformers looked out at the reality of packing children into trailers staffed by long-term substitute teachers and decided it was time to give parents other options.

The Nevada Constitution guarantees public funding for public education. Choice opponents filed suit against the Nevada program. Before the court injunction, the Nevada Treasurer's Office had received 8,000 applications to participate in the ESA program—less than 2 percent of the Nevada public school population. In the Nevada context of rapid population growth and public school overcrowding, choice programs will moderate the rate of growth in district schools rather than halt or reverse growth. Rather than some sort of public school apocalypse, the Nevada ESA program can play a productive role in moderating overcrowding.

The Nevada public education system isn't going anywhere, but it does need all the help it can get—the system lacks both physical facilities and the human capital needed to keep up with rapid enrollment growth. Not only does the state have plenty of students to go around, the U.S. Census Bureau projects that the number of Nevada residents will increase from 468,991 in 2010 to 765,572 in 2030.[19] In other words, there is no end in sight for Nevada's lack of physical space and teacher shortages.

The Nevada Supreme Court ruled upon the constitutional challenges facing the ESA program on September 29, 2016. The ruling decisively rejected multiple challenges to the constitutionality of the program. The Nevada Supreme Court also overturned the method that the Nevada legislature used to fund the accounts during the 2015 session.[20] The Nevada ESA program thus continues to exist in law, but currently lacks a funding source for the accounts. Nevada Governor Brian Sandoval subsequently announced the formation of a task force to develop a constitutional funding mechanism for the accounts. At the time of this writing, the funding source issue remains unresolved, but the underlying overcrowding problems in the Nevada public school system continue to mount.

ACADEMIC TRANSPARENCY, FINANCIAL OVERSIGHT, AND VENDOR ACCOUNTABILITY

ESA supporters must stand ready to answer three questions about how ESAs will work in practice. First, how will ESAs be evaluated to know whether or not students are learning? Second, how can states assure that parents spend account funds appropriately? Third, how can states prevent parents from being taken in by "fly by night" education service providers?

Parents who choose to participate in an ESA program have opted out of what is still largely a one-size-tries-to-fit-all system of schools with geographically defined attendance monopolies. People will argue endlessly about the accountability provisions that should be applied to the former public school system. Whatever their virtues (or lack thereof), public accountability systems were created to monitor the progress of single public schools—not the multiprovider system of education that ESAs create.

Through an ESA system, parents can use multiple service providers simultaneously. They can hire a certified tutor, enroll in massive-open online courses (MOOC) aimed at high school students, and also pay for a community college course. They can do all or none of these things in addition to either choosing to pay private school tuition or not.

So let's assume a student has chosen to do three of these things—say, hire a tutor, enroll in a MOOC, and pay for community college—in pursuit of a quality education. Which of these providers should be tasked with administering and being held accountable based on test scores?

If you answered "none of the above," give yourself a gold star.

A better system may be to let parents and students relate what they thought about the tutor, the MOOC, and the community college course, rather than asking students to take an exam. Policymakers should create transparent online platforms to collect the reviews of parents and students on major ESA purchases. If you hire a tutor, you should rate the tutor, and this rating can then serve as a resource to inform the decisions of other parents.

A second important question: how will we know whether ESA students are learning? The Nevada bill strikes an appealing balance in requiring the student to take a national norm reference exam. These tests—like the Stanford 10 and Iowa Test of Basic Skills—are not based upon state academic standards but instead measure the mathematics and reading achievement of students compared to a representative sample of peers.

The main aspiration of account based education lies in providing flexibility to parents, so such broad exams strike a balance between flexibility for parents and an appropriate interest on the part of the public for academic transparency. If parents desire to take state criterion based tests for their own information, these expenses can be allowable uses under the account.

Aggregated scores should be made public and gain scores properly studied by academic researchers. The responsibility for taking this test and providing the results should rest with the parent rather than any individual service provider. In addition, researchers should study account-based education on a variety of factors beyond just test scores—including but not limited to student–parental satisfaction, long-term educational attainment, civic involvement, and tolerance. There are more things in heaven and earth, Horatio, than are dreamt of in a standardized test score.

ESA programs should be viewed as an opt-out of the public school system, not as an extension of the public education practices that currently rule in private schools, community colleges, private tutors, and universities. The main point of the ESA experiment is to give parents the freedom to customize an education with the opportunity to build assets for future higher education use. In other words—we want parents to be set free. The public has a legitimate interest in the overall effectiveness of ESA programs, but that interest must be balanced with the autonomy of parents to meet the individual needs and interests of their child. National norm reference exams—like the Stanford 10, Iowa Test of Basic Skills and others—can serve as the basis for an academic evaluation of scores.

Finally, a note on financial accountability. Any publicly funded program will inevitably involve a level of misuse of funds—including the public school system itself. The question for ESA supporters is how to develop a rigorous system that prevents, deters, and punishes misuse without becoming tyrannical in the process.

Other chapters in this volume will have much more to say on this subject, but for now note that (fortunately) ESAs do not represent the first account mechanism financed by the government but utilized by private individuals. We have a rich set of experiences from other programs on which to draw in the ongoing effort to optimize account-based education.

For example, the federal temporary assistance for needy families (TANFs) program uses an account mechanism and has created an elaborate system to prevent, detect, and punish fraud among its beneficiaries. TANF is designed to give its participants the ability to purchase food rather than, say, poker chips, cigarettes or alcohol. The introduction of purchasing technologies through a debit card mechanism—vendor and product codes—dramatically reduced the incidence of fraud under the voucher (food stamp) mechanism.

Other account mechanisms with public policy implications include Health Savings Accounts, prepaid college tuition programs and others. Fortunately, ESA supporters not only have decades of experience upon which to draw from other policy arenas, but also a number of private vendors who have developed techniques and technologies to address both utility and financial accountability concerns.

ADDRESSING EQUITY IN AN ESA PROGRAM

The adoption of the Nevada ESA program elicited fierce critiques based upon notions of equity. David Osbourne, Senior Fellow at the Progressive Policy Institute and author of *Reinventing Government*, took to the pages of *U.S. News and World Report* to blast Nevada's embrace of the ESA program. Osbourne's critiques of Nevada's ESA program are best summarized when he wrote,

> It allows families to add to their education savings account to buy a more expensive education. Most parents want what's best for their children, so those who can afford it will do just that. Those who can't will not. And the education market will stratify by income, far more than it already does. In a decade, it will look like the markets for houses, cars and other private goods, with huge disparities based on wealth.[21]

Osbourne underestimates the level of crisis in the Nevada public school system. If we take some time to examine Nevada's test scores on the National Assessment of Educational Progress (NAEP—also known as the Nation's Report Card) we learn that it will not take a decade for Nevada's schools to mirror the disparities in the housing and car markets. Nevada's public school system is *already* far, far worse than the markets for cars and houses.

Let's take cars as our example: Whether you buy a Hyundai or a Mercedes, your car will drive off the lot. Examine Nevada's NAEP scores, however, and you find the opposite to be true. Only 17 percent of Nevada's Hispanic students scored proficient in eighth-grade reading in 2015. The same percentage of students eligible for free- and reduced-price lunch scored proficient. But of Nevada's middle- and high-income white students—clustered mainly in suburban schools—only 48 percent of eighth-grade students scored proficient in reading.

Osbourne has assumed a level of quality that does not exist in the actual Nevada public school system. If someone gave me a Hyundai, I'd be thrilled and let my teenage son drive it. If someone offered me a spot in a random Nevada district school for my son, I would politely decline the offer. All too often, public schools don't operate at even a minimal level of functionality—in other words, you can't drive them off the lot.

As mentioned earlier, the Nevada ESA provides additional assistance to low-income children, providing them with 100 percent of the average state funding in public schools ($5,700) and awarding higher-income students 90 percent of the state share ($5,100). Assuming an ultimate court victory, future legislative debates will almost certainly consider whether low-income children and other disadvantaged students should receive a greater subsidy—a topic worthy of deliberation and debate. Critics such as Osbourne, however, should note that an ESA providing a 12 percent greater subsidy for low-income children stands in stark contrast to the public school system—which in Nevada and elsewhere has a habit of providing more funds into wealthier children.

Parents in Incline Village, a posh community on the shores of Lake Tahoe, are likely satisfied with their generously funded public schools. If, however, some of them would like to take advantage of a $5,100 account rather than a $13,000+ public expense in the district, more power to them. Perhaps it will open spots for out-of-district transfers for children whose parents work in Incline Village but cannot afford to live there.

Spending per pupil, for instance, in Incline Village High School stood at $13,248 per child compared to a statewide average of $8,274 in 2013–2014.[22] Osbourne lamented that high-income parents will be able to supplement their $5,100 ESA, while ignoring that high-income parents, like those in Incline Village, can already supplement the $13,248 spent at their schools by hiring private tutors, coaches, SAT test prep classes, and so on. The Nevada ESA program at least gives the most public funds to the kids who start with the least.

The controversy stirred by the Nevada program points toward the need for a serious discussion regarding the topic of educational equity. The elected representatives of each state will need to wrestle with these issues. The public school system tends to give a number of systemic advantages to wealthy children—often including higher levels of funding and access to more experienced and higher quality teachers.

This constitutes an uncomfortable reality to be sure, but a reality nonetheless. Different democratic bodies will decide how to address the equity issue differently. All parents pay school taxes, and should have every publicly funded learning opportunity available to them. Every student can access district, magnet, charter, and public universities without facing discrimination on the basis of family income. Public education has long operated on the principal that everyone pays in, and all age-eligible children can participate. Addressing equity concerns by providing additional assistance to disadvantaged students remains an area for ongoing consideration and debate in the design and revision of ESA programs.

ESA advocates, however, have the opportunity to fashion a system far more mindful of equity issues than that currently practiced in the public school system. While all children should be eligible for an ESA program, ESA policy crafters have the ability to reflect equity concerns in a much more meaningful way than currently practiced in public education. A state spending $12,000 per child could provide up to $14,000 for low-income children in an

ESA, and $7,000 to the highest income children. The higher-income children in essence can generate the savings needed to provide additional assistance to lower-income children, and the state could still realize savings.

ACCOUNT-BASED CHOICE PROGRAMS: A JOURNEY OF DISCOVERY

The oldest account-based choice program, ESAs, has only made it to the ripe old age of five at the time of this writing. It would be foolish indeed for any supporter to claim that advocates of such a young and radically different approach have everything figured out. Quite the contrary, they have a great deal to learn. What advocates do have at the moment are five experiments in liberty, and thus, the opportunity to observe and learn.

The problems in transitioning to a parent-directed system from one determined solely by government loom large. How should ESA policies ensure the integrity of funds and prevent fraud? Do existing funding weights for the public school system adequately reflect equity concerns, or should policymakers depart from them in crafting ESA programs? Should policymakers pursue a reimbursement or a pre-approved provider system—and what are the implications of each? What techniques, organizations, and allowable account uses can assist parents in navigating a much-expanded universe of choices? How can parents hold service providers accountable—and, perhaps, vice versa? What level of academic transparency do participants owe to the public? How can public schools be included as vendors in a system of education that utilizes voluntary exchange as its guiding principal?

A decentralized process of multiple teams of individuals, all grinding away on problems over time, creates the primordial soup for deeper understanding. That soup has begun to bubble with ESAs, but it will need to cook for some time to know how to best proceed. In regard to that process, your humble authors of the present volume have endeavored to provide thoughts on how to design a more powerful mechanism for delivering K–12 results. With hard work and persistence, our fields may productively bloom despite a great many obstacles.

NOTES

1. "Iowans Who Fed the World—Norman Borlaug: Geneticist," *Herbert Hoover Presidential Library-Museum*, October 26, 2002, accessed June 02, 2016, http://www.agbioworld.org/biotech-info/topics/borlaug/iowans.html.

2. *Id.*

3. Charter school market share has grown to a significant figure in a small number of urban districts, most notably New Orleans, Detroit, and Washington, D.C., but at the time of this writing remained a single-digit share of the total number of public school students in a large majority of states with charter school laws. Private choice programs with broad and funded eligibility, and unencumbered various limitations to funding and/or student participation, have been much rarer still, with only Nevada having passed a broadly available program in 2015. A number of other private choice programs operate through tax credits, requiring a process of soliciting donations that has proven to be inherently incremental (in addition to usually being capped at a maximum dollar amount per year). Still other private choice programs focus on particular geographic areas (such as city-based programs in Milwaukee and Cleveland) or student subgroups (such as children with disabilities in several states).

4. Matthew Ladner, "Turn and Face the Strain: Age Demographic Change and the Near Future of American Education," Foundation for Excellence in Education, January 2015, accessed April 21, 2016, http://www.excelined.org/wp-content/uploads/ExcelinEd-FaceTheStrain-Ladner-Jan2015-FullReport-FINAL2.pdf.

5. Mark J. Perry, "The Magic and Miracle of the Marketplace: Christmas 1964 vs. 2014—There's No Comparison," *AEIdeas*, December 18, 2014, accessed April 21, 2016, https://www.aei.org/publication/magic-miracle-marketplace-christmas-1964-vs-2014-theres-comparison/.

6. Mark J. Perry, "Data Reveal That the Average Working American Is Better Off Today Than In the 1950s, and 'Wage Stagnation' Is a Myth," *AEIdeas*, January 29, 2014, accessed April 21, 2016, https://www.aei.org/publication/data-reveal-that-the-average-working-american-is-better-off-today-than-in-the-1950s-and-wage-stagnation-is-a-myth/.

7. Don Boudreaux, "Most Ordinary Americans in 2016 Are Richer Than Was John D. Rockefeller in 1916," *Cafe Hayek*, February 20, 2016, accessed April 21, 2016, http://cafehayek.com/2016/02/40405.html.

8. Aaron Churchill, "'Elected' School Boards and the Dangerous Illusion of Democracy," *The Thomas B. Fordham Institute*, March 03, 2016, accessed April 21, 2016, http://edexcellence.net/articles/%E2%80%98elected%E2%80%99-school-boards-and-the-dangerous-illusion-of-democracy?utm_source=Fordham%2BUpdates&utm_campaign=c131575ee8-.

9. Matt Ridley, *The Evolution of Everything: How New Ideas Emerge* (New York: HarperCollins, 2015).

10. Robert George, "The Birth of the Goddess Athena," *Encyclopedia of the Goddess Athena*, accessed April 21, 2016, http://www.goddess-athena.org/Encyclopedia/Athena/Birth.htm.

11. Ron Matus, "Berkeley Liberals and the Roots of ESAs," *Redefined*, September 09, 2015, accessed April 21, 2016, https://www.redefinedonline.org/2015/09/berkeley-liberals-education-savings-accounts/#sthash.rEtAHP29.dpuf.

12. Kane Pearl Rock, "Choice & Freedom," *Education Next*, July 14, 2006, accessed April 21, 2016, http://educationnext.org/choicefreedom/.

13. "Choice & Charter School Facts," The Center for Education Reform, accessed April 21, 2016, https://www.edreform.com/issues/choice-charter-schools/facts/.

14. Dan Lips, *Education Savings Accounts: A Vehicle for School Choice*, Goldwater Institute, 2005, http://www.amazon.com/Education-Savings-Accounts-Vehicle-School-ebook/dp/B0033AH2I2.

15. "FindLaw's Supreme Court of Arizona Case and Opinions," *Findlaw*, March 25, 2009, accessed April 21, 2016. http://caselaw.findlaw.com/az-supreme-court/1391598.html.

16. While there are a number of school choice programs with broader eligibility pools, very few of them have funded eligibility. For example, Arizona's original scholarship tax-credit program makes all students eligible, but the program raises a finite amount of money each year, and scholarship granting organizations have waiting lists for students. At the time of this writing only the school voucher programs in Indiana and Louisiana have both broader eligibility pools with funded eligibility than the Arizona ESA program.

17. Arizona Department of Education, "Laws & Statutes," *Empowerment Scholarship Accounts*, accessed April 21, 2016, http://www.azed.gov/esa/laws-statutes/.

18. Adam Nagourney, "Las Vegas Schools Groan From Growing Pains," *The New York Times*, October 06, 2014, accessed April 21, 2016, http://www.nytimes.com/2014/10/07/us/las-vegas-schools-groan-from-growing-pains.html.

19. Matthew Ladner, "Turn and Face the Strain: Age Demographic Change and the Near Future of American Education," Foundation for Excellence in Education, January 2015, accessed April 21, 2016, http://www.excelined.org/wp-content/uploads/ExcelinEd-FaceTheStrain-Ladner-Jan2015-FullReport-FINAL2.pdf.

20. To review the *Schwartz vs. Lopez* decision, see http://law.justia.com/cases/nevada/supreme-court/2016/70648.html.

21. David Osborne, "The Wrong School Choice: Nevada's New School Voucher Law Will Make Inequality Worse," *U.S. News and World Report*, July 06, 2015, accessed April 21, 2016, http://www.usnews.com/opinion/knowledge-bank/2015/07/06/nevadas-new-voucher-law-will-worsen-educational-inequality.

22. Nevada Department of Education, "2013-14 Accountability Report," accessed April 21, 2016, http://www.inclinehs.org/attachments/063_2013-14%20Accountability%20Report.pdf.

Chapter Two

The Constitutional Case for ESAs

Tim Keller

Arizona launched the nation's first education savings account (ESA) program in 2011 to replace two publicly funded private-school scholarship programs that were struck down in 2009 by Arizona's Supreme Court.[1] The court struck down the voucher programs because participants could use their scholarships only at private schools.[2] The court held that by limiting scholarships to use at private schools, the programs violated a state constitutional provision prohibiting appropriations of public funds "in aid of . . . private and sectarian schools."[3]

Arizona designed its ESA program to comply with that 2009 decision. The key to differentiating Arizona's ESA program from the unconstitutional voucher programs was ensuring that parents did not have to enroll their participating student in a private school. This innovative policy design withstood the inevitable legal challenge because parents had a choice not to spend their ESA funds on private school tuition. In upholding the ESA program under the same constitutional provision used to strike down the voucher programs, Arizona's intermediate court of appeals explained that the ESA program was not "in aid of . . . private or sectarian schools" because "none of the ESA funds [we]re pre-ordained for a particular destination."[4]

In addition to being constitutionally robust, ESAs also proved to be a popular policy design. ESAs quickly garnered interest from legislators around the nation. Since 2011, six state legislatures have passed ESA programs, although two of those programs were vetoed.[5] As ESA programs spread from one state to another, lawsuits aimed at shutting them down can be expected to follow.

As with legal challenges to traditional school choice programs, such as vouchers, lawsuits will be filed in state courts asserting violations of state constitutions. Why state courts and state constitutions and not federal courts and the federal Constitution? In 2002, the U.S. Supreme Court upheld, under the federal Constitution, school choice programs that allow parents to choose religious schools.[6] After that decision, the National Education Association's then-chief counsel, Robert Chanin, explained that choice opponents would "continue to challenge voucher and choice programs under state constitutions on whatever grounds are available to us—from lofty principles such as church-state separation, to 'Mickey Mouse' procedural issues like the single-subject rule."[7] True to Mr. Chanin's promise, ESA opponents have taken a "throw it against the wall and see what sticks" approach to challenging ESA programs in Arizona, Florida, and Nevada.

The legal history of Arizona's ESA program reveals how and why ESAs differ from other educational choice programs. It also explains how those differences matter for constitutional challenges in other states. Even though ESAs are distinct from other educational choice programs, lawsuits challenging the constitutionality of ESA programs will continue to be filed. These lawsuits will invoke a dizzying array of constitutional claims, from important constitutional principles, such as separation of church and state; to arguments that ESA programs violate a state's duty to establish a "uniform" public school system; to the various "Mickey Mouse" procedural arguments promised by Mr. Chanin.

It is thus essential that policymakers be aware of the most oft-cited constitutional provisions in opposition to ESA programs and whether their own state constitutions contain any of these provisions. Once policymakers understand the constitutional landscape, they can design an ESA program that will pass constitutional muster. While individual tailoring is important to drafting a constitutional ESA program, there are several universal components that every ESA program should incorporate. Policymakers need to be cognizant of these ideal common elements as they design future ESA programs.

THE LEGAL GENESIS OF ESA PROGRAMS

The nation's first ESA program was born out of necessity. It was also designed to satisfy the Arizona Supreme Court's restrictive interpretation of a relatively unique state constitutional provision. Arizona's ESA program proved to be not only constitutionally resilient, but it also proved very popular with policymakers nationwide. Indeed, only four years after the adoption of the nation's first ESA program, six more ESA programs have been passed— including a nearly universal ESA program in Nevada, which was immediately challenged in court after its passage and ultimately upheld as constitutional.[8]

The Birth of Arizona's ESA Program

In 2006, Arizona's Democratic Governor Janet Napolitano signed into law two small voucher programs. The programs, which served children with disabilities and children in the foster care system, were funded from two $2.5 million dollar appropriations from the state treasury. Both programs allowed parents to use their eligible student's voucher to pay for tuition at the private school of their choice. The programs were entirely neutral with regard to religion, meaning that parents could choose to enroll their child in any participating private school, regardless of whether the school was religiously affiliated or not. The programs did not allow state officials to take any cognizance of religion when approving participating schools. State officials could look only at nonreligious factors, such as employee background checks and other similar public health and safety matters.

Both programs were challenged in a single state court lawsuit filed by a handful of individuals, Arizona's teachers' union, and the American Civil Liberties Union of Arizona, amongst other groups closely aligned with Arizona's public education system.[9] After three years of litigation, during which time hundreds of families came to rely on the programs, the Arizona Supreme Court invalidated both programs.[10] The court ruled that the programs violated the Arizona Constitution's "Aid Clause," which says, "No tax shall be laid or appropriation of public money made in aid of any church, or private or sectarian school, or any public service corporation."[11]

Proponents of the voucher programs argued that the Aid Clause did not prohibit the programs because the money was appropriated "in aid of" families and not "in aid of" the private schools parents chose.[12] But the court rejected that argument and said the programs violated the Aid Clause because parents had "no choice" but to use their vouchers at private schools.[13] The court believed that requiring parents to use their vouchers at private schools was the equivalent of transferring "state funds directly from the state treasury to private schools."[14]

Despite this nonsensical conclusion, there were two silver linings for choice advocates in the court's decision. First, the court reaffirmed its prior ruling upholding Arizona's tax-credit-funded scholarship program because tax credits are private funds, and thus not an "appropriation of public money" under the Aid Clause.[15] Second, the court concluded its decision by stating that there "may well be ways of providing aid to these student populations without violating" the Aid Clause.[16] That conclusion was the first breadcrumb in a trail that ultimately led Arizona to adopt the nation's first ESA program.

The Arizona Supreme Court's rather vague, but hope-inspiring, conclusion caused Arizona's educational choice advocates to carefully review the Supreme Court oral argument concerning the voucher programs.[17] There was an exchange between the teachers' union's lawyer, Donald M. Peters, and then-Justice Andrew Hurwitz that was of particular importance. Justice Hurwitz asked Mr. Peters whether the Aid Clause would permit the state to provide parents with a more open-ended grant; one that they could use for a broader array of educational goods and services than just private school tuition. Mr. Peters' affirmative response that such a grant would be permissible may have been the reason for the court's concluding statement that a program could be designed to comply with the Aid Clause. The exchange was as follows:

> *Justice Hurwitz:* Do you agree that the state could pick this population of worthy parents and say to them "here's a grant for each of you for $2,500 to be used in pursuit of your children's education, spend it as you wish?"
>
> *Mr. Peters:* Yes.
>
> *Justice Hurwitz:* And if they spend it on a private or parochial school, or on a public school transfer, that would be okay?
>
> *Mr. Peters:* Yes. I think the dividing line is how much the state constrains the choice.
>
> ***
>
> *Mr. Peters:* Under the Aid Clause, that funding is for the most part only going to be used to pay one of two prohibited recipients. So the choice is constrained to the point that the odds are overwhelming that it's going to go to a prohibited recipient.
>
> *Justice Hurwitz:* So then why wouldn't that make illegal the program I just described, where we said to each parent, "here's money to use for your child's education?" Those who are going to public school would have no expenditure in any case.
>
> *Mr. Peters:* My assumption is that you can hire a tutor with it; you can do all kinds of things with it other than paying a private or religious school.

Regardless of whether this exchange was the impetus for the court's conclusion, it was certainly the starting point for designing Arizona's ESA program.[18]

The key constitutional element derived from the Arizona Supreme Court's interpretation of the Aid Clause is that families participating in the ESA program are not limited to enrolling their children in a private school. Instead, parents may use the funds deposited in their child's ESA for a wide array of educational goods and services including, if parents choose to exercise it, the option of paying for private school tuition. This design means that no funds can be said to be transferred "directly from the treasury to private schools."[19]

Predictably, in 2011, Arizona's ESA program was challenged in state court—by the same groups, same lawyers, and under the same legal theory that was successful in their challenge to the voucher programs for children with disabilities and children in foster care. This time, however, because of the careful legislative drafting that went into the ESA program, the result was different. As the Arizona Court of Appeals stated in its decision upholding Arizona's ESA program, "none of the ESA funds are preordained for a particular destination."[20] The decision of the Court of Appeals became final when the Arizona Supreme Court chose not to review the appeals' court's decision.[21]

ESAs DIFFER FROM OTHER TYPES OF SCHOOL CHOICE PROGRAMS

The primary difference between ESAs and traditional school choice programs is that participating families are not limited to using their funds to pay for tuition at a private school. Participating parents agree to provide their children with a basic education[22] and, to accomplish that task, they are permitted the flexibility to use the funds in their student's ESA to pay for any combination of educational goods and services authorized by the program. ESAs may include a variety of educational goods and services, including, but not necessarily limited to, tutoring, home school curriculum, supplemental materials (such as lab equipment or literature and history books), individual classes at public schools, online instruction, special education therapies and services, private school tuition and fees, and saving for college tuition. The ability to custom-build an education means that ESA programs move the needle from offering school choice to offering course and educational choice.

CATCHING FIRE: AN OVERWHELMINGLY POPULAR POLICY

The ESA concept has proved to be a popular policy design and has quickly garnered interest from legislators around the nation. Since Arizona adopted its program in 2011, six more states have passed ESA programs, though to date only four of those were signed into law (bringing the total number of operational ESA programs to five).[23] In 2016, at least ten more states considered bills to create new ESA programs.[24]

It is encouraging to see a relatively new policy innovation gaining such momentum, especially a policy with so much potential to bring about positive change in education. However, it is essential that policymakers examine their own state constitutional provisions, and the judicial decisions interpreting those provisions, in order to craft constitutionally defensible ESA programs.

Just as there is no one-size-fits-all approach to educating children, there is no one-size-fits-all approach to drafting a constitutionally defensible ESA program.

EYES WIDE OPEN: THE CONSTITUTIONAL CHALLENGES WILL COME

Since the beginning of the modern school choice movement in 1991, when state-Democratic Representative Polly Williams teamed up with Wisconsin Republican Governor Tommy Thompson to pass a small voucher program for inner-city students in Milwaukee,[25] there has not been a single day that an educational choice program has not been in court being challenged some place in this country.

The most common claim made against school choice programs is that they violate state constitutional provisions designed to ensure separation of church and state. Any properly designed ESA program should include religious affiliated educational service providers among an array of both nonreligious and religious choices given to parents.[26] However, this type of religious neutrality will almost certainly induce choice opponents to file legal challenges based on the various religious provisions in state constitutions. The two most common types of state religion clauses are "Blaine amendments" and "compelled support" clauses.[27] The proper interpretation of these state religion clauses is a significant unresolved issue under many state constitutions. Indeed, the existing interpretations of these provisions vary significantly from state to state.

Legal challenges to school choice programs also often assert that state constitutions restrict the use of public funds exclusively to supporting the public school system. Or, alternatively, that school choice programs will cripple the public school system's ability to adequately educate children, thereby undermining a state's obligation to establish and maintain a public school system. Indeed, these types of claims were a significant part of the litigation challenging Nevada's nascent, nearly universal ESA program.[28]

These and other state constitutional issues—such as the "Mickey Mouse" procedural claims Mr. Chanin promised—need to be examined by policymakers in each and every state before they start drafting ESA legislation. Any viable, successful, and constitutional ESA program must begin with a blueprint based on each state's unique constitutional landscape. As such, state constitutions must be scoured for the various provisions, discussed below, that opponents may use to challenge ESA programs. Policymakers must develop a thorough understanding of how those provisions have been interpreted and applied and then design ESA programs accordingly.

Blaine Amendments

State Blaine amendments present the most serious threat to ESAs and other educational choice programs in the thirty-seven states whose constitutions contain Blaine language.[29] Blaine amendments are characterized by their restriction on the use of public funds "in aid of" or "for the benefit of" "sectarian" schools. They were also "born of bigotry," specifically, anti-Catholic bigotry.[30] Understanding the discriminatory history that gave rise to Blaine amendments is crucial to their proper interpretation and application.[31]

Properly understood and construed, Blaine amendments should not present a barrier to any type of religiously neutral educational choice program, ESAs included. This is true, in part, because phrases like "in aid of" suggest an inquiry into who, or what, is the true beneficiary of the challenged governmental program. And the overwhelming majority of state courts that have examined who is "aided" or "benefited" by educational choice programs have concluded that it is the students themselves—not religious schools—who are the true beneficiaries.[32]

The name "Blaine" refers to James G. Blaine, who served as both a U.S. senator from Maine and as speaker of the U.S. House of Representatives. At the urging of President Ulysses S. Grant, Blaine proposed an amendment to the federal constitution in 1876 to prohibit states from appropriating public money to "sectarian" schools.[33] The term "sectarian" was widely understood at that time to mean "Catholic."[34] It was not merely a synonym for "religious," as it is often understood today.

The proposed federal Blaine amendment arose at a time when public schools were not the thoroughly secular institutions we know today.[35] Public schools were originally designed to be religious schools, except that their religion was a generic, nondenominational Protestantism that taught doctrines that most Protestant sects could agree upon.[36] Because they were unhappy with the Protestant orientation of the public schools, beginning in the mid-1850s, Catholics began creating their own schools and campaigning for a proportional share of public school funds.[37] These efforts outraged the Protestant majority.[38] In response to Catholic efforts to secure public funding for their schools, several states enacted proto-Blaine amendments to ensure that Catholic schools would not receive the same subsidies that the Protestant public schools received.[39]

After the Civil War, Catholics renewed their demands for a share of the public school funds. Blaine, who was eager to secure the Republican presidential nomination, introduced an amendment to prohibit public funding of "sectarian" schools. His proposed amendment was a "transparent political gesture against the Catholic Church."[40] It was part of a crusade manufactured by the contemporary Protestant establishment to counter what was perceived as a growing "Catholic menace."[41] It is no wonder that the U.S. Supreme Court has called for the Blaine amendments' legacy of anti-Catholic bigotry to be "buried now."[42]

Blaine's federal amendment narrowly failed to garner the required super-majority in the U.S. Senate to send it to the states for possible ratification, but a number of states thereafter adopted similar state constitutional language. Indeed, the language of the aforementioned proto-Blaine amendments, which preceded Blaine's proposed federal amendment, and the state Blaine amendments that passed after the failure of the federal amendment all contain similar language, which was designed to rebuff the efforts of Catholics to acquire institutional assistance for their parochial school system.

Blaine amendments, however, are not aimed at preventing states from providing families with religiously neutral educational aid. Efforts to invoke Blaine amendments to halt educational choice programs thus seek to expand the discriminatory reach of Blaine amendments from Catholicism to all religions. Courts should reject any interpretation of state Blaine amendments that would resurrect and expand the historical animus that animated their adoption.

Unfortunately, many states have construed their Blaine amendments to prohibit student aid programs that permit participants to use their aid at religiously affiliated private schools.[43] The existence of these negative precedents means that nearly every educational choice program that uses state funds—ESA programs included—will face Blaine challenges.[44] This is likely true even in states with Blaine precedent that distinguishes between student aid programs and institutional aid programs. Opponents will try to import negative precedent from other states in an attempt to overrule or undermine cases that permit student aid programs.

But, the question arises—given the Arizona ESA program's success in overcoming a Blaine precedent that struck down a voucher program—are ESAs more likely than other types of educational choice programs to withstand Blaine amendment challenges? The logic that allowed Arizona's ESA program to survive a constitutional challenge that the voucher programs could not survive might be extended to ESA programs in other states.

More recently, Nevada's nearly universal ESA program survived a legal challenge under a Blaine amendment worded very differently from the Arizona Blaine amendment considered by the Arizona Court of Appeals. Nevada's Blaine amendment states that "No public funds of any kind or character whatever, State, County or Municipal, shall be used for sectarian purpose."[45] In upholding Nevada's ESA program, the Nevada Supreme Court did not rely on precisely the same reasoning as the Arizona Court of Appeals.[46] The Nevada Supreme Court concluded that the ESA program's purpose was "educational" not "sectarian" and reasoned that "[o]nce the public funds are deposited into an ESA, the funds are no longer 'public funds' but are instead the private funds of the individual parent who established the account."[47]

While educational choice proponents will certainly advocate that other state courts adopt the reasoning in these two cases, each state's Blaine amendment must still be assessed based on the legal precedents in that state. There are at least two reasons for this. First, while the Nevada Supreme Court did construe ESA funds to be "private" once deposited into an individual's ESA, the program still relies on appropriations of state funds.[48] Thus, Blaine amendments that specifically mention appropriations of public funds will still likely be found to apply to publicly funded ESA programs.[49]

Second, some state supreme courts have relied on Blaine provisions to strike down programs that give parents a genuine choice between religious and nonreligious schools. Thus, giving parents "more choices" would not necessarily have changed the outcome of those cases. The reasoning in those cases acknowledged that not all of the funds in the challenged program would go to religious schools—but struck down the programs anyway because most of the funds were *actually* being used at religious schools. This "actual use" problem is not necessarily solved by ESAs because even though ESA programs provide a wide variety of uses to which the aid can be put, at this time, families will primarily spend their ESA funds on private school tuition.[50] Thus, if the bulk of ESA expenditures are on private school tuition, and if most of those private schools are religious,[51] then an ESA program in a state with Blaine law based on an "actual use" theory could still be struck down.

Accordingly, the best alternative in states with restrictive Blaine law is to consider using a tax-credit model for funding an ESA program.[52] Tax-credit-funded scholarship programs have proven immune from Blaine amendment challenges to date because tax credits do not involve any appropriation of public funds. Rather, tax-credit programs involve donations of private funds by private individuals (or corporations) to private charities that in turn award scholarships to families. Every case that has addressed the issue of whether tax credits are appropriations of public funds—nine in total—have concluded as a matter of law that tax credits are not public funds.[53] There is no reason why a state could not design and implement a tax-credit-funded ESA program.

Compelled Support Clauses

Compelled support clauses prevent, and in many cases ended (at the time of their adoption), the establishment of an official state religion. Most states modeled their compelled support provision after Pennsylvania's 1776 Constitution, which reads in part, "That all men have a natural and unalienable right to worship Almighty God according to the dictates of their own consciences and understanding: And that no man ought to or of right can be compelled to attend any religious worship, or maintain any ministry, contrary to, or against, his own free will and consent."[54] Such language is clearly aimed at prohibiting states from requiring mandatory church attendance and/ or compelling financial support in order to establish an official religion for the state.

Generally speaking, state courts have not invoked compelled support clauses to strike down educational choice programs. This is because compelled support language prohibits states from providing direct financial support for and/or requiring attendance at churches. They say nothing about providing religiously neutral financial aid to families to choose the school of their choice. There is one modern exception, however. In 1999, the Vermont Supreme Court held that Vermont's compelled support clause prohibits publicly funded tuition assistance to students choosing religious schools.[55] The court's holding misconstrues the plain language of the compelled support provision in two ways. First, it construed tuition assistance to students as "support" for the schools they chose to attend. And second, that such support, when used to attend religious schools, constituted support for a "place of worship." No other state court has similarly construed a compelled support clause.

Education Articles

Every state constitution contains an article dealing with public education. Most contain some sort of mandate to establish and maintain a public school system, and those states that do not do so in their constitution do so by statute.

There are three lines of arguments that educational choice opponents invoke when relying on public education mandates to challenge school choice programs. The first argument is that the imposition of a duty to operate and fund a public school system limits the authority of state legislatures to fund any educational alternatives outside of that system. In other words, opponents claim that the requirement to operate a public school system means that that system is and must remain the exclusive means of publicly funding education. But every state supreme court—except one—to consider this type of claim in the context of an educational choice program has rejected such "exclusivity" claims.[56] The reason exclusivity claims are rejected is that nothing in the plain language of such provisions suggests that they are setting forth the only means of delivering a publicly funded education.

Second, opponents will argue that ESA programs drain resources from public schools. This loss of resources, they will assert, will detrimentally impact public schools in a variety of ways, from public school closures to fewer electives. But the real question is whether ESA programs in any way impede a legislature's ability to meet its obligation to provide for a system of public schools. The answer to that question, is, of course, no. Public schools will no doubt remain firmly in place, and fully available to parents who wish to send their children to those schools, even after the passage of ESA programs.[57] As long as all students remain free to attend public school if they desire to do so, then a state is not violating its duty to provide a system of public schools.[58]

Finally, opponents will argue that the private schools that parents choose must be considered part of the public school system—meaning they must be subject to the same legal requirements as public schools. Treating participating private schools as public could require any amount deposited in the parents' ESA to cover the full amount of tuition—or be accepted as the full amount of tuition—due to the requirement that public schools be free.[59] But, with an ESA program, the state is not transforming private schools into public schools. Private schools remain private.[60]

"Mickey Mouse" Provisions

Choice opponents have been faithful to Mr. Chanin's promise to comb through state constitutions looking for any hook; any obscure provision upon which a sufficiently choice-hostile state court might seize to strike down a program. These include arguments that programs were improperly enacted by the legislature (e.g., because it was rolled into a larger bill, thus violating "single-subject" requirements, or that it constitutes a local or special law, as opposed to a general law); that it derives its funding from an improper source (state constitutions sometimes provide that certain pots of state money may only be spent in certain ways or that certain public education funds be subject to the "local control" of school district officials); or that scholarships constitute impermissible "gifts" to parents under "anti-gift" or "anti-donation" clauses, intended to prevent the type of corporate welfare often exhibited during the building of the railroads.

Single-Subject Provisions

Single-subject provisions were designed to prevent so-called "log-rolling," which is the practice of including disparate and unrelated "subjects" in a single bill in an effort to entice legislators who may oppose one aspect of a bill to vote in favor of another, more attractive aspect of the same bill. Florida's ESA program was challenged under Florida's single-subject provision because it was passed as part of a comprehensive education reform bill that, among other things, also expanded eligibility for Florida's tax-credit-funded scholarship program. The lawsuit was thrown out on grounds that the plaintiffs were not personally injured and therefore did not have "standing" to file the case.[61] There is a simple, straightforward way to avoid single-subject challenges: pass ESA programs as stand-alone bills rather than as part of comprehensive reform bills.

Special and Local Law Provisions

In addition to single-subject provisions, most state constitutions contain provisions requiring the adoption of general laws that are applicable statewide, rather than special or local laws applicable only to limited jurisdictions. Opponents have challenged school choice programs that are limited to certain cities, such as Milwaukee and Cleveland, or certain school districts, such as those rated as failing.[62] Generally speaking, these claims fail if there are valid reasons for limiting the scope of the legislation and the class of beneficiaries is capable of expansion.

Legislators need to articulate valid reasons for any limitations on eligibility they incorporate into ESA programs. Courts generally give legislatures considerable leeway in responding to perceived problems and needs and permit them to approach problems incrementally.

Restricted Funding Provisions

Many state constitutions restrict certain "pots" of money exclusively for use on public schools. Generally, these restricted monies are the interest and investment income generated from federal lands granted to the state at the time of statehood for the purpose of funding public schools. Of course, there may be other restricted funding sources as well. But even successful claims under restricted funds provisions may not be entirely prohibitive of ESA programs if there are other available funding sources.[63] Of course, there is no guarantee that ESA proponents will have enough political capital to tap a new funding source after a program has been declared unconstitutional. It is far better to avoid these questions entirely by carefully avoiding use of restricted funds from the outset.

Local Control Provisions

Similarly, local control provisions generally vest control over public education at the school board level. In 2004, the Colorado Supreme Court relied on a local control provision to invalidate a statewide school choice program because it directed school districts to turn over a portion of their locally-raised funds to nonpublic schools over whose instruction the districts had no control.[64] The only way to ensure compliance with local control provisions is to carefully structure the program. In many instances, this will mean ensuring that no local funds are utilized.

Gift Clauses

Finally, opponents may invoke anti-gift or anti-donation clauses, which are intended to prevent gratuitous giveaways to private individuals and corporations, to halt ESA programs.[65] Typically, programs are constitutional if they further a valid public purpose (such as education) and have a demonstrable benefit to the state (such as increased educational options for parents; increased competition and innovation in the educational marketplace; and even cost savings to the state from not having to educate ESA participants in the public school system).[66] In states with particularly robust anti-donation jurisprudence, lawmakers should consider designing ESA programs with cost-savings in mind to demonstrate both tangible and intangible benefits.

Unfortunately, this list of "Mickey Mouse" provisions is by no means exhaustive. Each state constitution must be studied to determine if it contains additional potential legal claims. Lawmakers, legislative staffers, state policy groups, and interested parents should also seek expert advice from constitutional lawyers with experience in drafting and defending ESA programs—such as the lawyers at the nonprofit Institute for Justice, who are always happy to review proposed educational programs and help bulletproof legislation free of charge.

COMPONENTS OF CONSTITUTIONALLY VIABLE ESA LEGISLATION

The primary appeal of ESA programs is the power they place in parents' hands to personalize an educational program for their children, rather than any sort of inherent or greater likelihood of withstanding constitutional challenge. However, there are at least four "universally" applicable components that will not only go a long way toward truly empowering parents, but may also strengthen the constitutional viability of ESA programs.

First, it should be clear that participating students do not need to enroll in a brick-and-mortar private school—or an online private school—as a full-time student. This means that the ESA agreement between the state and the parent, in which the parent promises to provide his or her child with a basic education, should, in and of itself, satisfy the state's compulsory education laws.

Second, to help parents provide their child with a basic education, and to entice entrepreneurs to provide innovative educational goods and services, policymakers should include as broad a range of educational options as possible. This includes the obvious: tuition, fees, and textbooks at private and online schools—but it should also include the authority to pay for individual classes and extracurricular activities at public schools. Participants should be able to pay for classes and materials at community colleges and universities while still in high school—but also save money for future college tuition. They should also be able to pay for college entrance and advance placement exams in addition to other tests to measure current achievement levels.

Parents should be able to access educational services outside of traditional educational institutions. This would include tutors—the qualifications for which should be defined as broadly as possible to permit a wide array of choices for parents. Students should be able to obtain special education and related services (such as speech and occupational therapy) without having to jump through hoops (such as being evaluated by their local education agency to determine if they are eligible for special education). Parents should be able to purchase not only curricula to use at home, but also the necessary supplemental materials to make particular curriculum work (such as lab supplies, additional reading materials, etc.). Lawmakers should also consider allowing parents to use their student's ESA funds to pay for transportation, consumable materials, and even electronic devices, software, and other learning aids.

Third, lawmakers should consider including a statutory right for participating parents to intervene as defendants in any legal or constitutional challenge to a program. Parents and students are the intended beneficiaries of ESA programs and they have discrete interests in the outcome of any lawsuit that seeks to strike down such programs. Indeed, in any legal challenge to an ESA program, it is the parents and students who have the most to gain or lose in the outcome of the case. They should be permitted the right to fully participate so as to have an independent voice in the litigation that is distinct from any named state defendants.

Fourth, while it is clear that educational choice programs do not constitute taxable income for purposes of federal law,[67] ESA programs should include language that the money deposited in each student's account is not taxable income for state income tax purposes.

ESA programs are just as likely as any other type of educational choice program to be subject to legal challenge. However, this reality should not curb enthusiasm for ESAs. In nearly every state, it is possible to design an ESA program that will have a high likelihood of withstanding a constitutional challenge. Policymakers must take the time to review their individual state constitutions for provisions that ESA opponents may invoke to halt the program. Then they must study their state's jurisprudence to understand how the courts interpret and apply those provisions. Taking these steps is essential to charting a course that will lead to a constitutionally defensible ESA program.

NOTES

1. Cain v. Horne (*Cain II*), 202 P.3d 1178 (Ariz. 2009).
2. *Cain II*, 202 P.3d at 1184, ¶ 26.

3. Ariz. Const. art. IX, § 10.

4. Niehaus v. Huppenthal, 310 P.3d 983, 988, ¶ 17 (Ariz. Ct. App. 2013).

5. Ariz. Rev. Stat. §§ 15-2401–15-2404 (2015) (Empowerment Scholarship Account Program); Fla. Stat. §§ 393.063 (2013), 1002.385 (2015) (Gardiner Scholarship Program); Miss. Code Ann. §§ 37-181-1–37-181-21 (2015) (Equal Opportunity for Students with Special Needs Program); S.B. 27, 109th Gen. Assemb., Reg. Sess. (Tenn. 2015) (Individualized Education Account Program); S.B. 302, 2015 Leg., 78th Sess. (Nev. 2015) (Education Savings Account Program). Montana Governor Steve Bullock vetoed the Special Needs Education Savings Account Program, H.B. 322, 64th Leg., Reg. Sess. (Mont. 2015); "Montana Governor Bullock Vetos Education Savings Account Legislation," *Excelined in Action*, May 1, 2015, http://www.excelinedinaction.org/disappointing-decision-by-mt-governor-bullock-to-veto-education-savings-account-legislation/. Virginia's Governor Terry McAuliffe vetoed the Parental Choice Education Savings Account Program, H.B. 389, 2016 Gen. Assemb., Reg. Sess. (Va. 2016); Patrick R. Gibbons, "Va. Governor Vetoes School Choice Bills," *redefinED*, April 7, 2016, available at https://www.redefine-donline.org/2016/04/virginia-governor-vetoes-education-savings-accounts-bill/.

6. Zelman v. Simmons-Harris, 536 U.S. 639 (2002).

7. George A. Clowes, "Voucher Wars Will Continue," *Heartland Institute*, July 1, 2003, http://news.heartland.org/newspaper-article/2003/07/01/voucher-wars-will-continue.

8. Schwartz v. Lopez, 132 Nev. Adv. Rep. 73 (Nev. Sept. 29, 2006).

9. Other associational plaintiffs included the People for the American Way, the Arizona Association of School Business Officials, the Arizona Federation of Teacher Unions, the Arizona Parent Teacher Association, the Arizona Rural Schools Association, Arizona School Administrators, Inc., and the Arizona School Boards Association. *See Cain II*, 202 P.3d 1178.

10. *Cain II*, 202 P.3d 1178.

11. Ariz. Const. art. IX, § 10.

12. *Cain II*, 202 P.3d at 1183, ¶ 23.

13. *Id*. at 1184, ¶ 26.

14. *Id*.

15. *Id*. at 1183, ¶ 22.

16. *Id*. at 1185, ¶ 29.

17. Archived video of the *Cain II* oral argument is available at http://supremes-tateaz.granicus.com/MediaPlayer.php?view_id=2&clip_id=1177.

18. Matthew Ladner & Nick Dranias, *Education Savings Accounts: Giving Parents Control of their Children's Education*, Goldwater Institute, 2011, 8–9. However, Dan Lips' 2005 white paper may have been the first detailed proposal of an ESA program. Dan Lips, *Education Savings Accounts: A Vehicle for School Choice*, Goldwater Institute, 2005.

19. *Cain II*, 202 P.3d at 1184, ¶ 26.

20. *Niehaus*, 310 P.3d at 987, ¶ 17.

21. Niehaus v. Huppenthal, 2014 Ariz. LEXIS 59 (Mar. 21, 2014) (denying review of *Niehaus*, 310 P.3d 983).

22. Ariz. Rev. Stat. § 15-2402(B)(1) (2015).

23. *See* note 5 above.

24. H.B. 84, 2016 Leg., Reg. Sess. (Ala. 2016); H.B. 243, 153d Gen. Assemb., Reg. Sess. (Ga. 2015); H.B. 427, 99th Gen. Assemb., Reg. Sess. (Ill. 2015); S.B. 93, 119th Gen. Assemb., 2d Reg. Sess. (Ind. 2016); H.B. File 2284, 86th Gen. Assemb. (Iowa 2016); S.B. 273, H.B. 620, 2016 Leg., Reg. Sess. (Ky. 2016); H.B. File 1529, 89th Leg. (Minn. 2015); S.B. 609, H.B. 2307, 98th Gen. Assemb., 2d Reg. Sess. (Mo. 2016); H.B. 916, Gen. Assemb., 2015–2016 Sess. (N.C. 2015); H.B. 2949, 55th Leg., 2d Reg. Sess. (Okla. 2016).

25. Clint Bolick, *Voucher Wars: Waging the Legal Battle over School Choice* (Washington, DC: CATO Institute, 2003),15–43.

26. The federal Constitution demands religious neutrality and therefore prohibits the wholesale exclusion of religious options from an otherwise generally available government aid program. *See, e.g.*, Everson v. Bd. of Educ., 330 U.S. 1, 16 (1947) (holding that the government "cannot exclude individual Catholics, Lutherans, Mohammedans, Baptists, Jews, Methodists, Non-believers, Presbyterians, or the members of any other faith, because of their faith, or lack of it, from receiving the benefits of public welfare legislation").

27. Richard D. Komer, "School Choice and State Constitutions' Religion Clauses," *Journal of School Choice* 3, no. 4 (2009).

28. *Schwartz*, 132 Nev. Adv. Rep. 73, slip op. at 16–18.

29. For a list of states with Blaine language in their constitution see Richard D. Komer & Olivia Grady, "School Choice and State Constitutions: A Guide to Designing School Choice Programs," *Institute for Justice and American Legislative Exchange Council*, September 2016, 16–102.

30. Mitchell v. Helms, 530 U.S. 793, 829 (2000) (plurality opinion).

31. Kotterman v. Killian, 972 P.2d 606, 624, ¶ 66 (Ariz. 1999).

32. *E.g.*, *Schwartz*, 132 Nev. Adv. Op. 73, slip op. at 24 (Nev. 2016); Meredith v. Pence, 984 N.E.2d 1213, 1228–29 (Ind. 2013); *Niehaus*, 310 P.3d at 987, ¶ 15; Griffith v. Bower, 747 N.E.2d 423, 426 (Ill. Ct. App. 2001); Toney v. Bower, 744 N.E.2d 351, 360–63 (Ill. Ct. App. 2001); *Kotterman*, 972 P.2d at 620, ¶ 46; Jackson v. Benson, 578 N.W.2d 602, 626–27, ¶¶ 81–82 (Wis. 1998).

33. Tyler Anbinder, *Nativism & Slavery: The Northern Know Nothings and the Politics of the 1850s* (New York, NY: Oxford Univ. Press, 1992), 271.

34. *Mitchell*, 530 U.S. at 828; *see also Zelman*, 536 U.S. 639, 721 (Breyer, J., dissenting) (explaining that references to "sectarian schools . . . in practical terms meant Catholic") (internal quotation marks omitted).

35. Lloyd P. Jorgenson, *The State and the Non-Public School: 1825-1925* (Columbia, MO: Univ. of Mo. Press, 1987), 69–72.

36. *Id.* at 60.

37. *Id.* at 83–85.

38. Anbinder, 95, 110–15.

39. *Id.* at 135–36.

40. Joseph P. Viteritti, "Blaine's Wake: School Choice, the First Amendment, and State Constitutional Law," *Harvard Journal of Law & Public Policy* 21, no. 3 (1998), 621.

41. Joseph P. Viteritti, "Choosing Equality: Religious Freedom and Educational Opportunity Under Constitutional Federalism," *Yale Law & Policy Review* 15, no. 1 (1996), 146; *see also* Steven K. Green, "The Blaine Amendment Reconsidered," *American Journal of Legal History* 36, no. 1 (1992), 38–96.

42. *Mitchell*, 530 U.S. at 829.

43. *See* note 29 above.

44. Historically, educational choice programs that serve children with disabilities have not been subjected to legal challenge as often as other types of school choice programs.

45. Nev. Const. art. XI, § 10.

46. Arizona's Aid Clause is unusual among Blaine amendments because it prohibits "aid" to both sectarian and non-sectarian schools and not just "sectarian" schools. Only Alaska, Hawaii, New Mexico, and South Carolina have similarly worded provisions. Alaska Const. art. VII, § 1; Haw. Const. art. X, § 1; N.M. Const. art. XII, § 4; S.C. Const. art. XI, § 4. Some state constitutions contain language prohibiting appropriations to schools not under the exclusive control of the state or public school officials, which could be seen as similar prohibitions. *See* Ala. Const. art. IV, § 73; Cal. Const. art. IX, § 8; Colo. Const. art. V, § 34; Miss. Const. art. IV, § 66; Neb. Const. art. VII, § 11 (1); and Wyo. Const. art. III, § 36.

47. *Schwartz*, 132 Nev. Adv. Op. 73, slip op. at 24.

48. While the Nevada Supreme Court did uphold the Nevada ESA program's constitutionality, the court also concluded that the legislature failed to appropriate any money to fund the ESA program. *Lopez*, 193 Nev. Adv. Op. 73, slip op. at 31 ("the record is devoid of any evidence that the legislature included an appropriation to fund the education savings accounts"). As of this writing, the Nevada legislature still has not appropriated any money to fund the program.

49. *Compare* Ariz. Const. art. IX, § 10 ("No tax shall be laid or appropriation of public money made in aid of any church, or private or sectarian school, or any public service corporation.") *with* Nev. Const. art. XI, § 10 ("No public funds of any kind or character whatever, State, County or Municipal, shall be used for sectarian purpose.").

50. Eighty-three percent of all ESA funds in Arizona were expended on private school tuition between the fourth quarter of 2013–2014 and 2014–2015. Jonathan Butcher & Lindsey Burke, "The Education Debit Card II," Friedman Foundation for Educational Choice, 2016.

51. And, in reality, the private school marketplace in all states is characterized by a preponderance of religious schools.

52. Jason Bedrick, Jonathan Butcher, & Clint Bolick, "Taking Credit for Education: How to Fund Education Savings Accounts through Tax Credits," *CATO Institute*, 2016.

53. Six cases involved school choice programs. Ariz. Christian Sch. Tuition Org. v. Winn, 563 U.S. 125, 144 (2011); McCall v. Scott, 199 So. 3d 359 (Fla. 1st DCA 2016) Magee v. Boyd, 175 So. 3d 79, 136 (Ala. 2015); *Kotterman*, 972 P.2d at 618, ¶ 40; *Toney*, 744 N.E.2d at 357; *Griffith*, 747 N.E.2d at 426. The other cases involved other types of tax credits. Manzara v. State, 343 S.W.3d 656, 661 (Mo. 2011); State Bldg. & Constr. Trades Council v. Duncan, 162 Cal. App. 4th 289, 294, 299 (2008); Olson v. State, 742 N.W.2d 681, 683 (Minn. Ct. App. 2007).

54. Neil Cogan, ed., *The Complete Bill of Rights: The Drafts, Debates, Sources, and Origins* (Oxford Univ. Press, 1997); *see also* note 27 above.

55. Chittenden Town Sch. Dist. v. Vermont Dep't of Educ., 738 A.2d 539 (1999).

56. *Schwartz*, 132 Nev. Adv. Op. 73, slip op. at 17–18; *Meredith*, 984 N.E.2d at 1224, n. 17; Hart v. State, 774 S.E.2d 281, 289–90 (N.C. 2015); Simmons-Harris v. Goff, 711 N.E.2d 203, 212 & n.2 (Ohio 1999); *Jackson*, 578 N.W.2d at 628; Davis v. Grover, 480 N.W.2d 460, 474 (Wis. 1992). *But see* Bush v. Holmes, 919 So. 2d 392, 405 (Fla. 2006) (striking down voucher program).

57. *Meredith*, 984 N.E.2d at 1223.

58. *Id. See also Davis*, 480 N.W.2d at 474.

59. Requiring private schools to accept the ESA amount as full tuition could discourage many private schools from participating, especially considering that the actual cost of educating students often exceeds tuition. For students whose parents cannot afford the difference, there are often private endowments and other discounts and scholarships that can level the playing field and make even the most elite private schools accessible to the most impoverished families.

60. *Meredith*, 984 N.E.2d at 1224; *Jackson*, 578 N.W.2d at 627.

61. *See* Faasse v. Scott, No. 2014-CA-1859 (Fla. Cir. Ct. Dec. 30, 2014) (dismissing case with prejudice), available at http://miamiherald.typepad.com/files/the-motion-here.pdf.

62. *E.g.*, *Davis*, 480 N.W.2d at 469.

63. For example, the Louisiana Supreme Court, in *Louisiana Fed'n of Teachers v. State*, 18 So. 3d 1033 (La. 2013), struck down a voucher program that relied on a constitutionally mandated public school funding mechanism, but left the state free to fund the program from annual appropriations from the state general fund.

64. Owens v. Colorado Congress of Parents, 92 P.2d 933 (Colo. 2004).

65. *Kotterman*, 972 P.2d at 621, ¶ 52.

66. *Toney*, 744 N.E.2d at 353; *Kotterman*, 972 P.2d at 621, ¶¶ 51–52.

67. U.S. Department of the Treasury: Internal Revenue Service, *Publication 970: Tax Benefits for Education* Cat. No. 25221V (2015), available at https://www.irs.gov/pub/irs-pdf/p970.pdf.

Chapter Three

Education Savings Accounts

The Great Unbundling of K–12 Education

Adam Peshek

In 2005, Dan Lips—then a policy analyst with the Heritage Foundation—wrote the report *Education Savings Accounts: A Vehicle for School Choice.*[1] In it, he detailed a vision for the future of educational choice where "instead of channeling children's education funding through the public education system, the government would deposit those funds directly into a child's [education savings account]" which could be used to pay for a school of their parents' choice "or pay for other qualified education expenses such as tutoring," with unspent funds accumulating that parents could eventually use for their child's college or a job training program. Lips noted that this proposed system of replacing the way the government funds education with a system of funding individual accounts represented a "revolutionary proposal."

Yet, this revolutionary proposal has come a long way in the past decade. By 2015, five states had enacted education savings account (ESA) programs. An additional sixteen states had ESA legislation proposed in that year alone. This chapter explores the growth of ESAs and examines the differences between the existing five programs. It addresses the administrative challenges and lessons learned so far, including how administrators are adapting tools and practices from healthcare, banking, and technology to create an entirely new way of operationalizing choice and customization. Finally, the chapter provides examples of how state leaders can move forward to create a parent-friendly, accountable, and dynamic education marketplace suited for the twenty-first century (figure 3.1).

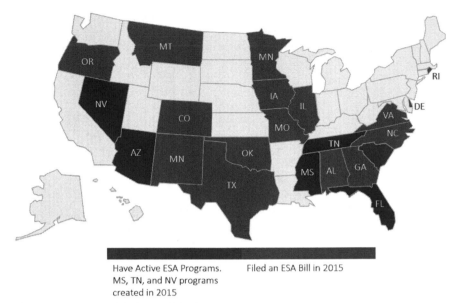

Have Active ESA Programs.   Filed an ESA Bill in 2015
MS, TN, and NV programs
created in 2015

Figure 3.1   ESA Legislative Activity in 2015.

DEMAND FOR CHOICE AND CUSTOMIZATION

Parent demand for more choice and customization is clear from polling. In 2013, EdChoice conducted a study of nearly one thousand Georgia parents whose children received a scholarship to attend a private school. The researchers, Benjamin Scafidi and James P. Kelly, surveyed this economically diverse set of parents to learn more about what they looked for in a school.[2]

Figure 3.2 shows the distribution of parents' top three reasons for choosing their child's school. Their responses show that parents have a wide array of priorities for their child's education. They care about discipline, safety, and the learning environment. Some parents place a high value on the influences and peer group that a child is surrounded by. Others place a challenging "every child must go to college" environment or high student test scores at the top of their list.

It would be difficult to characterize any of these responses as "wrong." The diversity of responses reflects an intuitive understanding that all children are unique and what is ideal for one child may not be the right approach for another.

Also in 2013, Dara Zeehandelaar and Amber Northern at the Fordham Institute began asking similar questions. They wondered: "Is it possible to segment the parent market into identifiable groups, each with distinctive preferences?" Working with the polling firm Harris Interactive, they approached

Response	Percent
Better student discipline	40.3%
Improved student safety	37.7%
Better learning environment	31.6%
Better education	28.9%
Smaller class sizes	25.9%
More individual attention	23.2%
Religious education	21.0%
Better college preparation	15.8%
Greater sense of community	15.5%
Better teachers	13.7%
More responsive teachers/administrators	10.2%
More attention to the unique needs of my child	6.9%
Better peer influences	5.8%
Higher standardized test scores	4.2%
Other parents concerned about child's education	3.8%
Greater respect for my rights as a parent	3.1%

Figure 3.2   Top Three Reasons Surveyed Parents Sent Their Child to a Private School.

More extracurricular opportunities	2.0%
More tutorial/supplemental learning services	2.0%
Less gang activity	1.9%
Other	1.9%
Less time wasted during the school day	1.3%
More opportunities for parental involvement	1.1%

Figure 3.2   *(continued)*

the topic as market researchers, surveying more than two-thousand parents nationwide to learn more about the educational goals for their children and the attributes they look for in schools.[3]

They discovered that most parents want their child to attend a school with "a strong core curriculum in reading and math; an emphasis on science, technology, engineering, and math (STEM); and the development of good study habits, strong critical thinking skills, and excellent verbal and written communication skills." But beyond these foundational responsibilities, Zeehandelaar and Northern developed six archetypes of parents based on their deeper preferences:

- Pragmatists—desire for real-world training.
- Jeffersonians—emphasis on instruction in citizenship, democracy, and leadership.
- Test-Score Hawks—valuing high test scores.
- Multiculturalists—parents who value learning how to work with people from diverse backgrounds.
- Expressionists—emphasis on arts and music instruction.
- Strivers—parents who prioritize their children being accepted to a top-tier college.

Implicit in both studies' findings is the acknowledgment that there is no perfect school. Some students thrive in a school with uniforms and a demerit system, while others do better in a more relaxed environment. One child may excel in a technology-rich school that relies heavily on computers, while their sibling may do better in a school that emphasizes history's great books and a learning environment that mirrors the classroom of their grandparents.

The goal of a school is not just about filling students' brains with the knowledge contained in the "eat your broccoli" STEM subjects. Or, as the band Radiohead once expressed with an ominous robotic voice, making sure that students are "fitter, happier, more productive . . . getting on better with associate employee contemporaries."[4] Education should also be about learning in the environment that is best suited to one's personal needs, without forcing that type of learning on all other students.

As John Katzman recently noted in a paper commissioned by the American Enterprise Institute (AEI), the role of competition in marketplaces tends to be overemphasized while the benefit of matching, or "fit," tends to be left out of the conversation. "There doesn't need to be an objectively best school, teacher, curriculum, or ed tech company," Katzman writes. "There is the right school for your son or daughter, or the right technology or curriculum for your school." Choice is not merely about entering the ring with four opponents and emerging as the last man standing. As Katzman notes, "In a marketplace, players differentiate themselves and optimize for their target audience."[5]

Yet, instead of catering to parents' unique demands for their child's school, our public system of education treats schools as interchangeable cogs in a system that sorts students based on their home address. While sorting based on zip code may be the ideal way to deliver mail, it is far from the ideal way to sort children for education.

Thus, the history of school choice in America has been an attempt to separate the government's role as both the funder and vendor of education. This effort has taken two primary forms: private school choice and charter schools. These policies do something small, yet radical: instead of receiving students based on attendance zones, they must attract and retain students. These policies have grown consistently for the past twenty years, with an estimated 2.9 million students in charter schools and 400,000 students in a private school choice program in 2016.

These policies are huge advancements, but they still require parents to choose one school building where all services are expected to be bundled. Yet, this whole-school model does not reflect the world we live in today. As John Katzman observes:

> If we tossed our entire education system out and rebuilt it from scratch with the present and future in mind, the result would likely bear no resemblance to what we have today. Our public K–12 system was founded with an Industrial Revolution-era mindset, and we should never have expected it to prepare an increasingly diverse student population for college. The only surprise is that anyone would continue proposing top down, one-size-fits-all processes to

improve on it. We need to test whether a civil approach to education reform—
where students and educators are empowered to find the schools and tools that
best fit their needs—might accomplish more.[6]

Enter ESAs. Through an ESA program, the state deposits a participating
child's education funds into an account that is managed by parents under state
supervision. With an ESA, parents are able to direct their child's funding to
the schools, courses, programs, and services of their choice. Funds can be
spent on tuition, tutoring, therapies for students with special needs, advanced
coursework or exams, online courses, savings for college, and many other
state-approved expenses. The goal of ESA programs is to allow parents
to plan for their child's unique needs and in the process create a personal
approach to education, where the ultimate goal is maximizing their child's
natural learning abilities.

An ESA allows education to be nimble, adapt to changes, and constantly
improve through micro experiments that need not apply to an entire school
system—a system that changes course with the efficiency and speed of a
sixteenth century Spanish galleon. With an ESA, one does not need to go to a
raucous school board meeting to determine what books to teach or not teach.
You do not need a lobbyist in the statehouse advocating for an increase in
music funding at the expense of computer science. You do not need a three-
year study committee to determine when it is most effective to teach a child
a foreign language. All you need is a parent who values one of these subjects
and an option to pursue it.

The key is customization. Parents are no longer relegated to just school
A or school B. A child can attend a private school and use funds to receive
speech therapy, or they can learn math and science online, English and history
at home, get tutored twice a week, and save any leftover funds for college.
Through an ESA, education is no longer "use it or lose it." Parents decide
where the best values are and have the ability to direct their child's funds in
the most efficient way.

Each state ESA law differs, but many of the common allowable expenses
include

- tuition, textbooks, and fees at participating nonpublic schools;
- tutoring;
- online learning programs and courses;
- curriculum and instructional materials;
- fees for specialized or advanced courses, testing, certifications, and college
  entrance exams;
- services for students with disabilities, such as therapy from licensed
  providers;

- dual enrollment;
- computer hardware, software, and assistive technology for students who require them for learning (such as a talking computer for blind students);
- contracted services provided by a public school or district, including individual classes and extracurricular programs;
- transportation (usually limited to $500–750 a year);
- fees for account management; and
- savings for future K–12 or higher education expenses.

The ability to save unused funds for future K–12 and/or higher education expenses creates an incentive for parents to judge all K–12 expenses not only on quality but also on cost. This is an important distinction between ESAs and traditional private choice programs.

THE PROGRAMS

The five existing ESA programs differ dramatically in both design and function. Figure 3.3 summarizes some of the key differences, each of which are discussed in detail in this section.

Student Eligibility

The most obvious starting point for state lawmakers is to determine what types of students are eligible to participate in the program, whether it is limited to current public school students, and whether to cap the total number of participants.

Nevada lawmakers took the boldest approach in 2015 when they passed the nation's first near-universal ESA program. Once fully implemented, any student in the state who was in a public school for at least one hundred consecutive days prior to applying will be able to participate, as well as entering kindergarteners and children of active-duty military members. This creates the most expansive private educational choice program in the country, giving eligibility to at least 93 percent of students in the state.[7]

The Nevada program initially launched on January 1, 2016 and the first dispersing of funds was scheduled to take place in February. However, groups opposed to the program filed lawsuits to block the program from being implemented. In September 2016, the Nevada Supreme Court ruled that while ESAs are constitutional, the funding mechanism used in the program's authorizing legislation is not. At the time of this writing, approximately 8,000 applications have been received for the program, which remains dormant until state lawmakers create an alternative funding mechanism.[8]

	Arizona	Florida	Mississippi	Tennessee	Nevada
	Empowerment Scholarship Accounts	Gardiner Scholarships	Education Scholarship Accounts	Individualized Education Accounts	Education Savings Accounts
Year Enacted	2011	2014	2015	2015	2015
Student Eligibility	• Special needs • 'D' & 'F' schools • Military • Foster care • Native Amer. reservations • Siblings	Certain disabilities (cerebral palsy, Down syndrome, autism, etc.)	Special needs (IEP) Capped at 500 new participants per year	Certain students with special needs (IEP)	Nearly universal eligibility
Prior Public School Enrollment Requirement	Yes (military exempt)	No	Yes	Yes (K exempt)	Yes (military, K-1 exempt)
Funding	Formula	Appropriation	Appropriation	Formula	*TBD*
ESA Amount	90% of state funds, plus charter school assistance and special needs weights	90% of state and local funds, with weights	$6,500	100% of state funds with special needs weights	100% of state funds for IEP and FRL 90% for all other students
Administrator	Dept. of Ed.	Nonprofits	Dept. of Ed.	Dept. of Ed.	Treasurer
Admin. Fee	3%	3%	6%	4%	3%
Account Structure	Debit Cards	Reimbursement, preapproval, purchase order	Reimbursement	Debit Cards	Reimbursement, preapproval, purchase order
Testing	None	State or national norm-reference test	None	State or national norm-reference test	State or national norm-reference test

Figure 3.3   ESA Programs Overview.

Arizona has opted for the slow-and-steady approach. When the state's Empowerment Scholarship Account program launched in 2011, it was limited to students with special needs. Since then, state lawmakers have expanded eligibility to include children in "D" or "F" rated public schools, military families, foster children, children living on Native American reservations, and siblings of participating students. This approach has allowed the program

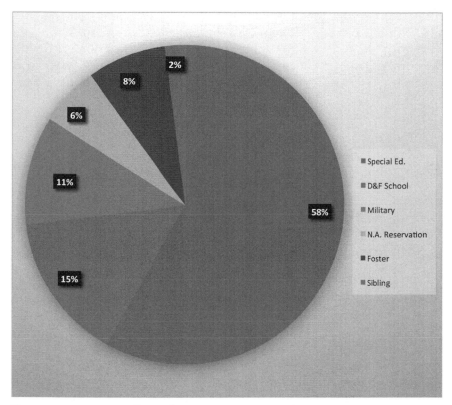

Figure 3.4   AZ ESA Enrollment by Category, 2015–2016.

to slowly grow to meet the needs of several unique student populations. The ability for siblings to participate allows families to educate their children in the same setting, should they choose. The program has effectively doubled in participation each year, starting with 144 students in 2011 and reaching 2,406 in 2015 (figure 3.4).

Mississippi, Tennessee, and Florida limit their programs to students with special needs. Mississippi's Education Scholarship Account Program gives eligibility to all students in the state with an individualized education plan (IEP) but caps enrollment at 500 new students each year. If more students apply than there are available spots, the state holds a random lottery.

Tennessee's Individualized Education Accounts were created to serve special needs students with an IEP who meet one of seven different disability types that reflect the more severe end of the disability spectrum. The state estimates that there are approximately 18,000 students who meet eligibility statewide.[9]

The Florida ESA program, Gardiner Scholarships, awards eligibility to roughly a dozen types of disabilities, including cerebral palsy, Down syndrome, autism, muscular dystrophy, and other conditions that represent the more-severe end of the disability spectrum. Identifying specific disabilities instead of vague IEP categories has allowed the state to take the unique approach of allowing students to gain eligibility through a diagnosis from a doctor. This allows current private and homeschool children with eligible disabilities to participate in the program.

The ability to include current private and homeschool students in the program is also unique to Florida. In all other ESA programs—and most private school choice programs—students must have prior public school attendance to participate. This requirement allows lawmakers to show that a program has no fiscal impact on the state's coffers: the state was already contributing to the child's education in a public school and allowing them to participate in the choice program merely changes where the money goes.

States often propose allowing students entering kindergarten or first grade to enter immediately into the program, without having to first attend a public school. The logic is simple: depending on the state, there is approximately a 90 percent chance that the state would be paying for the child's education in a public elementary school and giving them eligibility to participate should not increase the amount the state is paying for education. Additionally, requiring a student to go to a year of public school to gain eligibility, just to leave the school in their second year, is more disruptive and costly than letting them exercise choice to begin with. A state could easily extend this logic to students entering middle and high school (typically sixth and ninth grades). Though no state has proposed it yet, this approach could allow sizable eligibility while still giving schools a multiyear time horizon to plan for enrollment increases or declines, which they are already doing for natural enrollment changes.

Some states feel the need to cap enrollment. Instead of an arbitrary amount, states could also propose capping participation as a percentage of the state's total public school enrollment. This was proposed in a bill in Georgia in 2015, where lawmakers proposed capping participation to half of one percent of the state's total enrollment in the first year of implementation and one percent in the second year. This approach allows state lawmakers to avert arguments that a program will dramatically siphon students from public schools, while still creating sizable eligibility pools. In Georgia, for example, half of one percent of total public school enrollment was approximately 8,000 students—likely far more than would apply in the program's first year.

Account Funding

Three states—Arizona, Nevada, and Tennessee—fund ESAs at the amount the state would have spent on the child in a public school. In Arizona, ESA students receive 90 percent of what they would have received in a public school plus the additional assistance the state gives to students in charter schools. Since charters do not have the power to levy local taxes for education like school districts, the state provides $1,735 per charter student in grades K–8 and $2,022 per high schooler. While not completely equitable with public school funding, this amount helps split the difference. For students with special needs, the state also includes the various funding weights that a student would get, which can increase an ESA amount considerably, depending on the severity of the disability.

Florida has the most generous funding, awarding students the equivalent of 90 percent of all the state *and* local funding the student would have received in a public school as calculated through the state's funding formula, including any additional weights the student would receive based on the severity of their disability. Mississippi is the outlier, opting to fund their eligible students at a flat $6,500, regardless of their disability.

Program Funding

The easiest way to fund accounts is through the state's education funding formula. While there will be nuances across states, this is typically done by counting students in the enrollment figures of their resident school district for the purposes of calculating the aid that the state would have sent if they were attending their local public school. Then, the state either subtracts this amount from the state aid payable to the district or places that amount directly into the student's account. This process is easier administratively and ensures that there is no fiscal impact on the state, since it is merely reallocating existing funds. A version of this method has been created in Arizona and Tennessee. The Nevada program also went this route, though the nuances of its constitution and funding formula led the Nevada Supreme Court to determine that lawmakers could not do this type of redirecting without separately accounting for ESA students in addition to district students.[10]

For various political, legal, and administrative reasons, some states choose to fund the program through a direct appropriation from the legislature. This was the case in Florida, where lawmakers chose to fund the program outside of the education budget in order to fund eligible private and homeschool students. Had they not done this, the entrance of these students into the program would have increased the state's education budget since they were not previously paying for their education in a public school. While direct appropriations may be necessary due to a state's particular context, it almost always results in making the program a political target, with opponents attempting to defund the program each year.

Program Administrator

The best agency or organization to implement the ESA program will be different in each state. But, at a minimum, they need to have the capacity, drive, and desire to properly implement the program for the long term. This means an administrator that is open to trying new, innovative, and out-of-the-box approaches to implementation.

In some cases, that may be the state department of education. However, it is most often not. Many departments have proven to be antagonistic or indifferent to choice programs. Those that are not may still be unable to see the proverbial forest for the trees. They are often too close to the world of compliance and micromanaging educational initiatives that they ignore the big picture of building effective processes, while spending their time pondering over policy nuances that they assume were overlooked by lawmakers when crafting the program. A more fundamental task for an administrator is to create a system that is user-friendly while still safeguarding against the possibility of financial fraud.

Nevada's decision to administer the program through the State Treasurer's Office has proven successful. State treasurers regularly deal with flows of money, contract with financial vendors, and often run the state's college savings, scholarship, and prepaid tuition programs. From the start, the Nevada Treasurer's Office focused its attention toward the important questions, such as how many staff are needed to run the program effectively, how to operationalize parent accounts, ways to monitor for fraud, how to approve providers, and many other fundamental tasks.

Another administrative approach is to task qualified nonprofit organizations with implementation. This is a particularly good option in states with existing tax-credit scholarship programs, which are already administered by nonprofit scholarship organizations. This is the path that Florida has chosen, where two scholarship organizations are the primary administrators of the state's ESA program. The Florida Department of Education performs some administrative duties, such as maintaining the official list of approved providers, determining student funding levels, and various oversight responsibilities over the scholarship organizations. Most functions, however, are handled entirely by the scholarship organizations.

The nonprofit model has proven effective in Florida. Scholarship organizations' independence allows them to operate much more nimbly than departments of education. They can test new methods and improve in real time. Step Up For Students—the largest scholarship organization in the state—has been the primary organization for the state's tax-credit scholarship program for fifteen years, with nearly 70,000 students served in the 2015–2016 school year. Because of their size and experience, Step Up For Students has been able to effectively market the ESA program and provide a level of awareness that the first state with an ESA program, Arizona, has not been able to accomplish with a department of education administrator. Despite Arizona's program being in place longer and having a much larger pool of eligible applicants, the Florida program saw more enrollment in its first year (1,655 students) than Arizona had by its fourth (1,311).

If a government body is selected to administer the program, lawmakers should still allow them to contract with qualified nonprofits to implement some or all parts of the program. This will give the administrator the flexibility to outsource parts of the program to third parties who may be better equipped to administer them.

Administrative Fees

An administrative fee is a necessary part of an ESA program. As detailed below, ESAs are far more complicated to implement than traditional private school choice programs and require resources and manpower to launch and administer. All existing programs provide an administrative fee, ranging from three to six percent of total program funding.

As with a voucher or tax-credit program, an ESA administrator has to perform initial tasks like building a website, hiring staff, and creating resources for parents. But unlike a traditional choice program, an ESA program requires the administrator to establish application and eligibility guidelines for at least half-a-dozen types of nonschool providers, create the actual system of accounts and forms of payment, and contract with a financial institution or manager. All of these differences also lead the administrator to engage in much more detailed rulemaking than a voucher program.

Since many of the costs are greater in early years, another option is to create administrative fees that gradually taper off over time as administrators benefit from economies of scale. In a recent legislative proposal, lawmakers in Alabama proposed setting fees at 6 percent for the first three years of implementation and 4 percent thereafter.

Startup Funding

An administrator will also have significant expenses before students enroll and administrative fees begin to generate, so it is wise to provide startup funds before a program launches. The most obvious way to accomplish this is to provide funding in the authorizing legislation or in the state's budget. Tennessee allocated $199,000 in new state expenditures for three positions to manage the program: a director, a finance position, and an administrative assistant. In Nevada, the State Treasurer's Office went through the process of taking out a legislatively approved loan of $116,000 for certain parts of their administration.[11]

IMPLEMENTING ESA PROGRAMS

Administrative choices are particularly important because, regardless of how detailed an ESA bill may be, a great deal of a program's effectiveness will be determined in implementation. This is why, as noted earlier, administrators must possess the freedom and wherewithal to strategically plan for a user-friendly and appropriately regulated program.

The most fundamental task will be to determine the actual structure of the ESA account. When designing the account, the goal should be to balance two seemingly opposing goals. The first is to have effective controls in place to ensure that funds are only spent in approved ways. Especially in early years, ESA programs will be held under intense scrutiny and controlling for fraud is the most important key to a program's long-term prospects. Second, however, should be to create a program that is user-friendly. Creating burdensome systems that are difficult to use defeats the purpose of empowering parents to make choices for their children.

So far, states have taken one of two approaches—reimbursement/claims or debit cards—but a more effective method may be waiting to be executed.

Reimbursement Systems

On the burdensome end of the spectrum, states have employed reimbursement systems that require parents to make payments out-of-pocket and submit reimbursements to the state. This type of system is problematic for two reasons. First, it is unfair to parents who may not be able to afford to pay for tuition and services up front and wait for a reimbursement from the state. One way that states with reimbursement systems have attempted to alleviate this is by also including pre-authorization systems that allow a parent to submit expenses up front to have the administrator pay for the expense directly or fast track the parent's reimbursement claim.

The second problematic aspect of a reimbursement system is its scalability challenges. The claims processes needed for a reimbursement system are labor-intensive, time-consuming, and bureaucratic—especially once a program reaches several thousand participants. An example of this complexity can be seen in Florida, where the nonprofit organization Step Up For Students administers both the state's ESA program and tax-credit scholarship program. In the 2014–2015 school year, there were 69,950 students attending 1,533 participating schools under the tax-credit scholarship program.[12] In the same year, the organization had 1,579 students with 9,505 expenses and 1,923 preauthorizations submitted under the ESA program.[13] This goes from a private school scholarship program with one brick-and-mortar school for every forty-six participating students to an ESA program with seven expenses for every participating student.

Some have argued that a reimbursement system's main benefit is that it is less prone to fraud, since a human is reviewing each expense. This could be the case, but it is this author's opinion that human error is just as likely to occur, especially as enrollment grows and parents begin to acclimate to the idea of directing funds to various nonschool expenses.

ESA Debit Cards

Arizona adopted debit cards for their ESA program in 2011, and many ESA supporters have advocated for their use ever since. If reimbursement systems represent the burdensome end of the spectrum, debit cards represent the opposite end—allowing parents to spend funds relatively freely on the front end and submit receipts at the end of each quarter for administrators to reconcile purchases to accounts.

Use-restricted debit cards have a long history with government programs, including health savings accounts, food stamps, and many other programs. These systems rely on the use of merchant category codes (MCC)—a four-digit number assigned to a business by credit card companies once they are authorized to accept credit cards as a form of payment. The MCC is used to classify a business based on the type of goods and services it provides. For example, the MCC code for "elementary and secondary schools" is 8211, "child care services" is 8351, "medical services and health practitioners" is 8099, and others.

To operationalize its ESA program, the Arizona Department of Education has authorized thirty-seven different types of MCC codes.[14] In practice, this means that a parent can go to a "trade or vocational school" (MCC code 8249) and a debit card purchase will go through, but if they attempt to swipe the card at a liquor store (MCC code 5921) the card will be declined.

While this is more parent-friendly than a reimbursement model, it still has downsides. MCC codes are relatively broad and may not adequately distinguish between purchases that should and should not be made with an ESA account. For instance, at least one parent in Arizona was able to buy a big screen TV with their child's ESA funds because it was purchased at Wal-Mart, which meets the broad MCC code category of "discount stores."[15] MCC codes were never designed to limit a parent's ability to buy educational services and the only way to make them work practically for this purpose is to include similarly broad codes.

From the outset, the goal in Arizona was to eventually incorporate product-level codes into the system. In theory, this would allow a parent to go to an MCC-verified retailer and buy a foreign language product like Rosetta Stone but not a television. While this sounds good in theory, it seems unlikely to be possible in the foreseeable future. Product-level codes are possible in health-care because the use of health savings accounts, flexible spending accounts, and other consumer-directed health plans have necessitated the creation of a standard inventory list to comply with Internal Revenue Service requirements for transactions using these types of accounts.[16] That is why a shopper with an HSA can go to a drug store and a transaction will go through for medicine, but not for a magazine or a bottle of water. Until there is a large enough market for ESA transactions, the ability to get to product codes in any state is unlikely.

While it could be argued that the system is working since administrators are catching fraud after it happens, states would be wise to pursue a system that prevents misuse from happening in the first place.

Online Payment Systems

An online payment platform could prove to be the most effective option for account management. Through an online payment system, an administrator could limit payments to and from approved parents and vendors, track and approve all transactions in real time, allow parents to upload receipts immediately via a smartphone app, require both parties in the transaction to identify what the payment was for, and other advantages that give the administrator up-to-the-minute information on funding flows.

This system also has the potential to significantly reduce administrative costs. It makes accounting and auditing much easier, since the system automatically creates a paper trail of all transactions, which would otherwise need to be done manually by reconciling paper receipts with statements. Online payment systems can also limit the number of actual funded accounts that need to be maintained. Unlike a debit card system, which deposits money into individual accounts, an online payment system can facilitate the use of "notional" or shell accounts.

The Nevada ESA program provides an example of how this can work. The administrator of the program, the Nevada State Treasurer's Office, holds one omnibus bank account with all program funds. If the program enrolls 4,000 students who each receive $5,000, then one bank account would hold all $20 million. The Treasurer's Office is implementing a hybrid, quasi-online payment system that allows parents to be reimbursed, submit for preapproval, or use an online portal to direct funds to an approved school or provider.

The office has contracted with BenefitWallet, a company with experience in account management in fields like health savings accounts. BenefitWallet developed Nevada's online portal and interface, acts as the record keeper, and is the intermediary between the Treasurer's Office, the omnibus bank account, the parent, and the provider. A parent can log on to the ESA portal, review their account balance, and direct funds to the provider of their choice. Once this happens, the provider receives an email and must accept the payment and verify that it is for what the parent indicated. This process can also happen in the reverse, with the school or provider initiating the payment and the parent verifying. Once a payment is verified, the Treasurer's Office reviews and forwards to BenefitWallet, who then facilitates the payment from the omnibus account. All of this is done online through one seamless interface.

A difficult aspect of ESA administration deals with the ability for parents to purchase curriculum, instructional materials, limited amounts of school supplies, and other "grey area" purchases. As noted, Arizona administrators most often deal with these scenarios by requiring parents to submit receipts for review after a purchase has been made. If an unauthorized purchase is made, a parent is then required to reimburse the account. This is an inefficient process that can take weeks to finalize. A more efficient process could be the utilization of an online environment that allows administrators to tap into the various application programming interfaces (APIs) from online retailers that allow parents to access products through third-party websites.

An example of a firm that could be tapped for this type of system is ClassWallet, which uses cloud-based software and an online interface to create a parent- and administrator-friendly system. Parents can log in to their ClassWallet account to monitor their available funds, review purchases, send payments to participating providers, make payments through an online purchase order, or even use their concierge purchasing service to purchase approved items twenty-four hours a day.

ClassWallet has an e-commerce portal of more than forty-five (and growing) online retailers that could also be utilized. For example, a parent can go to Amazon.com through this portal and search for an item they need. But instead of sending them to the traditional checkout page, ClassWallet uses an API that takes the parent's shopping cart back to the administrator. From there, staff can either approve a purchase with a click of a mouse or even create specific rules, such as not requiring preapproval for specific items or those under a certain dollar amount.

One major benefit of this system is the ability to give administrators a real-time, product-level description of all purchases in their system, eliminating the need to reconcile paper receipts. It is conceivable that an administrator could even utilize an online marketplace to limit purchases to specific departments—for example, allowing purchases to happen within the book department but not automotive department—adding an extra layer of fraud prevention.

FUTURE OF ESA IMPLEMENTATION: ONE-STOP, FULL-SERVICE WEBSITES

An online payment system could be easily integrated into what could be the future of ESA implementation—a one-stop, full-service website managed by ESA administrators, where

- parents apply for the program;
- vendors apply and are listed for parents and the public to browse;
- parents monitor, manage, and pay for services;
- parents keep track of their child's "portfolio" of educational endeavors (schools they've attended, their grades, tutors they've visited, certificates they earned);
- administrators monitor the flow of money in real time;
- administrators utilize e-commerce platforms to narrow what parents are able to purchase;
- parents flag bad actors to help the state prioritize investigations;
- parents rate experiences with providers; and
- parents can participate in secure social forums to learn from the experiences of others.

Applications

One of the areas that ESA administrators have struggled with the most is the application process. Unfortunately, these applications often resemble the same systems in place before the advent of the internet: obtaining forms, filling them out by hand, copying forms of identification and various student records, and faxing or mailing them in.

As cumbersome as this is for the parent, it is even more difficult and time-consuming for administrators to go through these documents, enter written information into a database, follow up on mistakes, respond to parent requests for status updates, and properly identify and store this information. A full-service website would allow ESA administrators to rely on technology to streamline many of these processes.

Through an application portal, parents could complete the application process online for multiple children. If a parent neglects to input required information, the platform could automatically notify the parent and let them know that information is required before they can continue the rest of the application (applicants often leave out required information on paper applications). Through this portal, parents could upload required documents, edit existing applications as needed, check their status, and perform many other tasks that would otherwise require an administrator's time and effort.

Administrators could plug into existing student databases to automatically match a child's information to existing student records to seamlessly verify a student's eligibility. For instance, most programs will have at least a few eligibility requirements prior to enrollment in a public school, student IEPs, eligibility for the government's free or reduced-price lunch program, or many other characteristics that could be easily verified through existing databases.

In most scenarios, administrators would be wise to simply adopt existing systems developed by private firms. For instance, there are several companies that have created innovative and parent-friendly enrollment systems for charter schools. One company, SchoolMint, provides administrators with an online dashboard detailing the status of all applicants: who has been approved, declined, enrolled, waitlisted, and so on. With a click of a mouse, administrators can immediately send updates to individual parents, all parents with an incomplete application, all denied parents, and so on. They also provide the tools to conduct randomized lotteries in the event that more students apply than are able to participate. For entrepreneurial administrators, SchoolMint generates maps of where applicants are clustered, how parents first learned about the program, which type of marketing has brought in the most applicants, and many other analytics that can help improve awareness of the program. This could prove especially useful with efforts to inform disadvantaged populations, such as those that are low-income or where English is a second language.

Many more services like this exist and are readily available for administrators to use, often for less manpower and cost than would be needed to create an application system from scratch, and can be tailored to fit the needs of individual state programs.

Next-Generation Accountability

Accountability systems also have not caught up with the world we live in. ESAs can only be effective if parents function as informed consumers. Allowing a child to go to a different school, take an online class, or meet with a tutor is the first step, but for these programs to be effectively utilized, parents have to know what options exist. And for these options to have a positive effect on student learning, parents need to be able to filter based on the quality and characteristics of the available options.

But what does "quality" mean? In education, this usually comes down to performance on standardized tests. Yet, whether you think choice students should have to take a state test, a nationally norm-referenced test, or no test at all, one thing that everyone can agree on is that parents, by and large, are not using the available information to drive their decisions. It is hard to blame them. Most state accountability reports consist of confusing excel spreadsheets or incomprehensible PDF documents. Even the best state report cards focus on a small portion of the things parents care about—test scores, graduation rates, and maybe a couple of other objective academic metrics. Yet, as previously established, parents care about much more.

In 2014, Jon Valant wrote a paper commissioned by AEI in which he detailed "how people interpret and use information to choose products in general, how families use information when it comes to choosing a school, and how governments and other organizations should design and disseminate school profiles and performance reports."[17] Part of Valant's research included a survey that provided 1,000 participants with profiles of two existing schools in their zip code. Each school profile had information on the percentage of students in the school that scored proficient or better on state tests. However, one school profile included two positive comments from parents and the other included two negative comments. Whether a school profile included positive or negative comments was done at random using comments gathered from unidentified online sources. From this information, respondents were asked to judge the quality of each school on an A–F grading scale.

Valant reported that parent comments were "stunningly influential" and that "Seeing two positive parent comments rather than two negative parent comments led respondents to grade schools approximately two-thirds of a full grade higher (on average, about the difference between a C+ and a B)." He also found that "Respondents were significantly more likely to trust an independent nonprofit organization with providing public school academic ratings than their state government."

Valant's research indicates that parents care about the opinions of third parties, including other parents, more than they care or trust objective state data. This should not be surprising. It reflects how we largely live the rest of our lives, which is why businesses can literally succeed or fail based on the reviews of random people on services like Yelp, Trip Advisor, Amazon, and Google. If you find yourself hungry in an unfamiliar city, you are more likely to ask the opinion of a local or turn to a service like Yelp to help guide your decision. You are not likely to go to the local health department website to narrow your search by health ratings.

But you *should* be concerned. More than 48 million Americans get sick each year from food,[18] with 75 percent of this illness coming from restaurants, delis, and caterers.[19] In the battle against food-borne illness, city health inspectors have hundreds or thousands of restaurants under their jurisdiction, which quite often leads to inspectors visiting restaurants randomly, wasting time on clean restaurants, and missing the poor performing restaurants until it is too late.

The public is not disinterested with a restaurant's cleanliness, they just intuitively assume that recommendations from locals or random Yelp reviewers will give an approximate understanding of the cleanliness of a restaurant from the experiences of others. It turns out that this is a pretty good assumption. A recent study collected Yelp review data on restaurants and past city health inspection records to create a model that accurately predicts future inspection scores 82 percent of the time.[20] In other words, pairing available government data with reviews and opinions of consumers creates a good prediction of a restaurant's performance on city health standards.

Some cities are beginning to use services like Yelp to work smarter. Officials in cities like New York and San Francisco have acknowledged that the data they produce is not being digested by the public. So, they are beginning to partner with Yelp to list health scores when people search for restaurants.[21] Smart health officials are even using services like Yelp to narrow the restaurants that they target for surprise inspections. Unsurprisingly, they have found that this model has been tremendously helpful at finding violation-prone restaurants earlier.[22]

The lessons learned here for education oversight can be revolutionary. Supporters of choice in education are known to say "parents know best." But instead of making individual parents play an invisible game trial-and-error with their children, let's harness what we have learned to help inform other parents and build a true market for educational choice.

An ESA website can provide the platform to make this happen. Along with official state data, including test scores and graduation rates, ESA administrators can utilize the opinions of parents to evaluate schools and providers based on the dozens of nuances that cannot be captured in top-down accountability systems. (See John Bailey's chapter to learn more about some of the innovative ways administrators can use online platforms to drive accountability with parent opinions and other data.)

One of the longest-running selling points of school choice programs has been their potential to create healthy competition among providers, which would require them to innovate or go out of business. While an increase in parent choice will surely lead to more options, choice supporters must recognize that to see the benefit of competition, we need to create the infrastructure to help parents navigate and make informed choices.

ESAS' FUTURE POTENTIAL

This chapter provided a primer on the existing state programs, their similarities and differences, how administrators are tackling the challenges of implementation, and what states can do to provide a more parent-friendly and accountable system of choice and customization.

More and more, parents are demanding services and solutions that are unique to them, not standardized across the population. They want school offerings that fit their child's interests and abilities, as evidenced by the growing number of parents opting for schools of choice. This trend is likely to increase dramatically with the next generation of parents. Recent polling conducted for the American Federation for Children shows that Millennials support educational choice more than other generations.[23] This is not surprising: Millennials have grown up in a world where transportation is not controlled by a central dispatch or rental car company—they live in a world with Uber and car sharing. They balk at the concept of having to buy an album to get the one or two songs they actually want, or pay for hundreds of television channels they would never watch. They are coming of age at a time when an individual's genetics can be tested to see what diseases they may be predisposed to, the geographic makeup of their ancestors, and many other characteristics related to their unique DNA.

The world is moving at lightning speed toward customization, yet our K–12 education system still reflects the one-size-fits-all model that educated students hundred years ago. The dynamism that has occurred with the unbundling of other sectors will undoubtedly take place in K–12 education: the question is when, not if. States across the nation are embracing their roles as laboratories of innovation and are experimenting with ESAs as a way to inject this dynamism, choice, and customization into an outdated system of education.

When reflecting on the growing interest in ESAs, a quote from Bill Gates comes to mind:

> We always overestimate the change that will occur in the next two years and underestimate the change that will occur in the next ten. Don't let yourself be lulled into inaction.

In the world of policy, moving from an idea to enactment of a universal program in less than ten years is an astounding accomplishment. But the success or failure of this policy hangs in the balance. It is up to state lawmakers, administrators, and advocates to ensure that victory is not determined by the mere passage of a bill. Instead, they must work to put infrastructure and supports in place to ensure that these programs are built for the long-haul. The next few years can determine whether ESAs are built to serve a niche group of parents, or the catalyst for a total rethinking of the American education system.

NOTES

1. Dan Lips, "Education Savings Accounts: A Vehicle for School Choice," *Goldwater Institute*, November 15, 2005.

2. James P. Kelly & Benjamin Scafidi, "More Than Scores: An Analysis of Why and How Parents Choose Private Schools," Friedman Foundation for Educational Choice, November 2013, http://www.edchoice.org/wp-content/uploads/2015/07/More-Than-Scores.pdf.

3. Dara Zeehandelaar & Amber Northern, "What Parents Want: Education Preferences and Trade-offs," *Thomas B. Fordham Institute*, August 26, 2013, http://edexcellence.net/publications/what-parents-want.html.

4. Radiohead, "Fitter Happier," in *OK Computer*, Parlophone/Capitol Records, 1997.

5. John Katzman, "A Civil Education Marketplace," *American Enterprise Institute*, June 24, 2015, http://www.aei.org/publication/civil-education-marketplace/.

6. *Id.*

7. Arianna Prothero, "School Vouchers for All? Nevada Law Breaks New Ground," *Education Week*, June 4, 2015, http://blogs.edweek.org/edweek/charter-schoice/2015/06/school_vouchers_nevada_law_breaks_new_ground.html.

8. Sandra Chereb, "Nevada Supreme Court Strikes Down School Choice Funding Method," *Las Vegas Review-Journal*, September 29, 2016, http://www.reviewjournal.com/news/education/nevada-supreme-court-strikes-down-school-choice-funding-method.

9. Nathan R. James, "Legislative Update: 2015 Session" (presentation, Tennessee State Board of Education, Nashville, TN, June 9, 2015), https://tn.gov/assets/entities/sbe/attachments/6-9-15-WorkshopLegislativeUpdate.pdf.

10. Chereb, "Nevada Supreme Court Strikes Down School."

11. Neal Morton, "$116,000 Loan Approved to Build Nevada's Education Savings Enrollment System," *Las Vegas Review-Journal*, August 19, 2015, http://www.reviewjournal.com/news/education/116000-loan-approved-build-nevadas-education-savings-enrollment-system.

12. Florida Department of Education Office of Independent Education & Parental Choice, "Fact Sheet: Florida Tax Credit Scholarship Program," November 2015, http://www.fldoe.org/core/fileparse.php/5606/urlt/FTC_Nov_2015.pdf.

13. Step Up For Students chief financial officer Anne White, conversation with author, October 21, 2015.

14. State of Arizona Department of Education, "A Guide to Utilizing Your Empowerment Scholarship Account," (2015–2016 Edition), http://www.azed.gov/esa/files/2013/08/esa-parent-handbook.pdf.

15. Yvonne Wingett Sanchez, "Chandler Woman Indicted in Misuse of Sons' Scholarship Money," *The Arizona Republic*, October 6, 2015, http://www.azcentral.com/story/news/local/chandler/2015/10/06/chandler-woman-indicted-misuse-of-arizona-scholarship-money/73443902/.

16. "Debit Cards Used to Reimburse Participants in Self-Insured Medical Reimbursement Plans and Dependent Care Assistance Programs," Internal Revenue Service Notice 2006-69, July 31, 2006, https://www.irs.gov/irb/2006-31_IRB/ar10.html.

17. Jon Valant, "Better Data, Better Decisions," *American Enterprise Institute*, November 2014, http://www.aei.org/wp-content/uploads/2014/11/Better-Data-Better-Decisions-4.pdf.

18. Center for Disease Control and Prevention, "Estimates of Foodborne Illness in the United States," http://www.cdc.gov/foodborneburden/.

19. L. Hannah Gould et al., "Surveillance for Foodborne Disease Outbreaks—United States, 1998-2008," *Center for Disease Control and Prevention*, http://www.cdc.gov/mmwr/preview/mmwrhtml/ss6202a1.htm.

20. Jun Seok Kang et al., "Where Not to Eat? Improving Public Policy by Predicting Hygiene Inspections Using Online Reviews," http://homes.cs.washington.edu/~yejin/Papers/emnlp13_hygiene.pdf.

21. Poncie Rutsch, "Did That Restaurant Pass Its Health Inspection? Now Yelp Will Tell You," *National Public Radio*, March 27, 2015, http://www.npr.org/sections/thesalt/2015/03/27/395622262/did-that-restaurant-pass-its-health-inspection-now-yelp-will-tell-you.

22. Kathleen Hickey, "Cities Tap Yelp to Improve Health Inspection Process," *GCN*, March 2, 2015, https://gcn.com/articles/2015/03/02/yelp-city-restaurant-inspections.aspx.

23. American Federation for Children, "2nd Annual National School Choice Poll Released," January 28, 2016, http://www.federationforchildren.org/2nd-annual-national-school-choice-poll-released/.

Chapter Four

Public and Policymaker Perceptions of Education Savings Accounts

The Road to Real Reform?

Robert C. Enlow and Michael Chartier

In the past five years, education savings accounts (ESAs) have become the fastest growing form of school choice. Five states—Arizona, Mississippi, Florida, Nevada,[1] and Tennessee—have enacted ESA programs, and one state, Arizona, has expanded its ESA program no less than three times in five years. The passage of ESA programs—particularly when compared to the first five years after vouchers were introduced in Milwaukee, or the five years after the enactment of the first program in Arizona—is simply occurring at a faster rate.

This chapter explores why ESA programs are growing so quickly, and why many legislators appear to be enamored with ESAs as a policy option. The first section, part I, addresses what makes ESA programs more politically palatable to policymakers. In other words, what is a legislator's motivation to pass an ESA program, what are the challenges of passing ESAs, and what makes them politically different from school vouchers and tax-credit scholarships?

The best sources for this information are legislators themselves. Therefore, this chapter presents data gathered from six focus groups with state legislators from around the country. In addition, in-depth interviews were conducted with three state legislators who sponsored successful ESA legislation, including legislators from Arizona, Mississippi, and Nevada.

The second section of the chapter explores the public's perception of ESA programs compared to other types of educational choice. Does polling show that public support for ESAs is higher or lower than other school choice mechanisms? Who supports ESA programs the most, and does the public prefer programs with more universal student eligibility or eligibility based on income? To answer these questions, public polling is the best source; in particular, polling conducted from 2014 to 2016 by EdChoice, the American Federation for Children, and Education Next.

PART I: ESAs AND STATE POLICYMAKERS—A
POPULAR POLICY OPTION

To understand why state policymakers are introducing and enacting ESA programs, answer why ESAs have grown so quickly in recent years, and appreciate the challenges facing ESAs as policies, EdChoice conducted six focus groups with state legislators from twenty-three states specifically focusing on how they view and comprehend ESAs. Two focus groups were held in each of the cities where EdChoice sponsored a state legislator-training seminar in 2015—Seattle, Boston, and Nashville.

They were conducted by an independent outside facilitator, Bellwether Research and Consulting, and were composed of between six and ten legislators per group. Focus groups included male and female Republicans (thirty-one) and Democrats (three). Nineteen of the states represented in the focus groups are actively pursuing ESA legislation. In addition to the focus groups, personal, in-depth interviews were conducted with the three lead sponsors of recent (2015) ESA legislation in Arizona, Mississippi, and Nevada to discuss their motivation for introducing and spearheading ESAs. Efforts, though unsuccessful, were also made to interview the lead sponsors of ESA legislation in Florida and Tennessee.

Overall, state legislators support ESA policies for a number of reasons; chief among them being that ESAs empower parents to create a customized and individualized approach for their children. It is this feature of ESAs that policymakers hope will lead to systemic education reform not achievable through other forms of educational choice.

Customizing Choice

The sponsor of Arizona's recent legislation to expand the state's ESA program, Sen. Debbie Lesko (R-AZ), put it this way when she said, "All children are different and we should have as many options as possible to improve education for our children."[2] By sponsoring Arizona's ESA legislation, her goal was to make available the broadest number of educational options to improve the education system as a whole, and to give parents the ability to customize the educational process to better match it to the needs of their child.

When examining the way legislators view vouchers, tax credits, and ESAs, it's helpful to put the focus on an individual child as the most effective lever to change in the entire educational system. According to Sen. Scott Hammond (R-NV), author of Nevada's nearly universal ESA bill, legislators and advocates need to hone in on the needs of every child. "I've been hearing about individualizing education plans since I got into public education . . . it dawned on me years ago that eventually every single child will have an IEP, and this is it."[3] A typical teacher, he said, has a wide range of skill sets in her classroom—including children on the low, middle, and high end of the spectrum.

Previously, those teachers aimed for the middle of the class with the hopes of reaching the broadest number of students possible. Unlike this approach, ESAs allow educators and parents to individualize the approach to education. It also allows parents to be flexible with how the funds are utilized. This is not in the vein of what works for schools, but in the vein of what works for an individual student. As Sen. Hammond added, "We've done so much in the work of research on how children learn, and we discovered that children learn in all kinds of different ways and yet we keep trying to create the perfect school." To the state legislators who were interviewed, ESAs provide the flexibility to match an educational opportunity directly to the learning needs of a child.

A Bargaining Chip for Parents of Special Needs Students

For policymakers, this same line of thought especially applies to special needs students, who typically need and are used to a more customized approach to their education. Hence, it is not surprising that most of the existing ESA programs are programs focused on special needs students. According to a memo from Bellwether Research and Consulting, who conducted legislator focus groups, "ESA legislation focused on special needs students is a model that seems to work as it minimizes resistance . . . opening up the option to special needs students is the way to start."[4] For policymakers, the opposition to educational choice has a far more difficult time arguing against options for special needs.

Representative Carolyn Crawford (R-MS) believes that the situation is even worse for special needs students in Mississippi. The Magnolia State has some of the lowest educational proficiencies, ranking forty-third in the most recent rankings based on the results of the National Assessment of Educational Progress.[5] To Rep. Crawford, it's critically important to empower parents of special needs students to be advocates in their own children's educational future, as they are often the most underrepresented in the complicated negotiations for services from the public school. "Our parents had to have an option, a bargaining tool or something," Crawford said.[6] To her, ESAs allow a parent an escape valve to avoid an educational environment, in this case the public school, which is not meeting the needs of his or her children.

Rep. Crawford's concern that parents and children are powerless in their current educational environment was bore out of very personal experiences she had with the public school system. Her own daughter, Emily, has an individualized education program (IEP) and is required to receive special education services. Rep. Crawford and her husband, a special needs educator, encountered numerous challenges in getting appropriate services for Emily. "It dawned on me," she said, "that this system is fighting my husband and I, who know the law . . . What are they telling other parents?"[7]

She felt strongly that parents needed more power, which is why her first piece of legislation was aimed at giving parents of special needs students a bargaining chip, as she was deeply committed to the special needs community. "And so when I came up to the legislature," Crawford says, "the first piece of legislation that I had signed into law was a bill to allow IEP meetings to be recorded. That way, parents have documentation of some of the unprofessionalism that was going on in these meetings and what parents were being told."[8]

The dissatisfaction that Rep. Crawford identified is evidenced in a report from EdChoice regarding parental satisfaction with the ESA program in Arizona. In the 2013 report, *Schooling Satisfaction: Arizona Parents' Opinions on Using Education Savings Accounts*, the data showed that almost 50 percent of parents surveyed showed some level of displeasure with their previous education provider or school.[9]

This finding stands in stark contrast to the report's other main finding, namely that 100 percent of parents surveyed indicated that they were "satisfied" with the ESA program, and of that, 71 percent were "very satisfied" with how the program treated them. Given this, a strong majority of parents participating in the Arizona ESA program must feel that ESAs allow providers to be directly accountable to them, and vice versa.[10] Legislators like Rep. Crawford have been keen to provide this level of accountability to parents, and to provide an extra "bargaining chip" on their behalf.

Real Systemic Reform

When passing ESA programs, it is also important to the policymakers who were interviewed and who participated in focus groups that educational choice leads to systemic reform—actually improving the kinds and quality of educational providers in the system. ESA programs do not simply seek to redress the injustice of the current educational system, particularly for low-income families or families with special needs students, but they empower and develop a new system in which *every* student's needs can be met.

In this sense, the best way to ensure that all parents truly have a bargaining chip is to ensure that ESA programs are as broad and universal as possible. A broader eligibility pool of both applicants and providers will create the competition necessary to improve public schools or, better yet, create a brand new system of education. The more people that are eligible for ESAs regardless of their zip code or income level, the more people can advocate for their own children, allowing more children in the United States to receive the education that is best for their individual needs.

This desire for systemic reform through ESAs was evident in all of the interviews with state legislators. As Rep. Crawford said, "I know our public schools would work harder to do better and to come up with more creative teaching methods."[11] She added: "I thought of it as an encouragement for our public schools to, you know, start getting their ducks in a row and to encourage those districts that were not doing what they're supposed to be doing to step up."[12]

Throughout the interviews about their sponsorship of ESA policies, legislators had an eye towards improving the public school system. Sen. Hammond went even further, saying:

> The thing that I like about [an ESA] is that it wasn't a voucher where you gave all the money to an institution and said here you go, take the child. You're saying to the parents, here is the money, now find a school that works for your child or a combination of educational services that work for your child . . . And that's what the ESA did; the ESA is a whole new system, it's a whole new thought process . . . This is a whole new mindset.[13]

What is interesting is that there is already evidence to suggest that the competitive effects envisioned by Rep. Crawford and Sen. Hammond are occurring in small and targeted voucher programs, but not at the scale necessary to rapidly transform K–12 education. In the most recent literature review of the effects of educational choice, the data show that of the twenty-three studies conducted that examined the competitive effects of school choice on public schools, twenty-two found that public schools actually improved their test scores due to the choice measures.[14] Yet, even with this data on vouchers and tax credits, the legislators we interviewed felt that ESAs offer a faster and even more effective way to achieve parent-centric, systemic education reform.

A Path to Broad Eligibility

The question over whether educational choice programs should be limited to low-income families or to all families has been an ongoing debate for over twenty years. Some believe that there are many reasons to limit programs based on income: it is easier to get votes, the optics are better, and it rectifies injustices in the current educational system. However, there are just as many reasons to support universal student eligibility, and ample evidence that income limits have not worked.

Over twenty years of experience in promoting school choice has shown that it is just as difficult to garner votes for an income-limited program— be they vouchers, tax-credit scholarships or ESAs—as it is for a universal program. Moreover, there is a practical and political argument for universal student eligibility: a larger pool of beneficiaries makes it easier to sustain choice programs over time, given that the majority of legislators who support school choice don't represent areas most affected by the injustices of the current system.

In the legislator interviews and focus groups, universality was key to their views and opinions on ESAs. As previously mentioned, legislators who participated in focus groups conducted by Bellwether Research and Consulting felt that "opening up the option to special needs students was the best way to start."[15] However, once an ESA was passed, there was a strong appetite to expand the pool. "Those who have already done this are looking for ways to widen the pool of eligible students," as Bellwether's analysts explained.[16]

This theory has been put into practice in Arizona, where legislators have been working to expand the program beyond only special needs students to all students. Every year since its inception, Arizona's ESA program has added to its student eligibility pool, including children from military families, children who attend failing schools and children on Indian reservations. In 2016, instead of trying to expand the program incrementally, the legislature attempted to make the program universally available to all children, not just children from low-income families.

Senator Lesko from Arizona put it this way: "Last year [2015] I tried to expand [our ESA program] and was not successful when we limited it to low-income areas . . . So, it was kind of interesting to me that last year we had a limited expansion and I couldn't get the votes and this year it's just expanded basically to everyone phasing it in and we got the votes."[17]

In Nevada, the legislature passed a nearly universal ESA program, which is currently on hold pending a new funding allocation from the state.[18] Ironically, one of the biggest criticisms about the ESA program came from the private school community who did not like the rule that students must have attended a public school for at least 100 days before they can apply for the program. This rule essentially creates universal eligibility to current public and charter school students while it excludes current private school students from participating. According to Bellwether's findings from the focus groups, "the educational savings accounts have proven to be very popular—so much so that parents are pushing to do away with the 100 days in public school requirement, which legislators will consider at their next session."[19]

Nevada state senator Scott Hammond argues that coupled with this universality, ESAs have the opportunity to usher in a radical, new educational system that moves towards a more parent-focused and parent-involved system: "I'm very convinced that once a parent is involved in choosing an education and finding the right solution for their child, they're totally invested . . . And so that to me was really important, we needed a system that did that."[20]

He added that ESAs provide direct accountability to parents and further incentivize them to become involved in their child's education. They can hire and fire schools, teachers, tutors, and content providers as they so choose. This freedom, in turn, allows them—and even demands them—to become more involved in their child's education.

Ultimately, through the focus groups and interviews, it became clear that ESA programs are popular with many state legislators because they offer greater customization for parents and flexibility for students, and because they are seen as a way to give parents more power in the education process. Moreover, they offer a meaningful path to both systemic education reform and broader eligibility for all families to participate. But, like all attempts at serious education reforms, particularly new reforms, there are challenges. What are those challenges, and what did policymakers point to as impediments to introducing and enacting ESA programs?

The Challenges—Really Opportunities—of ESAs

Same Old Arguments

A consistent theme in our interviews with legislators was the fact that opponents used the same arguments against ESAs as they do against vouchers and tax credits. "ESA programs spend public money to privatize education"; "there is no accountability for private schools"; "ESAs will hurt public schools." These are the same arguments that legislators have heard for over twenty years in the educational choice wars with other forms of school choice.

Ironically, the fact that the arguments used against ESAs were and are the same arguments used against other forms of educational choice proved to be a positive thing in the case of Arizona's ESA program. Senator Lesko described it this way when she stated, "these arguments that the opposition brings up are the same arguments that . . . were used against charter schools and . . . open enrollment, and look how popular all that is now. And, I think this resonates with some of my . . . fellow Republicans."[21]

In Nevada, Senator Hammond faced all the old arguments as well, but spent time on two in particular. The first was the critique that educational choice drains money from public schools. Hammond countered this argument by showing fellow policymakers how much money was being left on the table and put back into the traditional public school system. "We had to explain to them that we are not exactly doing that, [taking money away] we are still leaving several dollars on the table per student in every single school when a student leaves."[22] When each child uses an ESA, the federal and local property tax money remains with the school. The child only takes the state portion of his or her pupil funding.

The second argument against the Nevada program was a new argument based on the universality of the bill: that low-income families who need educational choice most will lack the know-how to enroll, while wealthier families will flock to enroll. Opponents argued that because wealthier families in rich suburban areas have access to greater information, poorer families will be at a disadvantage during the sign-up phase. How are inner city students going to discover the program? Additionally, other equity arguments arose such as the amount of funding tied to each account, which is 100 percent or 90 percent of what the state would spend on average per student, depending on family income.

Opponents argued that the amount would not cover the cost of tuition at private schools, and since families could add personal funds on top of the ESA, low-income families would be further disadvantaged. Likewise, even if it would cover tuition, there were few private schools located in low-income areas. While recognizing that he didn't know all the answers, Senator Hammond and advocates used the experiences with broader eligibility voucher and tax-credit programs in Indiana, Georgia, and Arizona to counter this argument and show that even when programs allow wealthier families to participate, they disproportionately serve low-income families. Senator Hammond also argued that "there will be organizations that come in and make sure that they [low income families] will receive word." He added, "Now we know it is happening."[23]

Opponents of educational choice have been slow to update their talking points. While they're using the standard arguments they've used for twenty years to defend the status quo, ESA supporters are successfully shifting to a parent-centric, not school-centric, argument. Senator Lesko, and the other legislators that proposed ESA legislation, are not thinking about the *system* of schools. Rather, they are thinking about the *delivery of education* and how policymakers can help parents customize their child's education. In so doing, ESA proponents are reframing the arguments for educational choice.

The "Newness" of ESAs

Despite the early and rapid success of ESA programs, they are a relatively new concept. Legislators often think, "my school district is doing well—and if it ain't broke, don't fix it." But in reality, schools are often not as good as policymakers think they are. In a study titled *Still Not as Good as You Think*, Lance Izumi revealed some eye-opening details: "In nearly 300 California public schools in middle-class and affluent neighborhoods, more than half the students in at least one grade level failed to score at the proficient level in English or mathematics on the annual state examination."[24] It also misses the point that even the best performing schools cannot meet the needs of every single student that is assigned to that school. Those children require something different because their assigned school doesn't provide the services, classes, or atmosphere they need.

Additionally, the newness of ESA legislation often scares lawmakers. Representative Crawford of Mississippi put it this way: "People are so scared of change. This is something that's brand new. I mean, being one of the first couple states to pass something like this . . . is just an amazing step for Mississippi. Especially when you consider that we really only spent two years debating this legislation, which in legislative years is really a short amount of time."[25]

Legislators are often reluctant to be the guinea pig for other states when it comes to passing new and untested legislation. Rather, they want fully formed and perfectly implementable solutions, not confusion, or misperceptions, the kinds of which are possible with a new policy like ESAs. As the Bellwether focus group demonstrated, the confusion between an ESA, a Health Savings Account, and a voucher led some legislators to believe that parents, not the state, deposited their own personal funds into the account and then spent that money on approved education expenses.

As Bellwether noted, "the familiarity with ESAs was uneven among legislators and the difference between what an ESA is and how it can be used and what a voucher is and how it can be used was not clear for some of the focus group participants."[26] These misunderstandings caused some legislators in the focus groups to believe, and not entirely incorrectly, that only parents with financial means—those with excess funds to put into such accounts— would be able to access the program. But these issues are simple to fix with basic information and education. As Senator Hammond noted, "it didn't take a whole lot of education, but it did take a few moments sporadically during the session to explain."[27]

Because ESAs are new and not very well known, ESA proponents must work with legislators to ensure the nuances of any legislation are understood. Rep. Crawford spoke of her continued effort to educate other legislators outside of session, a sentiment that was echoed by every other legislator interviewed. Again, Sen. Hammond remarked: "What they didn't realize was the difference between an ESA and a voucher program . . . there were a couple of times I had to explain it during a caucus meeting, for example, or go down to an individual office and explain the differences and why this was going to be great for the state of Nevada."[28]

The Need for Outside Organizations

This brings up a broader point—the role outside organizations must play in the ESA policymaking process. Throughout the interviews, ESA sponsors expressed gratitude for the work of outside organizations. This is legislation 101: every legislator who passes a school choice bill needs help. That help often comes in the form of support from parents, lobbyists, think tanks, and other advocacy groups. Each of these groups adds a different level of information and credibility to the movement inside the state house. Countering misinformation, educating policymakers, sharing parent stories, providing research, and building coalitions are a key part of what outside groups bring to the advocacy table.

According the ESA sponsors in Arizona and Nevada, think tanks and advocacy groups such as EdChoice, the Goldwater Institute, the American Federation for Children, the Foundation for Excellence in Education and the Institute for Justice helped lend credibility to the legislators who sponsored ESA legislation. In Arizona, Senator Lesko spoke highly of the Goldwater Institute and their help as one of the main driving forces behind ESAs. "We have the Goldwater Institute here and they helped design the language of the Empowerment Scholarship Accounts," she said.[29]

Additionally, Senator Scott Hammond mentioned the educational work of EdChoice. Back in 2014, EdChoice hosted a conference in Salt Lake City attended by the senator, who stated that this was one of the most important events in prompting him to introduce ESA legislation. It also allowed his fellow legislators to be educated on the concept of ESAs. "What was really good is several legislators including Mr. (Pat) Hickey attended that conference in Salt Lake."[30] What no one could have known at the time, but what we know now, is that Assemblyman Hickey was one of the key actors in getting the ESA passed at the end of the session.

The Need for Leadership Support

In addition to outside forces, the success of any legislation depends on support from leaders in state executive and legislative branches. Senator Lesko spoke of how Arizona Governor Doug Ducey, a strong school choice supporter, was able to help sway or pacify certain members who were nervous about voting on particular school choice bills. "I think part of it has to do with Governor Ducey who is . . . publically supportive of school choice. I think that's helpful with some of our members."[31]

Likewise, Senator Hammond's legislation benefitted from the good relationship he had with Governor Brian Sandoval, who is a supporter of educational choice but who also wanted to pass a tax increase to raise public K–12 revenue in the same year ESAs were being debated. However, many legislators were hesitant to raise taxes unless there was something that would offset that vote. These legislators ultimately found that in SB 302, which later became the Nevada ESA program.

Senator Hammond also had a unique relationship with the Assembly Majority Leader Paul Anderson. In Nevada, most legislators have roommates where they live during session. It just so happened that Assemblyman Anderson and Senator Hammond were roommates during the 2015 legislative session. While together, Senator Hammond was able to talk through legislative strategy with a member of the other house and come up with ways to help ensure passage: "I also talked to him several times . . . But every night that he and I talked we would go into what this would do and how his caucus really wanted this, how do we get what the governor needs, what we need to get out . . . [T]hey really wanted to make this part of the end game."

Lastly, Mississippi Representative Carolyn Crawford, the lead sponsor of the ESA legislation, had her own strategy for legislative leadership. Put simply, it was to do the right thing and be viewed as a tireless advocate for children with special needs. Representative Crawford is a former social worker whose husband is a special needs educator. As such, she was an important resource for other legislators. Her background gave her credibility, which gained her the trust of both leadership and her colleagues, and which gave her the ability to shape the legislation to what she knew would work. "I got their vote because they know that I wouldn't present something that I didn't think was needed," she said.

As with all legislative efforts, and especially in the ESA legislative efforts in Arizona, Mississippi, and Nevada, leadership support was important. But, while leadership support was instrumental in passage of this bill, there were other hurdles that needed to be overcome.

Fewer Rural and Democratic Legislators Support ESAs

Oftentimes, the biggest opponents of educational choice are rural legislators. The reasons are many, but they generally fall into a few categories. Because public schools are typically the largest employer in smaller towns, rural legislators often vote the way that their school district superintendents feel will best benefit the public schools in their area. When a rural legislator hears that money is coming directly out of the pockets of the teachers, nurses, and school administrators of the people that buy groceries, houses, and cars in their district, it has an outsized impact on his or her decision-making. Moreover, rural legislators point out that there are few private schools in their area, and that even if an ESA program were enacted, children in their district would have limited options for using the ESA funds.

This proved to be the case in the focus groups held by EdChoice. According to the Bellwether analysis, "Legislators from rural states face particular challenges . . . Many rural states lack options or infrastructure for school choice and supportive legislators encounter resistance from colleagues who think school choice would benefit just a few of the most populous counties and not them."[32] From this memo it is clear that rural, suburban, and urban legislators feel as though options in rural areas of the country are lacking. Moreover, it is difficult to convince rural legislators to support school choice programs when opponents are claiming that school choice, or in these cases, ESAs, will siphon funding from their public schools while at the same time students in their district will not be able to fully utilize the ESA program.

The legislators interviewed for this chapter—all Republicans—were also disappointed by the lack of support from their Democratic colleagues. No Democrats voted for the ESA program in either Nevada, Arizona, or Mississippi. Perhaps Senator Hammond from Nevada said it clearest when he commented, "Their response was that they still can't break away from their natural alliance with the Nevada association of law [the trial lawyers], the education associations, all the unions . . . they just could not break away from that." While this sentiment was unique to Senator Hammond in Nevada, the teachers unions, along with almost all the public school establishment groups, likewise opposed ESAs in both Arizona and Mississippi.

Yet at least privately, there have been some cracks in the Democratic opposition. Both Senators Lesko (AZ) and Hammond (NV) mentioned that they had meaningful conversations with Democrats. Senator Lesko mentioned that there was one Democratic senator who believed that children with special needs should be able to stay in the program until age twenty-two and so he supported that addition even though he would not support the universal ESA.

Senator Hammond told a story of a Democrat colleague who wanted to vote yes on the bill but could not because it became an issue for the caucus. He "could not break away from his caucus and this became a caucus vote."[33] This is not to say that Democrats have not supported school choice; there has been support in the programs in Rhode Island, Florida, Tennessee, and Iowa, but in a state with ESAs, there has been no real support from Democrats. Policymakers, who were interviewed or participated in focus groups, felt that ESAs were a very effective way to empower parents with greater educational options that will hopefully transform the K–12 education system. But what about their constituents?

PART II: THE PUBLIC PERCEPTION OF ESAs

Charter schools, vouchers, and tax-credit scholarship programs have been around for more than twenty-five years, and there is plenty of data on the public support for and perceptions of these policies over a long period of time. ESA programs are relatively new, yet there has also been strong polling data conducted over the last three years. This section will compare the polling data on ESAs to date with the polling data on charters, vouchers, and tax-credit scholarships to gauge the various levels of public support across programs.

Are ESAs more popular than other forms of choice? Is the intensity of support different, and what can we learn from the public's perception of ESA programs? Do Democrats and other subgroups favor ESAs? The majority of this data will be drawn from polls undertaken by EdChoice, but it will also include data from the 2015 EdNext Poll on School Reform and a survey sponsored by the American Federation for Children titled *Arizona School Choice*

The data show several important themes. First, overall support for ESAs in 2015 is higher than support for charter schools, vouchers, or tax-credit scholarships. Second, both the intensity of support for ESAs—that is the difference between those who strongly favor and oppose the policy—and the margins of support—that is the difference between total support and total opposition to the policy—are higher than for charters, vouchers and tax-credit scholarships. Third, and finally, a majority of Democrats support ESAs and support is especially high among Latinos.

Overall Higher Support for ESAs

Today, when looking at overall support for ESAs, there is slightly greater public support for ESA programs than for charter schools, vouchers, or tax-credit scholarships. According to the *2015 Schooling in America Survey* conducted by EdChoice, public support for charter schools, after a definition is provided, is only 53 percent. Public support for vouchers is at 61 percent, while support for tax-credit scholarship programs is 60 percent.[34] These findings are mirrored by the 2015 EdNext Poll that found 51 percent support for charter schools after a definition is provided and 55 percent support for tax-credit scholarships.[35] Yet, despite their newness, public support for ESAs stands at 62 percent favor with only 28 percent oppose, according to the *2015 Schooling in America Survey.*[36]

While total support for ESAs is only slightly above total support for vouchers, it is important to note that the intensity of support for ESAs is significantly higher. Intensity of support relates to the difference between those who say they strongly favor a policy and those who strongly oppose the policy. The intensity of support for charter schools is only +10 percent. Voucher intensity is +13 percent and tax-credit scholarship intensity is +12 percent. But, the intensity of support for ESAs is at +16 percent, which is the highest of all the options.[37] (see figures 4.1, 4.2, 4.3).

This trend of strong intensity continues with Hispanics. According to *Latino Perspectives on K–12 Education and Schools Choice*, the intensity of support for charters, vouchers, tax-credit scholarships and ESAs stands at +14, +26, +29, and +30 percent, respectively.[38]

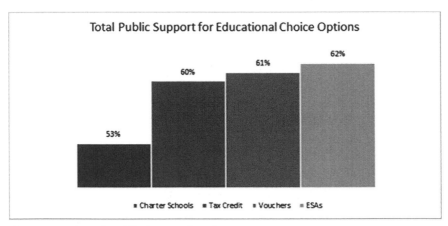

Figure 4.1   Overall Public Support for ESAs.

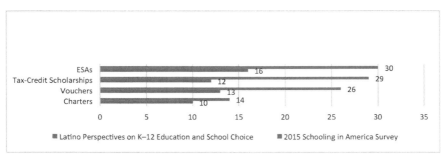

Figure 4.2   Comparing the Intensity of Support for Choice Program Types, Between the General Public and Latinos.

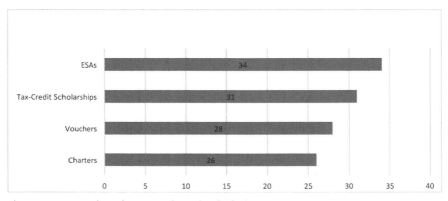

Figure 4.3   Margins of Support for School Choice Program Types.

The margin of support for the various school choice reforms also shows an advantage for ESAs. Margins of support relate to the difference between total support and total opposition. According to the *2015 Schooling in America Survey*, the margin between total support and total opposition to charters, vouchers, and tax-credit scholarships is +26, +28, and +31 percent, respectively. The margin of support for ESAs, however, is +34 percent. With the exception of tax-credit scholarships, this trend is the same from EdChoice's 2013 and 2014 surveys.[39] The margin of support was higher for ESAs than for charter schools or vouchers.[40]

Support for ESAs Among Democrats

As previously noted, there has been little support for ESAs from Democratic legislators in the five states that have passed ESA programs to date. The polling data, however, shows a different story. Multiple polls find that Democrats favor ESAs over other forms of school choice. According to EdChoice's *2015 Schooling in America Survey*, support for charter schools among Democrats is at 47 percent, with 35 percent in opposition.[41] These numbers are mirrored by the 2015 EdNext Poll, which found 40 percent support for charter schools among Democrats, with 25 percent of Democrats in opposition.[42]

In the EdChoice survey, vouchers had the support of 54 percent of Democrats and were opposed by 38 percent of Democrats.[43] The same survey found that Democratic support for tax-credit scholarships was also 54 percent with 33 percent in opposition.[44] ESA programs, however, found significantly higher support among Democrats. Sixty percent of Democrats support ESA programs while only 30 percent are in opposition.[45]

State Polling and Support for ESA Programs

So far, the national, statistically representative polls have shown that support for ESAs is higher than support for other types of choice. This is almost universally true across all demographics and subgroups according to the nationally representative sample of 1,002 respondents. ESA programs are simply viewed more positively than charters, vouchers, or tax-credit scholarships. But, how are they viewed at the state level, and what data do we have on parent satisfaction and use of ESA programs?

As figure 4.4 shows, a review of state surveys conducted by EdChoice in the past five years shows that with the exceptions of Rhode Island and Iowa, the margin and intensity of support for ESAs is high. Four states—Indiana, Alaska, North Carolina, and Texas—have margins that are higher than +28 points and intensity above +15 points. An additional seven states have margins

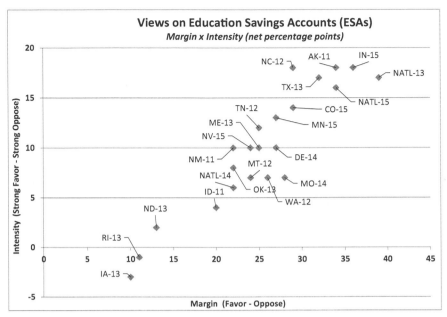

Figure 4.4   Views on Education Savings Accounts (ESAs).

above +20 points and intensity greater than +10 points. The rest of the states all have margins greater than +10 points, and only Rhode Island and Iowa have intensities that are negative.

A closer look at the poll numbers in Nevada and Arizona are also illuminating. In Arizona, a 2015 poll conducted in Arizona by WPA Opinion Research for the American Federation for Children found strong support for all types of school choice. Their conclusion: "Voters across the state and key demographic groups are favorable of the concept of school choice and they support policies that help give parents the ability to choose schools for their children. Additionally, voters believe that parents of all Arizona children should be able to send their child to a school of their choice, and have their tax dollars follow them."[46]

This support is also evidenced by a 2013 report authored by Jason Bedrick and Jonathan Butcher entitled *Schooling Satisfaction: Arizona Parents' Opinions on Using Education Savings Accounts*. This is the only survey of its kind, in which parents polled were actually using ESAs at the time of the poll. The survey, which was a self-selected survey of parents utilizing ESAs, found that:

Parents using an ESA are more satisfied with their children's current education compared with their previous public school: The majority of respondents reported being "very satisfied" with the accounts (71 percent); 19 percent reported being "satisfied"; and 10 percent said they were "somewhat satisfied." No parent responded as neutral or reported any level of dissatisfaction with the accounts. Those results show high levels of satisfaction even after accounting for our limited sample size and margin of error.[47]

In Nevada, the poll results are not as clear as in Arizona. In March 2015, EdChoice conducted a poll of 602 registered voters in Nevada, *The Nevada K–12 and School Choice Survey*, and found much higher levels of support for charter schools than for vouchers, tax-credit scholarships, and ESAs. In fact, among registered voters, support for ESAs was the lowest, with only 58 percent total support for ESAs compared with 71 percent support for charters, 64 percent support for tax-credit scholarships, and 61 percent support for vouchers.[48] This trend holds true across most demographic groups as well. Whites, Democrats, and parents all expressed greater support for charter schools than vouchers, tax credits, and ESAs. The notable exceptions were African Americans and Hispanics.

African Americans in Nevada supported vouchers and tax credits more than charter schools, and their support for ESAs was basically the same as their support for charters (57 percent vs. 59 percent). Hispanics, however, proved to be the anomaly. Their support for ESAs stood at 74 percent favor compared with 66 percent support for charters, 58 percent support for vouchers, and 56 percent support for tax credits. Moreover, the intensity of their support was off the charts. It was +36 points for ESAs compared to +24 points for charters, +23 points for vouchers and only +19 for tax-credit scholarships.[49]

Overall, the polling results presented in this chapter point to a couple simple takeaways. First, while the support for ESAs is only slightly higher than support for other types of educational choice, the intensity of support for ESAs among the general public is much higher. Second, support for ESAs is significantly higher among almost all demographics, but particularly Hispanics.

THE POPULARITY OF ESA PROGRAMS

In closing, the purpose of this chapter was to examine the politics and polling related to ESA programs to better understand policymakers' and the public's support for this newest form of school choice. On the legislative side, what is evident from the interviews previously mentioned, as well as from the focus groups, is that ESAs enjoy some notable advantages in the policymaking arena today. Their flexibility provides policymakers with a way to reframe the debate around parents and not schools, giving parents greater bargaining power. Unlike vouchers and tax credits, they are also seen as a meaningful way to achieve systemic reform and as a real pathway to universal educational choice.

The challenges of ESAs were also evident. ESAs are new and there is a lack of awareness on how they function, and how they should be implemented. And despite the successes in Arizona and Mississippi, there is consensus among the policymakers who were interviewed or who participated in focus groups that more needs to be done to message ESAs effectively, particularly since ESAs seem to confound some of the same old arguments against choice. It will be necessary in the future to see if these impressions are confirmed by a larger group of policymakers.

On the polling side, there is clear evidence that ESAs enjoy wide public support—even more than vouchers and tax credits. Not only does the public support ESAs, but there is even greater support between two specific demographic groups—parents and Hispanics. Moreover, parents who used ESAs in Arizona are much more satisfied than they were in their previous environment.

All this bodes well for the future of ESAs. As Milton Friedman said, "We have so far only seen the early fruits from the introduction of vouchers, from giving parents a choice. The best is yet to come as competition and the market work their wonders."[50]

Maybe with ESAs, the best is already here.

NOTES

1. At the time of publishing this book, the Nevada ESA program was blocked by an injunction from the Nevada Supreme Court for an inappropriate funding mechanism. The Nevada ESA program remains state law, and may continue pending a new funding source. All references to Nevada in this chapter relate to lawmakers' perceptions and public polling data about ESAs.

2. Debbie Lesko, interview via phone by Robert Enlow, February 22, 2016.

3. Scott Hammond, interview via phone by Robert Enlow, February 23, 2015.

4. Bellwether Research, "Memo for the Friedman Foundation for Educational Choice," 2015, 2.

5. Carolyn Crawford, interview via phone by Michael Chartier, February 24, 2016.

6. *Id.*

7. *Id.*

8. *Id.*

9. Jonathan Butcher & Jason Bedrick, "Schooling Satisfaction: Arizona Parents on Using Education Savings Accounts," Friedman Foundation for Educational Choice, 2013, 13.

10. *Id.*

11. Carolyn Crawford, interview.

12. *Id.*

13. *Id.*

14. Greg Forster, "A Win-Win Solution: The Empirical Evidence on School Choice," Friedman Foundation for Educational Choice, April 17, 2013, 1.

15. Bellwether Research, "Memo," 2.

16. Bellwether Research, "Memo," 2.

17. Debbie Lesko, interview.

18. For additional information on the state of the Nevada ESA program at the time of this book's publishing, see chapter two, The Constitutional Case for ESAs, by Tim Keller.

19. Bellwether Research, "Memo," 2.

20. Scott Hammond, interview.

21. Debbie Lesko, interview.

22. Scott Hammond, interview.

23. *Id.*

24. Lance Izumi, Vicki Murray, & Rachel Chaney, "Still Not as Good as You Think: Why the Middle Class Needs School Choice," *Pacific Research Institute*, 2009, 1.

25. Carolyn Crawford, interview.

26. Bellwether Research, memo, 2.

27. Scott Hammond, interview.

28. *Id.*

29. Debbie Lesko, interview.

30. Scott Hammond, interview.

31. Debbie Lesko, interview.

32. Bellwether Research, "Memo."

33. Scott Hammond, interview.

34. Paul DiPerna, "2015 Schooling in America Survey," Friedman Foundation for Educational Choice, June 30, 2015.

35. Michael Henderson, Paul Peterson, & Martin West, "The 2015 EdNext Poll on School Reform," *Education Next*, 2015, 1–15.

36. DiPerna, "2015 Schooling," 33–55.

37. *Id.*

38. Paul DiPerna, "Latino Perspectives on K–12 Education & School Choice," Friedman Foundation for Educational Choice, September 10, 2015, 33-64.

39. Paul DiPerna, "2014 Schooling in America Survey," Friedman Foundation for Educational Choice, June 26, 2014; Paul DiPerna, "2013 Schooling in America Survey: What Do Mothers Say About K–12 Education?" Friedman Foundation for Educational Choice, May 8, 2013.

40. DiPerna, "2015 Schooling," 33–55.

41. *Id.*

42. Henderson, Peterson, & West, "The 2015 EdNext Poll," 1–15.

43. DiPerna, "2015 Schooling," 33–55.

44. *Id.*

45. *Id.*

46. Matt Gammon, "Memo on Arizona School Choice Survey," American Federation for Children, 2015, 4, http://www.federationforchildren.org/wp-content/uploads/2015/10/AFC_AZ-Education-Survey_Memo_v1_151019.pdf.

47. Butcher & Bedrick, "Schooling," 2.

48. Paul DiPerna, "Nevada K–12 & School Choice Survey," Friedman Foundation for Educational Choice, March 2015, http://www.edchoice.org/wp-content/uploads/2015/07/1-NEVADA-Poll-Full-Report-WEB-3-11-15-1.pdf.

49. DiPerna, "Nevada."

50. *School Choice Ohio*, "Celebrating Milton Friedman," July 30, 2010, http://www.scohio.org/home/blog/2010/07/30/celebrating-milton-friedman/.

Chapter Five

The ESA Administrator's Dilemma

Tackling Quality Control

John Bailey

I know no safe depository of the ultimate powers of the society but the people themselves; and if we think them not enlightened enough to exercise their control with a wholesome discretion, the remedy is not to take it from them, but to inform their discretion by education. This is the true corrective of abuses of constitutional power.

—Thomas Jefferson

America is unique in its commitment to offer students education for at least twelve years. To accomplish that promise, our nation's leaders created a system that borrowed heavily from systems and structures that arose during the Industrial Revolution.[1] A key feature of these systems was the standardization that grew out of mass production. As *The Economist* notes, mass production systems typically sacrifice aspects of customization by taking "the initiative for choosing products out of the hands of the consumer and puts it into the hands of the manufacturer."[2] Production costs are lowered through standardizing products made in limited varieties at reasonable level of quality. Henry Ford captured the essence of this when he said "Any customer can have a car painted any color that he wants so long as it is black."

It makes intuitive sense that these lessons would heavily influence the structure of a system of education that had to scale to cover students across the country. Students could be grouped into grades, bundled into schools, organized within districts and overseen by state regulators. Standardized curriculums, textbooks, and experiences were a way to lower costs while providing a reasonable level of quality. Michael Horn, author of *Disrupting Class*, observed that, "Society created our current system of age-graded classrooms to serve a large number of students in the most economically efficient way possible by standardizing the way we teach and test."[3] The institutions within this system control most aspects of the learning experience, including what courses are offered, the pace of learning, what counts for credit, and which resources or services are available to students. But by and large, there has been—until recent times—little in the way to customize education for students in a cost-affordable, high-quality manner.

Mass production is now giving way to mass customization thanks to new technologies, global suppliers, and Internet-based distribution channels. Starbucks alone claims to offer more than 80,000 drink variations.[4] Music once could only be consumed by purchasing mass produced albums that were distributed through physical stores. Today, individuals have access to more than thirty million songs on Spotify that have been combined by users into more than two billion different playlists. As Americans become more exposed to a broader array of customization of products and services in every facet of their lives, they begin to develop expectations that everything will be customized for their tastes and preferences.

The cultural demand for customization is reaching education. Today's students have access to an incredible array of educational experiences that are growing to meet a broad set of children's educational, social, and health needs. More than 6,400 public charter schools—a 47 percent increase since 2006—offer different approaches and styles to serving different kids. However, some of the most exciting educational opportunities are emerging outside of the traditional school setting. Nearly one in four families currently has a child enrolled in an afterschool program, a 60 percent growth from 2004 to 2014.[56] As of June 2015, there were over 80,000 educational apps available in the Apple app store. There are more than 1,000 free online courses offered through just Coursera and EdX. Libraries, once measured by the number of books they held, are now access points to other learning repositories, such as the 850 online courses offered in the Los Angeles public library system.[7] Since 2002, the number of American Camp Association day camps has increased by 69 percent and resident camps have increased by 21 percent, offering children the chance to explore performing arts, sciences, the outdoors, and more. The Maker Movement is combining 3D printing, robotics, and computer programming into organized activities for children inside and outside of school.

These new opportunities are colliding with an education system of institutions and regulations that still assume the only way to deliver education is through public schools. That is still true, but less so given the rise of these other educational services and student supports. Parents can assemble a network of different education providers where a student takes some classes at a school, attends a special needs therapist, receives one-on-one tutoring, learning computer program from Code.org, and takes a few classes through Coursera.

There is already an emerging consensus that our education system needs to change to become more student centric. In 2013, the Aspen Institute Task Force on Learning and the Internet convened twenty leaders from the business, technology, and education communities to explore how young people learn today and recommend the new systems and structures that are needed to support that type of learning. A key finding of the Task Force was that in most instances, education is only formally recognized and credentialed when it happens inside a school. This long-held model is struggling to engage a new generation of students for whom learning is happening all the time—online, offline, in classrooms, as well as after school, in camps, with tutors, or with apps. The Task Force went on to recommend that education be organized around the student, harnessing the ecosystem of providers, courses, and services that can be tailored to the individual needs and interests of students.

Less than a year after the Aspen Task Force released its report, another diverse group of education leaders came to a similar conclusion. Signatories included no less than the head of the National Education Association (NEA) and American Federation of Teachers (AFT) along with KIPP, 50CAN, Disney, and the Hume Foundation. Their consensus vision of learning included the notion of "open walled learning," which acknowledges that learning happens not just within the hours during the school day but at any time and in any place. The report talked about a "network" of institutions, experiences, businesses, and organizations serving students. The financial resources supporting these opportunities will be allocated "in ways that support the whole child, ensuring that each child has access to and receives the necessary educational, social, emotional, and health supports and services, regardless of economic circumstances."[8]

While the visions are compelling and recognize a new reality, our traditional system of funding and regulating education is still stuck in more traditional paradigms. Parents are forced to "pay out of pocket" for many opportunities and most of these education experiences will not be recognized or credited as part of a child's formal education.

Other sectors have faced similar challenges and evolved to meet the needs of consumers. For example, the healthcare system has evolved to support patients assembling their own networks of primary care doctors, pediatricians, optometrists, dermatologists, allergists, dentists, cardiologists, and other specialists. The average patient will have more than eighteen different doctors over his or her lifetime.[9] A key reform enabling this stitching together of different doctors has been flexible spending accounts (FSA) and health savings accounts (HSA), which provide the flexible funding needed to empower this consumer driven healthcare. New dependent care reimbursement accounts help families save and manage childcare or eldercare expenses.[10]

Education leaders are drawing upon the lessons learned from these other sectors to explore similar consumer directed accounts that support parents who want to assemble the best portfolio of services for their child. These education savings accounts (ESAs) allow parents to pay for a variety of education services and supports, including tuition, tutoring, therapy for students with disabilities, instructional materials, online courses, a-la-carte public school courses, and savings for future college costs.[11] Doug Tuthill, the president of Step Up for Students, which manages the Florida ESA, calls it "a funding mechanism aligned to customization."[12]

While ESAs provide the funding flexibility to take advantage of a broad array of education opportunities, ESA administrators are confronting the dilemmas with how to regulate such a broad market to provide student protections, guard taxpayer funds from fraud, and also promote quality. Past approaches are insufficient for the challenges that lie ahead with thousands of different providers, services, and resources. With such rapid change, it will be impossible to identify every possible risk and bad actor through traditional approval processes. Policymakers will instead have to shift to managing and mitigating risk using new tools and systems to inform better decisions and target regulatory intervention where it is most needed.

CHALLENGES OF THE TRADITIONAL SYSTEM

The current top-down K–12 regulatory regime is insufficient to keep up with the diversity of providers and the challenges and opportunities they present. There are four primary challenges with the way the current regulation tries to address quality. First, it relies almost entirely on gating mechanisms that approve who can serve students. Second, regulations are unevenly applied, with different actors held to different standards. Third, state regulators with limited resources cannot keep up with the pace of new innovations and resources being introduced to the market. Fourth, regulations rarely sunset and, as a result, accumulate to the point of not only stifling teacher creativity but also walling out innovation outside the classroom.

Guarding the Gates

On the first point, the current system tightly guards who is part of the system. Instead of seeing the public education system as a network of different providers that serve the public good, it limits those who can serve students primarily to public schools. The system of services rests almost entirely at the discretion of what the school offers or the providers it contracts with.

New service providers or school models face high regulatory walls with narrow gates. Almost half the states have some form of textbook adoption system, in which a committee selects or recommends what books and other instructional materials can be used in classrooms. Regulations attempt to address the quality of online learning by restricting student eligibility, limiting the number of providers, or establishing lengthy approach processes. Public charter schools face state caps, growth restrictions, and student caps. As Robert Frost observed, "Before I built a wall I'd ask to know, what I was walling in or walling out, and to whom I was like to give offence."[13] Too often in education, our regulations wall out student opportunities.

Uneven Standards

Second, regulators create an uneven playing field by holding different providers to different standards of quality. Often, nonprofit entities are given a lighter regulatory touch compared to those offered by for-profit entities. In higher education, for example, the Obama Administration has established a regulatory framework aimed at protecting students from poor programs. However, only for-profit higher education institutions are held to these new "gainful employment" metrics. The similar "consumer protections" are not applied to nonprofit and public institutions, even though there are numerous programs and institutions in that segment that would not meet the bars.

There is a similar unevenness in the elementary and secondary sector as well. Policymakers in Chicago, Illinois have established both state and city charter school caps.[14] These limitations are rarely framed as limiting student options. Instead, the unions and protectionist leaders use the language of "consumer protection" in much the same way taxi commissions claim their banning of Uber protects consumers.

Yet there is a remarkable double standard applied to persistently failing traditional schools within the system. Consider the example of Fenger Academy High School in Chicago. In 2014, Fenger had just 1 percent of its students meet or exceed proficiency in reading and mathematics and only 54 percent graduated.[15] Tragically, this has been the pattern for over a decade despite new principals, rounds of School Improvement Grant funding, and more than 200 pages of comprehensive school reform plans.

The regulatory regime creates an uneven playing field for providers and even less fair protections for students. The regulators claim charter caps are needed to "protect" students from KIPP, but little protection is offered to the generations of students being so poorly served by Fenger.

Pace of Innovation

Third, state instructional resource approval processes are woefully inadequate for the pace of innovation today. Take for example textbook adoption processes, all of which were put into place before the advent of mobile devices and the Internet. Modern instructional resources confound archaic definitions and category descriptions. Many adoption processes require publishers to have repositories to stock products, a requirement that misses that digital resources are stored online in virtual data centers around the world.[16]

Even if such adoption processes were more flexible for new digital resources, it would be impossible to review on a continual basis the hundreds of thousands of resources, many of which are tweaked or updated daily. The Khan Academy offers a library of over 9,000 video tutorials on everything from arithmetic to SAT preparation. LearnZillion offers 4,000 lessons used by more than 300,000 teachers. And the OER Commons offers a growing library of 50,000 learning materials that teachers can use for their classrooms.

The free language app Duolingo is illustrative of the dilemma facing today's regulators. It offers fifty-four different language courses across twenty-three languages using a combination of gaming techniques, crowdsourcing, machine language learning, and voice recognition. One study suggests that using the app for a little more than thirty hours could lead to the equivalent of a university semester of language education.[17] But state regulatory systems struggle to know what to do with it. Is it a textbook? A course? A supplemental resource? Even if it could be considered for textbook funding, many state adoption cycles are out of sync with Duolingo's innovation cycle. The last time the Oklahoma adoption process was open for foreign languages was in 2009—a full two years before Duolingo was invented.[18] In the time since, the app has amassed over a hundred million users around the world— just in time for next year's state approval process.

Barriers Without a Sunset

Fourth, the accumulated regulatory red tape amassed over decades has stifled teaching and created barriers to entrepreneurs seeking to solve educational problems. Regulations rarely sunset and often preserve a view of the world at the time it was introduced. As a result, the regulatory system perpetuates itself. Today's teacher faces more regulations guiding everything from their credentials to use of class time to what resources they can use in class. None of these individual regulations are a problem by themselves. All were intended to protect children or ensure quality instruction. The problem is their cumulative effect. The Show-Me Institute's Michael McShane and colleagues note, "No raindrop thinks it is responsible for the flood. Individually, each regulation could be sensible and meaningful, but when combined with hundreds of other requirements, the sum becomes incoherent and onerous."[19]

SMART TOOLS FOR SMART REGULATION

In a world that changes much faster than the minds of the people who regulate it, the challenge in the modern education system is to have a nimble, flexible system that can accommodate new providers and approaches while constantly monitoring for potential bad actors and low quality. John Katzman, the founder of innovative education companies including Noodle, Princeton Review, and 2U, suggests, "Any conversation about educational quality should assume a quickly changing world where we are still learning about how to teach. It also requires that we are open to changing the structure of learning. Today, that means focusing on adaptive learning and breaking education into smaller units. But what will we know in six months or two years about brain development or technology that we don't know today? And how will we be able to adapt that new knowledge to better help students?"[20]

ESAs need a flexible regulatory system to match the flexibility of funding they provide parents. But how does an ESA administrator ensure those serving students are of high quality? If a top-down approach is too rigid, what is an appropriate alternative?

The answer is by embracing the key dynamics that make markets work so effectively. In education, markets are typically used to illustrate the power of competition, but there is a complementary side deserving more attention, which is the customization of supply to unique needs expressed in demand. Marketplace economies thrive when actors differentiate and optimize in meeting customer needs. It is this primary mechanism that has helped to make America's higher education the envy of the world. Institutional diversity ranges from large to small, from liberal arts colleges to specialized engineering schools.

Nobody is suggesting that the answer to these challenges is zero regulation. But regulators need to work smarter, leveraging new technology platforms and services to make markets work more efficiently, identify problematic providers, and provide both the regulators and parents with better information to make more informed decisions. John Katzman argues, "Markets are powerful places, and hold their players intensely accountable." Enhancing the accountability mechanisms of markets can address quality without being overly prescriptive or stifling innovation.

Leverage Platforms to Foster Quality Markets

A primary enabler of this new regulatory model is leveraging the next wave of technology platforms that use mobile devices and the Internet to create market platforms of tools and services that facilitate exchanges between providers and consumers. These systems facilitate listings, searches, reviews, financial transactions, background checks, and reporting complaints or violators.

These platforms provide a basic layer of consumer protection. Verifying someone's identity and conducting background and credit checks help create confidence that the person you're transacting with is legitimate. It is these features that allows individuals to trust staying in a stranger's home using Airbnb or get into a stranger's car using Uber.

These platforms also help to manage quality. Features like ratings and reviews help to create some transparency. Providers have incentives to provide high quality service or risk receiving low ratings, which in turn can lower their ranking or even result in their removal from the service. Uber, for example, deactivates drivers who have less than a 4.6 rating out of 5.

Ratings and reviews are a critical feature to all market platforms. Nearly nine in ten consumers have read online reviews to determine the quality of a local business, and 39 percent do so on a regular basis. Eighty-eight percent of consumers say they trust online reviews as much as personal recommendations.[21] More than 28 percent of parents choose a doctor based on their neighbors' recommendation. That number jumps up to 46 percent if the doctor also had good reviews on any one of the dozens of physician rating sites such as Healthgrades, RateMDs, or Vitals.[22]

Rather than fight this trend, ESA administrators should embrace it. Ratings and reviews help build trust and serve as a crucial foundational layer of quality control. They can also provide another data point for the search and filtering elements, helping to elevate those results that are more highly rated.

There is an added advantage to crowdsourced ratings and reviews. They can help ESA regulators stretch their limited resources by surfacing potential bad actors. City health departments are using Yelp reviews to flag potential violations allowing inspectors to narrow their search for possible violators.[23] Many of these systems also allow users to click on a button to report potential violations or other problems. In a similar fashion, bad reviews or ratings can help identify potentially bad education actors without regulators treating every actor as if they are bad.

These platforms can help facilitate ESA transactions, including providing a searchable listing of eligible ESA products and services, conducting background checks on tutors, facilitating ratings and reviews (including aggregating reviews from other sites), and facilitating the financial transactions which also can have built-in fraud protection services.

Approval Reciprocity

ESA administrators should consider leveraging inter-state reciprocity agreements to formally recognize the approvals, authorizations, and licensing of providers granted in other states. This mechanism is already used in three areas of education.

The first is teacher certification. Most states have established agreements or contracts that make it easier and more efficient for educators certified in one state to be credentialed in another state. The National Association of State Directors of Teacher Education and Certification (NASDTEC) developed an Interstate Agreement for Educator Licensure, which provides a mechanism for teachers, administrators, and support professionals licensed in one state to be accepted in another. More than forty-seven states have signed the agreement.[24]

Another example is the State Authorization Reciprocity Agreements (SARA), which calls for a single set of baseline standards and procedures to regulate the approval of postsecondary distance education programs. The reciprocity system will ensure institutions can easily operate distance education programs in multiple states as long as they meet the regulatory requirements of their home state.[25]

The SARA model is particularly relevant to the ESA discussion. The rapidly expanding universe of online courses offered by postsecondary institutions faced outdated federal regulations that would require thousands of institutions to contact and work through as many as fifty-four states and territories, and, sometimes, with multiple regulatory agencies in those states.

There is an elegance in the way SARA helps provide greater efficiencies while still providing quality controls. It is vastly more efficient for providers by offering them a uniform set of quality standards across all states. It is also less costly for states, many of which do not have the resources or capacity to perform their own individual reviews of thousands of providers.[26]

The SARA model offers a useful framework for ESA administrators searching for a mechanism to recognize approvals and disapprovals of different education providers in other states. Nevada could use a reciprocity agreement to formally recognize the online learning courses approved by the state departments of education in Florida, Texas, and Louisiana. Similar agreements could be used to recognize the approval of instructional materials, tutors, and other services.

Finally, all fifty states have voluntarily signed the Interstate Compact on Educational Opportunity for Military Children.[27] The Compact addresses key educational transition issues encountered by military families, including

- Enrollment: Schools should accept unofficial records of new enrolled students rather than waiting to receive an official transcript.

- Placement: If a child was receiving special education services at the old school, the new school should place the child in a comparable program.
- Attendance: Districts should allow children to miss school to attend deployment-related activities.
- Eligibility: Students should be able to continue at the grade level in which they were enrolled in their previous school, regardless of age.
- Graduation: Schools should waive specific course or exam requirements for students transferring during their senior year if necessary to allow the student to graduate on time.

Similar reciprocal agreements can be used by ESA administrators to recognize the approvals granted in other states of tutors, online learning providers, certified teachers, and instructional resources. Doing so frees up valuable administrative time and resources to focus instead on the monitoring of providers in their state and sharing information related to participation, performance, and violations with other state ESA administrators.

Accountability with School Choice

The school choice movement has struggled with how to best embrace private school choice with public accountability. Nearly all sides agree that parent choice is by its very nature an accountability check and balance. Schools will have to pay attention to quality once they face the pressure of parents being able to take a child out of a school and enroll him or her in another school.

The debate within the community has centered on the question if choice alone is sufficient enough accountability for public funds or if additional regulations are needed to help with equity, protect children, and also protect taxpayer investment.

One side of the debate argues that requiring private schools to use state assessments and accountability measures will create too many administrative burdens for private schools, which will keep many of the good ones from participating. Mandating the use of state assessments, for example, may restrict private school autonomy over curriculum and limit their ability to innovate. There is an understandable concern that too much top-down accountability and regulation will limit school leadership.

On the other hand, these schools are serving students using taxpayer dollars, which demands a level of transparency and comparable measures to know how well students are being served. Without these comparable measures, it is often difficult if not impossible to know the true impact of choice programs.

Paraphrasing President James Madison in Federalist 51, if all schools were angels, no regulation would be needed. Or as the Fordham Institute's president Michael Petrilli has explained, "Bad schools happen. They happen in the public sector, the charter sector, and, yes, the private sector. And . . . the answer cannot be 'let the market figure it out.' Because it hasn't, and it won't—and somebody must."[28]

The best solution is what has become known as a "sliding scale" approach which offers a flexible approach to regulation. Under this approach, a school's obligation to greater transparency and accountability accommodations goes up as the number of students participating in choice programs rises. This respects the independence of private schools that participate in choice programs in a limited way, but also allows for greater accountability for schools that serve more students through existing choice programs.

Even with this approach, states should be cautious in the accountability burdens placed on schools. A basic framework should require the following:

- accreditation that includes a review of the school's academic rigor and performance;
- documentation of financial sustainability;
- operation for a defined period of time prior to participation in the choice program;
- allow private schools that accept choice program students to use a nationally norm-referenced assessment as an alternative to the state assessment. For example, Florida allows private schools participating in the scholarship tax-credit program to choose from a list of nationally norm-referenced exams, or they can choose to administer the state assessment; and
- reporting the results to either the state or a third-party research entity. Florida results are shared with the University of Florida, where they are tabulated and released in an annual statewide report on the program.

This flexibility with the assessments helps provide a basic level of transparency without interfering with the curricular decisions of a school. The Foundation for Excellence in Education's director of educational choice Adam Peshek prefers this approach for a number of reasons: "It provides information on student learning, it allows private schools to maintain their autonomy, it does not stifle innovation, it avoids the slippery slope of regulatory creep, and it provides choice—which is the goal of these programs to begin with."[29] As an aside, states will need to confront this within their traditional school system given that the new federal Every Student Succeeds Act (ESSA) permits individual districts to use nationally recognized high school exams.

Frederick Hess, resident scholar and director of education policy studies at the American Enterprise Institute, says this option "strike[s] a balance between safeguarding institutional autonomy, providing families with what they need to be informed consumers, and ensuring some appropriate degree of public accountability." Under this approach private schools that receive only a small portion of their revenue from public course through choice programs would have minimal obligations and accountability regulations imposed on them. Those whose budgets have greater dependency on public funds would face stricter accountability measures. This is a reasonable ask to make of schools and a bargain used elsewhere, such as in higher education where a similar sliding scale of regulation is applied depending on the level of public investment with not just financial aid (the postsecondary equivalent of vouchers in K–12) but also general public investment in, say, a state system of higher education or community college system.

This sliding scale approach provides the regulatory framework for ESAs as well. More expensive services, such as school tuition, could be subjected to greater levels of both approvals to serve students as well as accountability measures. Lower cost services, such as a five-dollar app, would be left primarily to the quality tools built into the market platforms. The sliding scale approach provides agility for the regulator without sacrificing quality while also providing greater scrutiny for those services that cost more.

PUTTING IT ALL TOGETHER

ESA administrators have the chance to design their regulatory approach using these new tools and systems that can help them with providing maximum flexibility for parents while still remaining committed to quality.

Tiered Accountability

The only viable option for ESA administrators facing the challenge of thousands of financial transactions across tens of thousands of educational products and services is to embrace an approach that uses tiers of quality controls with a sliding scale accountability system for the most expensive services.

Tier I: Market Platforms Can Provide Two Fundamental Components of Quality Control

The first tier of accountability is the core account management services to prevent fraud, waste, and abuse. There are numerous services that now provide the backend support for consumer directed accounts, including HSAs and transportation benefits. These account management services include claims processing, fraud monitoring, and managing eligible expenses. Adam Peshek's chapter explores the account management services being utilized in state ESA programs and how these new service providers can support ESA administration.

The second key component is transparency. Market platforms can standardize key pieces of information about eligible ESA services and resources, from simple directory information to other forms of quality indicators such as evaluation results, assessment trends, certifications, background checks, staff credentials, and accreditation information. Pricing information is an essential element as well, particularly in services such as tutoring, online courses, and education therapies. For schools, ESA administrators can also use the indicators reported as part of school report cards and accountability systems, including summative grades or rankings.

Tier II: Ratings and Reviews

ESA administrators should use the functionality of market platforms to provide basic ratings and reviews for all approved services and products. ESA administrators should seek to leverage entities that have already amassed ratings to help seed their state listings, drawing upon GreatSchools for school reviews, Graphite for app reviews, and Noodle for tutor and other educational services. The ESA platform should then encourage additional ratings by requiring parents to rate and review a purchased service before they make their next financial transaction, similar to the practice used by Uber. These ratings would help to inform not only parent decisions among the options offered but also to help ESA administrators identify potential bad actors for more targeted reviews and actions.

Tier III: Approvals and Sliding Scale Accountability

The top tier of accountability requirements should be reserved mostly for schools that involve authorization (such as charter schools), approvals (such as online courses), or where a single provider consumes the majority of a parent's ESA. Within this level, ESA administrators can still use the sliding scale accountability framework to provide maximum flexibility to the schools while still ensuring a level of overall quality.

The use of reciprocity agreements can also save ESA administrators time with the approving of online course providers, education therapists, and other service providers. Reciprocity agreements still allow for approval, but they create efficiency in allowing the approval to be done once and for the entity to be introduced onto the market platform where its quality can be tracked and measured overtime. Reciprocity should also involve data sharing, so that a provider's outcome and quality ratings in one state can be shared with ESA administrators in another state.

The strength of this three tiered approach is that it builds layers of quality while preserving maximum flexibility. It allows ESA administrators to focus their monitoring efforts on more expensive services, such as schools charging tuition, and not getting bogged down with approving ten-dollar apps. At the same time, the fraud protection services and quality ratings can still help to flag potential bad actors that may deserve some additional scrutiny. The sliding scale system for participating schools respects institutional independence while still providing some reasonable accountability mechanisms.

It also helps ESA administrators make decisions related to the removal of providers from participating in the program. Products or services that fall below a certain rating could be flagged for additional review or automatic removal. Schools that struggle to demonstrate positive student outcomes could be removed from the program.

It also can formally recognize the quality controls within other programs. Charter schools could still have their charters revoked based on the state's authorizing requirements. Online courses that are subject to state approval could also be removed if they fail to meet key performance measures. In this way, the ESA program can not only embrace but benefit from the existing quality controls already provided under other reforms.

Partner First

ESA administrators should also consider which parts of their systems need to be built and which parts are better outsourced to existing platforms. States often try to build web services that try, but often fail, to match the quality of service provided by outside providers. Instead of building competing services, states could adopt a "partner first" approach where they contract with those that have developed core competencies or audiences.

Take for example user-generated feedback systems. Many state government leaders are learning that adding ratings and reviews to their web services is easier than actually generating the ratings. Silicon Valley is guided by a rule of thumb known as the "1/9/90 Rule" which suggests that only 1 percent of users will actively create content. Another 9 percent will participate by commenting, rating or sharing the content. The remaining 90 percent consume and read the content.[30] In other words, most people won't contribute reviews; they'll simply read them.

This is clearly evidenced in early state efforts to provide rating functionality. Florida, for example, maintains a list of more than 11,000 approved online courses and gives parents the chance to rate them on a scale of 1 to 5 stars, along with feedback on issues such as ease of registration, course quality, and overall satisfaction. Yet only forty-two courses have received a single review. This is not to be critical of the Florida Department of Education. It is simply to illustrate the challenges facing a state agency in not just offering the functionality of ratings but building the audience needed to populate it.

A "partner first" approach is more compelling for services that require not only technical functionality but access to audiences. Building some of this web functionality is easier compared to building the audience to use it and generating the content. GreatSchools, an online platform that provides school quality information, has developed not only a core competency in providing a searchable index of 200,000 schools, but in the process has amassed more than one million parent ratings. GreatSchools has spent decades focused on search engine optimization (SEO) strategies, partnerships with realtors and newspapers, and other marketing efforts, which has led to their ability to interact with nearly half of all parents in the country. GreatSchools' monthly visitor traffic dwarfs that of state school report cards. Even if a state could build a website that matches GreatSchools' functionality, it would be virtually impossible to recreate the parent ratings or build the audience.

ESA administrators should also explore additional ways to incentivize or cultivate reviewers. Common Sense Media offers teachers the chance to earn up to $250 in an Amazon gift card for reviews of apps, games, or websites.[31] Yelp provides businesses the chance to offer customers a "check in offer" to review a discount for checking in and reviewing a business. Uber requires riders and drivers to rate each other before the next trip.

These best practices should be applied to ESA rating systems by creating incentive programs to generate parent and teacher reviews which can then help populate the catalog of approved services. In addition, financial reimbursement could be linked to reviews, just as the Uber platform provides.

Critics suggest that such review and rating systems are vulnerable to providers who may just pay individuals to provide fake glowing reviews or high ratings. The concern is legitimate and one of the reasons why review sites are continuously developing new techniques and tools to identify fake reviews. Some analyze words, Internet addresses, and the velocity of reviews submitted. Companies including Amazon have also taken fake reviews to court in an effort to curb abuse.[32]

However, these platforms have also turned to their communities to help police the fake reviews. A visit to Yelp or Amazon allows users to report potentially fraudulent reviews and also "vote up" helpful reviews. This not only has the benefit of using the community to police the site but also helps to elevate the most helpful reviews to the top. Amazon also offers a "verified purchase" designation for reviews of products that are actually purchased through Amazon.[33] A similar check can be included in ESA systems since the back engine systems supporting the ESA transactions and financial management would know if a parent used their ESA to purchase the reviewed product or service.

Embrace Open Data

ESA administrators should also embrace strategies involving open data as a means by which to support better decisions, both by parents as well as other state administrators. Government entities that turn big data into open data empower not just new entrepreneurs but citizens and consumers as well. The majority of definitions of "open data" include two features: the data must be available for anyone to use and it must be licensed in a way that allows for its reuse.

Open data can support ESA administration in a few ways. First, just providing the data in machine-readable formats help support services like Noodle and GreatSchools that currently have to go through difficult steps to "scrape" data off websites, clean it, and then put it to use in their system. Second, open data sets can support quality control efforts across state lines. Larger data sets combined with increasingly sophisticated analytical tools and the power of the crowd can help regulators better utilize limited resources and reduce the burden of compliance on citizens and business.

Parent Navigators

Finally, some parents will need assistance to assemble a portfolio of educational services for their child, both in matching student needs with providers as well as helping parents make sense of the various quality information available to inform their decision. This again is not a unique need to education. Some individuals need their primary care doctor to help coordinate their other healthcare treatments and specialists. Many need financial advisors to assist in putting together the best portfolio of retirement investments based on their age, retirement goals, and risk.

With rapidly expanding choices, better guidance systems will be critical to ensuring that families can put together the right portfolio of opportunities and customized pathways to ensure better preparation. The role of school guidance counselors may evolve to provide this support. State ESA administrators could also provide this as a service. For example, the Louisiana Department of Education offers families with toll-free Course Choice Counselor Assistance that provides one-on-one access to experienced, certified professional school counselors who can help with course selection and registration.[34]

Here too, Internet-based approaches can help. The financial advisory service sector is being democratized with new startups such as Betterment, NerdWallet, FutureAdvisor, Motif Investing, Personal Capital, Wealthfront, and Aspiration that help families with managing their savings and retirement funds, track investment goals, and provide other financial advice. In education, Noodle is aggregating information to help families discover and choose education opportunities ranging from tutors to summer camps to master's programs. Naviance is providing the academic equivalent of a "GPS" for students to help them with course selection and planning for college. Parchment allows students to securely track, store, and share credentials they earn, be it high school transcripts or course certificates.

These services will evolve to better support the full range of choices students face, while ESA administrators can help accelerate their development by incorporating them into ESA programs.

MARKET PLATFORMS FOR EFFECTIVE QUALITY CONTROL

The new era of personalized learning offered by a diverse array of providers is an opportunity, not a threat to student success. It is a means by which to accommodate the rapid growth of diverse educational opportunities and student support services to help achieve the public good of public education. The arrival of sophisticated market platforms can help ESA administrators provide important student protections as well as quality controls. Indeed, the arrival of consumer directed accounts in other sectors has led to a growing number of tools and services to help make these markets work better not just in their efficiency but also in managing quality.

The ESA programs that succeed in the future will be those that leverage these market platforms to offer better transparency, quality control through ratings, and a sliding scale of accountability that requires more of the providers that charge the most or serve the most students participating in choice programs. This approach respects a minimum role of government while still preserving essential functions to protect students and taxpayers. It also embraces the use of transparent information to make markets work better and more efficiently. In addition, it allows ESA administrators to identify potential bad actors for more focused inquiries versus treating every provider as if they are a potentially bad actor.

It is also important to end this chapter on a note of humility. This system is far from perfect. But if the education sector were to agree to not offer ESAs until every part of it had been adjusted to weed out each and every worst actor, ESAs would never be available to support students. The system described above relies on layering different levels of quality control while also using the community and market platforms to track quality and bad actors. More importantly, these platforms are rarely static, with new improvements made on a daily basis, allowing for iterative improvements made toward the goal of better empowering parents and supporting high quality decisions. ESA administrators need to start from somewhere and improve their methods, structures, and systems over time. This approach offers a starting point from which to begin those efforts.

NOTES

1. The author thanks Sarah Runge, Erin Lockett, and Adam Peshek for providing research and support for this chapter.

2. *The Economist*, "Mass Production," October 20, 2009, accessed April 15, 2016, http://www.economist.com/node/14299820.

3. Michael Horn, "Why Traditional Education Reformers Struggle with Blended Learning," *EdSurge*, March 7, 2016, https://www.edsurge.com/news/2016-03-07-why-traditional-education-reformers-struggle-with-blended-learning.

4. *The Huffington Post*, "FACT: There Are 80,000 Ways to Drink a Starbucks Beverage," March 4, 2014, http://www.huffingtonpost.com/2014/03/04/starbucks_n_4890735.html.

5. Afterschool Alliance, "America after 3PM: How Are Kids Spending Their Time Afterschool?" accessed April 15, 2016, http://www.afterschoolalliance.org/AA3PM/.

6. National Center for Education Statistics, "Selected Statistics from the Public Elementary and Secondary Education Universe: School Year 2012-2013," accessed April 15, 2016, http://nces.ed.gov/pubsearch/pubsinfo.asp?pubid=2014098.

7. "Los Angeles Library to Offer High School Diplomas," 89.3 KPCC, January 9, 2014, http://www.scpr.org/news/2014/01/09/41466/los-angeles-library-to-offer-high-school-diplomas/.

8. Education Reimagined, "A Transformational Vision for Education in the US," 2015, http://education-reimagined.org/wp-content/uploads/2015/10/A-Transformational-Vision-for-Education-in-the-US-2015-09.pdf.

9. *PR Newswire*, "Survey: Patients See 18.7 Different Doctors on Average," April 27, 2010, http://www.prnewswire.com/news-releases/survey-patients-see-187-different-doctors-on-average-92171874.html.

10. Eli R. Stoltzfus, "Access to Dependent Care Reimbursement Accounts and Workplace-Funded Childcare," *Beyond the Numbers* 4, no.1 (2015), Bureau of Labor Statistics, http://www.bls.gov/opub/btn/volume-4/access-to-dependent-care-reimbursement-accounts-and-workplace-funded-childcare.htm.

11. Foundation for Excellence in Education, "Education Savings Accounts (ESA): Innovation and Customization," accessed April 15, 2016, http://www.excelined.org/wp-content/uploads/ESAs-Policy-Summary-12.20141.pdf.

12. Arianna Prothero, "Some States Put Parents in Charge of Student Spending," *Education Week*, February 24, 2015, http://www.edweek.org/ew/articles/2015/02/25/some-states-put-parents-in-charge-of.html.

13. Robert Frost, http://www.bartleby.com/104/64.html.

14. National Alliance for Public Charter Schools, "Measuring Up," accessed April 15, 2016, http://www.publiccharters.org/law-database/caps/; Denisa R. Superville, "Chicago Teachers' Union Rejects District Contract Offer," *Education Week*, February 1, 2016, http://blogs.edweek.org/edweek/District_Dossier/2016/02/chicago_teachers_union_rejects.html.

15. Illinois State Board of Education, "Fenger Academy High School," Illinois Report Card 2014–2015, accessed April 15, 2016, http://www.illinoisreportcard.com/School.aspx?source=Trends&source2=Parcc&Schoolid=150162990250012; Caitlin Emma, "Here's Why $7 Billion Didn't Help American's Worst Schools," *Politico*, November 3, 2015, http://www.politico.com/story/2015/11/failing-schools-education-white-house-214332.

16. Melissa Ezarik, "The Textbook Adoption Mess–And What Reformers are Doing to Fix It," District Administration, March 2005, http://www.districtadministration.com/article/textbook-adoption-mess-and-what-reformers-are-doing-fix-it.

17. John Grego & Roumen Vesselinov, "Duolingo Effectiveness Study," Duolingo, December 2012, accessed April 15, 2016, https://s3.amazonaws.com/duolingo-papers/other/vesselinov-grego.duolingo12.pdf.

18. Oklahoma State Textbook Committee, "World Languages K–12 Approved Titles: July 1, 2009–June 30, 2015," accessed April 15, 2016, http://oktextbooks.ok.gov/textbook_pdf/langk12.pdf/.

19. Michael Q. McShane, Jenn Hatfield, & Elizabeth English, "The Paperwork Pile-Up: Measuring the Burden of Charter School Applications," *American Enterprise Institute*, May 19, 2015, http://www.aei.org/publication/the-paperwork-pile-up-measuring-the-burden-of-charter-school-applications.

20. John Katzman, "A Civil Education Marketplace," *American Enterprise Institute* (paper presented at conference on June 24, 2015), http://www.aei.org/wp-content/uploads/2015/06/Katzman_FINAL.pdf.

21. Myles Anderson, "88% of Consumers Trust Online Reviews As Much As Personal Recommendations," Search Engine Land, July 7, 2014, http://searchengineland.com/88-consumers-trust-online-reviews-much-personal-recommendations-195803.

22. David A. Hanauer et al. "Parental Awareness and Use of Online Physician Rating Sites," AAP Gateway, September 2014, http://pediatrics.aappublications.org/content/early/2014/09/17/peds.2014-0681.abstract.

23. Michael Luca & Luther Lowe, "City Governments Are Using Yelp to Tell You Where Not to Eat," *Harvard Business Review*, February 12, 2015, https://hbr.org/2015/02/city-governments-are-using-yelp-to-tell-you-where-not-to-eat.

24. National Association of State Directors of Teacher Education and Certification (NASDTEC), accessed April 15, 2016, http://www.nasdtec.org/.

25. Commission on the Regulation of Postsecondary Distance Education, "Advancing Access Through Regulatory Reform: Findings, Principles, and Recommendations for the State Authorization Reciprocity Agreement (SARA)," April 2013, http://www.sheeo.org/sites/default/files/publications/Commission%20on%20Regulation%20of%20Postsecondary%20Distance%20Education%20Draft%20Recommendations%20FINAL%20April%20_0.pdf.

26. National Council for State Authorization Reciprocity Agreements, accessed April 15, 2016, http://www.nc-sara.org; "Leading in an Era of Change, Making the Most of State Course Access Programs," Foundation for Excellence in Education, July 2014, http://digitallearningnow.com/site/uploads/2014/07/DLN-CourseAccess-FINAL_14July2014b.pdf.

27. Military Interstate Children's Compact Commission, accessed April 15, 2016, http://www.mic3.net/.

28. Michael J. Petrilli, "The Problem with 'Bad Voucher Schools Aren't a Problem,'" *Education Next*, January 17, 2014, http://educationnext.org/the-problem-with-bad-voucher-schools-aren't-a-problem/.

29. Foundation for Excellence in Education, "Over-Regulation in Louisiana's Voucher Program," January 5, 2016, http://www.excelined.org/2016/01/05/over-regulation-in-louisianas-voucher-program/.

30. Susan Kuchinskas, "The 1/9/90 Rule: What You Need to Know," American Express Open Forum, May 25, 2011, https://www.americanexpress.com/us/small-business/openforum/articles/the-1990-rule-what-you-need-to-know/.

31. "Write a Review and Receive an Amazon Gift Card," Common Sense Education, accessed April 15, 2016, https://www.commonsense.org/education/transform.

32. Jackie Wattles, "Amazon Sues More Than 1,000 Sellers of 'Fake' Product Reviews," *CNN Money*, October 19, 2015, http://money.cnn.com/2015/10/18/technology/amazon-lawsuit-fake-reviews/.

33. "About Amazon Verified Purchase Reviews," Amazon, accessed April 15, 2016, http://www.amazon.com/gp/help/customer/display.html%3FnodeId=201145140; Megan Rose Dickey & Kim Bhasin, "Yelp is Going to Extreme Lengths to Crack Down on Fake Reviews," *Business Insider*, November 27, 2012, http://www.businessinsider.com/yelp-fake-reviews-2012-11.

34. Louisiana Department of Education, "Course Choice Professional School Counselors Informational Webinar," accessed April 15, 2016, https://www.louisianabelieves.com/docs/counselor-toolbox-resources/professional-school-counselor-webinar.pdf?sfvrsn=2.

Chapter Six

State Education Agencies, Regulatory Models, and ESAs

Gerard Robinson

Education savings accounts (ESAs) arrive on the national scene at a time when school choice is one of the most important social movements since the civil rights campaigns of the 1950s. Addressing similar themes of equality and access, ESAs promote the idea that all parents have a right to enroll their child in an educational setting that fits his or her needs. But unlike traditional solutions to fix education, ESAs put parents in the driver's seat, rather than state bureaucrats. As other chapters in this volume note, ESA programs have expanded greatly since the first program passed in 2011. As more ESA laws are enacted across the nation, it is important that state policymakers and agency leaders reflect upon how existing ESAs have been designed and implemented, and how processes and programs could be improved to help ESAs meet their great expectations in the future.

Proponents of ESAs point to a variety of great expectations for how ESAs will expand school choice and increase opportunity for students and families. On face value, ESAs are similar to charter, voucher, and tax-credit scholarship programs in two ways. First, ESAs empower parents with a choice to pick a school that best fits their child's needs. Second, ESAs use public funds to pay for the cost of attending that school. But the distinguishing factor between ESAs and other choice programs is that parents can customize their child's K–12 education even *beyond* schools with the use of a debit card or bank account they control—not a state department of education, a nonprofit scholarship organization, or a school principal. With state-allocated funds, parents have access to a restricted-use account that they can use toward a range of educational services, including tuition, tutoring services, special education therapies, and other state-approved expenses.

The opportunities made available through ESAs excite reform-minded state lawmakers and families—but frighten the education establishment—as

ESAs will upset traditional schooling in America as we know it. ESA proponents should therefore expect continued opposition, explicitly in public debate and in the legislative process, but also in state regulations and bureaucratic politics. The creation of the Milwaukee Parental Choice Program (MPCP) provides a glimpse into these dynamics that may be helpful to those considering ESA legislation.

The purpose of this chapter is to inform lawmakers and school choice advocates about the regulatory models that will help ESA programs achieve their goals. To do so, it analyzes how state administrative agencies (SAAs) adopt regulations for ESA programs. But before turning to ESAs, the first section of the chapter considers how lessons from MPCP, which began the modern school choice movement in America, can inform legislators' understanding of how a choice program can clear legislative and judicial opposition but still be affected by bureaucratic group politics and state regulations.

The chapter then describes how SAAs such as state departments of education create regulations for public and private education, and provides an overview of ESA programs and their administrative oversight in the states that have adopted ESA programs to date—Arizona, Florida, Tennessee, and Mississippi. Nevada enacted the fifth ESA program in 2015, but that program is suspended pending a new appropriation from the state.[1] The chapter concludes with general principles for how SAAs can help, and not hinder, the success of ESA programs moving forward.

LESSONS FROM THE PAST[2]

An uncommon political alliance between a black, inner-city Milwaukee state representative, Polly Williams, and a white Republican governor, Tommy Thompson, led to the enactment of the MPCP on April 27, 1990.[3] At the time, Milwaukee had a high dropout rate and was observing disappointing outcomes in student achievement that decades of additional money, redrawn attendance zones, and busing policies had promised to fix. With a shrinking pool of high-paying, blue-collar jobs, and a growing population of chronically unemployed and lower-skilled young people, officials felt that something radical needed to be done, and fast.

MPCP's intent was to allow low-income parents to opt-out of sending their children to Milwaukee public schools. MPCP is a means tested program, meaning that eligibility is based on socioeconomic class, not a student's performance. Therefore, students living in a household with an annual income of 185 percent of the federal poverty level were eligible to receive a publically funded voucher worth $2,466 to pay for education at a private school.[4] Wisconsin Supreme Court Justice William Callow defined it more succinctly: "The purpose of this experimental legislation is to determine if it is possible to improve, through parental choice, the quality of education in Wisconsin for children of low-income families."[5]

Following the enactment of the program, approximately 300 MPCP students enrolled at seven nonsectarian private schools during the 1990–1991 school year. By 1995, enrollment had quadrupled to over 1,200 students. Although parental demand for vouchers was high, the supply of private schools was low because religious schools were not included in the MPCP program. One reason for this was constitutional. Article I, section 18 of the Wisconsin Constitution states:

> The right of every person to worship Almighty God according to the dictates of conscience shall never be infringed; nor shall any person be compelled to attend, erect or support any place of worship, or to maintain any ministry, without consent; nor shall any control of, or interference with, the rights of conscience be permitted, or any preference be given by law to any religious establishments or modes of worship; nor shall any money be drawn from the treasury for the benefit of religious societies, or religious or theological seminaries.[6]

In 1995, choice advocates successfully lobbied the Wisconsin legislature to amend the MPCP law in two significant ways. First, the legislature acknowledged that a parent—not the state—selected the school for his or her child's education. Therefore, the legislature was not funding religious schools and was not in violation of the state constitution. Catholic, Lutheran, Jewish, and Muslim schools began accepting voucher families for the first time. Second, the new law replaced the 1,500-student enrollment cap with an enrollment formula that raised it to approximately 15,000 students.

The Wisconsin Education Association Council, the Milwaukee Teachers Education Association, the People for the American Way and others challenged the amended law on the grounds that giving public money to religious schools violated the Wisconsin constitution. The National Association for the Advancement of Colored People alleged in its lawsuit that MPCP violated the equal protection clause of the state and federal constitutions because it advanced segregation in city schools. Ultimately, none of these allegations persuaded the court to stop the program. In 1998, the Wisconsin Supreme Court ruled in a 4–2 decision that low-income parents could spend public tax dollars to enroll their children in religious schools in Milwaukee through MPCP.

As of September 2015, MPCP included 27,619 students in 117 schools, with the majority being religious.[7] The program provides a voucher worth $7,214 (grades K–8) and $7,860 (grades 9–12) to parents with a household income up to 300 percent of the federal poverty level, which is $73,401 for a family of four. The demand for enrollment is still high, and research demonstrates the positive effects of MPCP on student achievement and high school graduation rates.[8] To broaden the reach of parental choice beyond Milwaukee, the Wisconsin legislature approved a voucher program for Racine in 2011, and a statewide voucher program in 2015.

For twenty-five years, Wisconsin lawmakers have successfully cleared judicial and legislative obstacles to keep MPCP alive. Still, opposition to its growth is ubiquitous, at times, even stemming from the state's own educational administrative agency that is responsible for regulating public and private education, the Wisconsin Department of Public Instruction (DPI).

DPI has written rules and regulations for MPCP since 1990. Its responsibilities include choosing which private schools participate in the program; establishing academic standards; setting minimum qualifications for teachers; evaluating vendors; and sponsoring MPCP workshops for families and schools. Though some principals and families believe DPI is an asset to MPCP, others have accused DPI of hindering the growth of MPCP through overregulation or agency politics, particularly during the program's initial years of implementation. For example, DPI approved a short, two-week window for private schools to sign up for participation in MPCP; failed to comply with a statute that required DPI to "[e]nsure that parents and students . . . are informed" about MPCP in a timely manner; rejected applications for minor technicalities such as a missed middle initial in a parent's name; and, in some cases, adopted an annual reimbursement policy for transportation costs when a monthly reimbursement option would have helped them receive their money sooner. To complicate matters, the DPI superintendent of public education (the state education chief) *joined* the teachers union in a lawsuit against MPCP during the early implementation of the program.[9]

Claims of DPI's hostility toward MPCP go beyond the initial years of the program, however. This quote from a 2013 report summarizes this concern well:

> The most significant area DPI holds sway over schools in the Milwaukee and Racine parental choice programs are through the interpretation and application of state statutes governing the use of vouchers. Choice schools are required by law to produce numerous annual audits for review by DPI officials. It's through that nuts-and-bolts process that many in the choice community believe the department's hostility toward voucher schools is most apparent.[10]

Of course, there are varying opinions about whether DPI is a help or a hindrance to MPCP. However, the big takeaway is not about DPI: rather, it is that even when state lawmakers successfully clear judicial and legislative obstacles to enact a choice program, an SAA can potentially create a new set of bureaucratic and political challenges.

Generally speaking, SAAs' regulatory duties fall into three categories: legislative, executive and judicial.[11] Legislative functions include writing regulations, which for ESAs include the creation of a reimbursement policy for education service providers, a process for states to determine and validate allowable educational expenditures such as private school tuition or special education classes, and clear eligibility requirements for provider participation. The executive function of an SAA includes implementation of program requirements, which for ESAs include the distribution of public funds to education service providers as well as establishing contracts with financial institutions for distributing debit cards to families. Lastly, the judicial function allows an SAA to take on responsibilities such as removing service providers from an ESA program for financial malfeasance or for failure to comply with transparency guidelines. The next portion of the chapter discusses the primary SAA for school districts around the country: the state department of education.

THE STATE DEPARTMENT OF EDUCATION

In fifty states and the District of Columbia, the state department of education (DOE) is the primary SAA responsible for setting administrative standards for public schools. Its delegation of responsibility includes adopting regulations for curriculum and assessment standards, qualifications for teachers, and implementation of federal laws such as the Every Student Succeeds Act. A DOE is more than a regulator of public schools; it is a partner as well. For example, a DOE provides seed money to help a school board plan for the implementation of a new STEM program, submits a grant application to the U.S. Department of Education or a national foundation on behalf of urban or rural districts for professional development programs for teachers and principals, and offers technical support to magnet schools and charter schools.

Similar to public schools, a DOE is the primary SAA responsible for setting administrative standards for private schools, which includes choice programs like vouchers and tax-credit scholarships. In addition to regulating private schools, a DOE often supports them financially as well. Since the enactment of the Elementary and Secondary Act of 1965, the federal Department of Education has partnered with state and local school boards to allocate Title I funds to independent and religious private schools to pay for education services for low-income students, and to allocate Title II funds to provide professional development for private school teachers.

Putting ESAs in the context of an SAA is important because DOEs have a large role to play in the regulation and administration of private school choice programs. Unsurprisingly, four of five existing ESA programs have selected the DOE to be at least one of the SAAs tasked with administering the state's ESA program. In three states, it is the only SAA that can do so. Although the DOE-as-regulator-approach-model has many benefits and challenges, some state lawmakers have selected an alternative SAA to oversee such programs, such as a Department of the Treasury. The next section of this chapter illustrates the administrative and regulatory approaches that govern the ESA programs in Arizona, Florida, Tennessee, Mississippi, and Nevada.

EXISTING ESA REGULATION MODELS

Lawmakers in the five states with ESA programs have chosen a variety of different models for implementation given the complex nature of transferring state funds directly into the hands of parents, and overseeing how those funds are used (see figure 6.1). The diverse array of regulatory approaches to governing ESAs reflects this reality. This section contains four models: (1) a DOE model in Tennessee and Mississippi; (2) a non-DOE model in Nevada; (3) a dual agency and a multiple scholarship organization model in Arizona; and (4) a dual agency with a single scholarship organization model in Florida. Following the description of the existing state models is another option that policymakers could consider for future ESA programs: a single agency with a multiple scholarship organization model.

DOE Model: Tennessee and Mississippi ESAs

The Tennessee legislature enacted the *Individualized Education Account Program* (IEA) in 2015 to help families with special needs children pay for educational costs including private school tuition and contracted services with a public school. The Tennessee DOE is the state agency responsible for all regulatory and administrative management of IEA.[12] These duties include approving a list of participating nonpublic schools and education providers and suspending or terminating any of them from the IEA program for failure to comply with program requirements; preparing a quarterly allocation of state funds to a student's IEA; providing parents with a written notice of allowable expenses and their responsibilities; adopting policies for conducting or contracting an annual or random review of IEAs; and establishing an online and anonymous fraud reporting service.

The Mississippi legislature enacted the *Equal Opportunity for Students with Special Needs Program* in 2015 to provide parents the opportunity "to withdraw their child with special needs from the public school system to use scholarship money to help defray the cost of private school tuition or other specific allowable activities."[13] Similar to the Tennessee law, the

Mississippi DOE is tasked with regulating and managing the ESA program. The Mississippi DOE's duties include notifying low-income parents about ESAs; managing online applications; conducting audits; approving or denying applications within twenty-one days of receipt; and depositing money into a student's ESA.

What are the benefits of the DOE model? First, a DOE provides regulatory consistency to ensure that rules for choice programs do not conflict with traditional public school regulations. Second, a DOE has years of experience in creating and amending public and private school programs, which no other state agency has. Third, DOE staff, many who have worked in the agency for

STATE	ELIGIBILITY	AGENCY
Arizona	<ul><li>Special needs students</li><li>Students enrolled in a school graded as a "D" or "F" by state accountability system</li><li>Child of a parent or guardian killed while on active duty in the armed forces</li><li>Ward of the state or juvenile court (i.e., a child in foster care)</li><li>Sibling of a student currently enrolled in the ESA program</li><li>A student remains eligible for an ESA through high school graduation</li></ul>	<ul><li>Department of Education</li><li>Office of the State Treasurer</li></ul>
Florida	<ul><li>Special needs students</li><li>Any student over 3 years of age</li><li>A student remains eligible for an ESA through high school, or to 22 years of age (whichever is first)</li></ul>	<ul><li>Department of Education</li><li>Scholarship Foundation Organization (the SFO can retain up to 3 percent of funds to administer the ESA)</li></ul>
Tennessee	<ul><li>Special needs students</li><li>Students enrolled for two semesters in a public school</li><li>Student that received an IEA within the previous year</li><li>A student remains eligible for an ESA until she or he returns to a public school, through high school graduation, or to 22 years of age by August 15</li></ul>	<ul><li>Department of Education</li></ul>
Mississippi	<ul><li>Student with an IEP in use for 18 months</li><li>A student remains eligible for an ESA until she or he returns to a public school, through high school graduation, to 21 years of age, or if a parent fails to verify program eligibility every 3 years</li></ul>	<ul><li>Department of Education</li></ul>
Nevada	<ul><li>Special needs students</li><li>Student enrolled in a public school for 100 days</li><li>Student in a household less than 185 percent of federal poverty</li></ul>	<ul><li>Office of the State Treasurer</li></ul>

Figure 6.1   ESA Programs in Five States.

several years, possess institutional knowledge that can help incoming board of education members and the state chief manage the ESA program.

One particular benefit of the DOE model in Tennessee and Mississippi is these states' long histories of DOEs overseeing rulemaking for private schools. The IEA is the first private school choice program in Tennessee, so it is understandable for the DOE to be the state regulatory and administrative agency of ESAs. The ESA is the third private school choice program in Mississippi, and the DOE manages all three.

However, the challenges are also threefold: slow adoption of innovation; more regulation instead of less; and a monopoly mindset. First, a DOE may not pivot as quickly as an innovative school choice law requires because it takes time to clarify how legislative intent should be translated into rules and regulations that govern it. This is also true for traditional public schools, but the speed of adoption may be even slower for a choice program because DOEs often incorporate providers outside of the public sector for implementation. Second, a DOE can impede the accomplishment of legislative goals by overregulating a choice program. Third, DOEs are accustomed to having a monopoly over Pre-K–12 education and, thus, may be disinclined to adopt regulations that incorporate new education providers.

The DOE-only model resembles the regulatory model that forty-three state DOEs use for charter school laws. Fifteen DOEs also use this approach for private school voucher programs such as the Louisiana Scholarship Program for low-income students.

Non-DOE Model: Nevada ESAs

One alternative to a DOE-only model is to place all regulatory and administrative authority in another state agency entirely. Unlike Tennessee and Mississippi, the Office of the State Treasurer of Nevada is designated as the SAA for the Nevada ESA program, and maintains all of its regulatory and administrative authority. In 2015, the legislature enacted an ESA law for families with "children enrolled in a public/charter school to choose a different option to meet their educational needs."[14] Unlike Tennessee and Mississippi, where DOEs are responsible for the management of the ESA program, the Nevada DOE is responsible for the collection of student enrollment and achievement data. All Nevada families with children enrolled in a public school for one hundred consecutive days qualify for an ESA—not just targeted populations like in Tennessee or Mississippi.[15] It is worth noting that Nevada's 100-day enrollment rule is open to nearly all its students.[16]

The benefit of a state treasurer's office, rather than a DOE, as the regulator and administer of an ESA program is that it reduces the likelihood that a conflict of interest may arise. The DOE in a state is organized around supporting and regulating public schools, and in some cases may be suspect of, or hostile to, an ESA program. In such cases, the DOE may not necessarily be the best administrative agency to house an ESA program that is designed to provide alternatives to public schools. By contrast, the state treasurer's office is, at face value, a neutral actor for this program. Although the Nevada Supreme Court required that the legislature create a new funding source for the ESA program in its September 2016 ruling, the Nevada Office of the State Treasurer remains the SAA responsible for the administration of ESA funds to families.

Comparatively speaking, Nevada's non-DOE model resembles the regulatory model 9 state SAAs use for tax deduction laws. For instance, the Illinois legislature enacted the Tax Credit for Educational Expenses Program in 1999. The state department of revenue administers the program, not the DOE. In 2013, more than 302,000 parents claimed up to a $500 credit on their state taxes for education expenses for a child enrolled in a public, private, or home-school program. A parent must submit the appropriate paperwork to the department of revenue and then he or she receives a tax deduction directly from the revenue department.[17]

One rationale for not placing a tax deduction (or ESA) program in a DOE is practical—the financial benefit goes directly to families—not schools, as in the case of a voucher program like MPCP. Therefore, DOE oversight is not necessary. Another rationale is political—a DOE tends to overregulate a choice program under its supervision.

Dual Agencies and a Multiple Scholarship Organization Model: Arizona ESAs

One alternative to a DOE-only model in Tennessee and Mississippi, or a non-DOE model in Nevada, is to share regulatory and administrative authority between two SAAs. Lawmakers in Arizona selected a dual agency model to oversee its ESA program when it enacted the *Empowerment Scholarship Program* (ESP) in 2011. The goal of the program is to "provide options for the education of students in this state" who are enrolled in a school with a D or F grade.[18] To meet this objective, the legislature authorized the Arizona Department of Education (DOE) and the Office of the State Treasurer (OST) with a dual role in supporting ESP. The DOE is responsible for adopting "rules and policies necessary for the administration of empowerment scholarship accounts."[19] These rules include the authority to conduct or contract for an annual audit of empowerment scholarship accounts; to remove a parent or a child from ESP for a violation of school or program rules; to refer fraud cases to the state's attorney general; and to determine the eligible enrollment period. In contrast, OST's role with ESP is primarily administrative. It contracts with private financial firms to manage the empowerment scholarship accounts, and oversees the funds DOE deposits with the state treasurer every quarter.

The benefit of the dual agency model is that it enables agencies to regulate within their area of expertise; meaning, a DOE regulates the educational components of a school choice program, while a department of revenue regulates fiscal matters. The benefit of a multiple SSO model is that it empowers parents and private schools to shop for the best fit. Simultaneously, the challenge with this model is that some parents and private schools may not know how to shop and evaluate which SSO is the best fit for their child. Instead, the scholarship organization with the best marketing brochure may get the most business.

Comparatively speaking, Arizona's dual agency model resembles the regulatory model 9 states use for tax-credit scholarship laws. For instance, multiple stakeholders are involved in the administration of the Georgia Education Expense Credit scholarship program enacted in 2008.[20] The process begins with the state DOE approving student scholarship organizations (SSOs) that are qualified to receive tax-credit-eligible-contributions. SSOs such as the G.O.A.L. Scholarship Program work with families and schools to ensure students use the tax credit to the benefit of children. Lastly, the state department of revenue establishes rules for the distribution of scholarship funds to SSOs.[21]

Dual Agencies and a Single Scholarship Organization Model: Florida ESAs

An alternative model is to have two state agencies and a single scholarship organization support an ESA program. This has been done with other school choice programs. For instance, the Florida legislature enacted the Tax Credit Scholarship Program (FTC) in 2001 to allow the DOE and the department of revenue to partner with a nonprofit scholarship-funding organization (SFO) to administer the FTC. In Florida, the leading SFO is Step Up for Students. Under this partnership, a SFO is responsible for reviewing applications and awarding scholarships up to $5,677 for low-income families or students in foster care to pay tuition and fees at private school, or $500 to attend a public school located outside of her or his zoned district. Therefore, the SFO helps to ensure "that all parents, regardless of means, may exercise and enjoy their basic right to educate their children as they see fit."[22] The Florida Department of Education (FLDOE) determines SSO eligibility, and the Florida Department of Revenue adopts rules that govern the FTC.[23]

When the Florida legislature enacted the state's ESA program—the *Gardiner Scholarship Program* (GSP)—in 2014 to "provide the option for a parent to better meet the individual educational needs of his or her eligible child," it modeled the program after the FTC regulatory structure.[24] Unlike the agency-managed ESA programs in Nevada, Arizona, Mississippi, and Tennessee, a SFO is responsible for reviewing applications, determining who is eligible for the program, and managing parent accounts. The FLDOE approves GSP service providers; it requires each nonprofit scholarship organization to verify expenditures before its spends money; investigates complaints about violations by GSP providers or scholarship organizations; requires quarterly reports from GSP providers and scholarship organizations; and evaluates student enrollment lists in public and private schools to avoid a duplication of payments. The legislature also authorized the Florida Commissioner of Education with certain powers that allow him or her to "deny, suspend or revoke" a student's participation in the program or funds to spend within it, if a child's "health, safety, or welfare" is threatened. The commissioner can also "deny, suspend or revoke" a private school, an eligible postsecondary institution, or an approved service provider from participation in GSP.

The benefit of having a single, nongovernment SFO working with parents and schools is that the program can continue to grow and thrive despite a change in governor, the dominant political party in the legislature or the DOE commissioner. A single SFO can also provide programmatic consistency by, for example, maintaining consistent standards for reviewing applications and determining eligibility for the program. In addition, an SFO can sustain ongoing relationships with families that can help families identify high-quality programs and services that effectively meet their child's needs. The challenge is that a single SFO could adopt a monopoly mindset, meaning it could essentially morph into a DOE for private schools. In addition, an SFO can become so close to private school leaders and families that it no longer serves as an objective evaluator of the quality of services provided. Lastly, the absence of a competitor SFO can lead to less innovation that is present when multiple players are in the game.

An Alternative Model

State lawmakers will consider other ESA regulatory approaches in the future, but they will inevitably adopt some of the models described here. In addition to these models, here is one to consider moving forward: a single agency and multiple scholarship organization model. A single agency model requires a state to keep regulatory authority for an ESA in one SAA—a DOE, revenue department or other—and authorize multiple nonprofit scholarship organizations to work directly with families and schools—not a state bureaucracy. The general benefits and challenges of a single agency model in Tennessee, Mississippi, or Nevada were already identified in previous sections. However, an additional benefit not already mentioned is that a single agency model provides one-stop-shop accountability, meaning the legislature, parents, and education service providers have one agency to address its grievances. This can minimize a web of regulatory and administrative confusion associated with more than one agency managing an ESA.

One benefit of having multiple, nongovernment scholarship organizations working with families and schools is that they can grow the program through grassroots outreach. Multiple scholarship organizations can also provide a niche market for families looking for a religious education. In Virginia, the *Education Improvement Scholarships Tax Credit Program* allows foundations to provide scholarships to faith-based private schools. For instance, the Association of Christian Schools International has a foundation to support students at its member schools, as do Jewish and Catholic foundations.[25]

One challenge with having multiple scholarship organizations is a competition of different messages that could result in a marketing overload for families. Another challenge is that a single agency will have multiple scholarship organizations to oversee, which can be a bureaucratic nightmare for the agency and all involved parties. Therefore, state lawmakers should carefully design ESA legislation to include the necessary funding and contractual authority necessary to equip a single agency with the professional, technical, and managerial competencies needed to manage its collaboration with multiple scholarship organizations.

Examining the tradeoffs and benefits of various regulatory models for ESA programs reveals that the optimal approach is likely to remain contested within state legislatures. Although a state agency regulating ESAs can provide essential structure, clarity, and oversight, these agencies can also serve as potential hindrances to ESAs achieving their great expectations, and as MPCP shows us, they can also be subject to political winds that hinder program growth. Lawmakers must make a state-specific analysis of the challenges and advantages of the particular regulatory model that will best serve the families and students within their state. As lawmakers consider the best model for ESAs, the next section contains four recommendations a state can adopt to support them, in whatever regulatory form the programs take.

GENERAL PRINCIPLES FOR REGULATING ESAs

With at least twenty-two legislatures introducing ESA bills between 2010 and 2016, the importance of regulatory frameworks to ESA success is vital.

Therefore, I offer four general principles to lawmakers considering ESA legislation should keep in mind.

1. *Regulatory Oversight Should Honor the Spirit of a School Choice Statute*

ESAs seek to empower parents to meet the needs of their children. As a means to achieving this goal, lawmakers and ESA supporters often seek extensive autonomy from government oversight for schools and providers as they work to serve the needs of students. Given the goal to maximize the freedom of schools and providers, lawmakers should instruct administrative agencies to minimize the regulatory burdens that they impose on schools and providers. This can be accomplished by enacting legislation that reduces the need for a wide variety of regulations to implement the program or to amend an existing rule to make the program work better.

For example, regulators of the D.C. Opportunity Scholarship Program (OSP) amended its rules to include applications in English and Spanish to attract more low-income families to the program, and adopted a protocol for program administrators to communicate with families and students about OSP updates and application deadlines. In Arizona, the DOE amended a rule in 2013 to make it easier for families to renew or postpone renewal of a child's special need as described in her or his Individual Education Plan (IEP) or a Multidisciplinary Evaluation Team (MET) report.[26] Making policy shifts of this type is an example of a regulatory agency aligning its rules or procedures to honor the spirit of the law.

2. *Regulatory Oversight Should Support Parental Entrepreneurialism*

What makes ESAs truly entrepreneurial is that they provide ordinary parents an opportunity to spend their tax money in the manner of their choosing. This includes shopping for the right set of educational options for a child, be it in a private or public school, online or with a tutor. However, a roadmap and guardrails must accompany parental entrepreneurialism.

A roadmap guides parents on how to maximize the benefits of ESAs for their child. One example is an ESA handbook for parents, which two states use. The Arizona DOE's parent handbook is available online and in hardcopy for families, explaining all allowable ESA expenses, which include private school tuition and credential requirements for tutors, as well as procedures to fill out ESA expense reports for reimbursement.[27] The Nevada Office of the State Treasurer's parent handbook contains similar information.

Guardrails seek to prevent misuse of ESA funds and to establish quality controls for ESA-funded programs and services. For example, parents with students in the Tennessee ESA program must sign an agreement with the DOE promising to use funds properly, to not enroll a child in a public school as a full-time student, and "to provide an education for the participating student in at least the subjects of reading, grammar, mathematics, social studies, and science." The Tennessee law also requires parents of a child enrolled in grades 3–8 to ensure that she or he annually takes a nationally norm-referenced test or the Tennessee comprehensive assessment program. An exception is made for some special needs students for whom an annual assessment is not appropriate.[28]

3. *Regulatory Oversight Must Avoid Overly Prescriptive Mandates*

For innovation to flourish for ESAs, an SAA must not be overly prescriptive in enrollment and paperwork requirements for private schools. A 2014 study of the regulatory impact of state statues on twenty-three choice programs in twelve states provides insight into this issue. Of the 575 regulations governing school choice programs between 1990 and 2014, at least 130 were implemented during the first year and ninety were implemented in year two and beyond. Year-one regulations usually impact admissions, enrollment, student eligibility, and tuition policies. By contrast, year two and beyond regulations usually impact paperwork and reporting data requirements.[29] An example from MPCP illustrates this point.

The legislation that created MPCP in 1990 created fifty-five additional regulations for participating private schools. In year one, MPCP had four regulations for admissions, enrollment, student eligibility, and tuition, and six in year two and beyond. By comparison, MPCP had two regulations for paperwork and reporting data in year one, and twenty-five in year two and beyond.[30] The author of the study concluded that MPCP is the most regulated choice program of the twenty-three in the study. By contrast, the Arizona ESA program is the least regulated program in the study.

4. *Regulatory Oversight Should Support Parental Involvement for Student Achievement*

Writing ESA regulations to support parental choice is part of the school choice equation; encouraging parents to be involved in their child's education is the other. Existing research has shown that parent involvement can boost the academic outcomes of students. According to a 2005 meta-analysis by William H. Jeynes, students living in a home with involved parents had an "academic advantage" of higher grades and test scores than less involved parents. Reading and communicating to a child mattered a great deal to student achievement, but parental expectations actually had a greater effect on student outcomes. In a 2012 meta-analysis, Jeynes identified four programs that had statistically significant, positive effects on student achievement: share reading (parent and child reading together); a parent–teacher partnership; checking homework; and increased communication between parents and teachers.

In addition to encouraging parents to be involved in a child's education, regulators must trust parents to make the right decisions for their children. Naturally, some parents will make better decisions than others. Yet, this is nothing unique to ESA parents: parents with children in traditional public schools or voucher schools make decisions every day. But as the first program to authorize parents to invest their tax dollars in educational services themselves, lawmakers and SAA leaders should do all they can to help families succeed in an ESA marketplace. This requires government to both trust parents and give them room to succeed, while also allowing them to make mistakes.

REGULATING TO HELP ESAs FLOURISH

Like other school choice programs, each ESA law is created within the context of a state's constitution, codes, and funding formula. Once a legislature enacts or amends an ESA law, a state administrative agency—DOE, department of revenue or alternative model—is tasked with implementing the program and is ultimately responsible for answering the "now what?" questions that surface during the implementation process. While these questions post challenges, they also present opportunities for states to experiment with several regulatory models, and learn from how other states that have adopted ESA programs to date have regulated them.

Each regulation model has its benefits and drawbacks. The key goal, nonetheless, is to allow ESA programs to flourish by avoiding excessive bureaucracy or unnecessary hurdles. Several agency options appear capable of striking this delicate balance, but it will require careful and deliberate implementation by policymakers and agency leaders. No matter the regulatory structure that states select, the important thing is that state officials are able to support ESA programs so they can be of use to the families and students who rely upon them.

NOTES

1. In 2015, Nevada became the fifth state to create an ESA program and the only one with a universal model. However in September 2016, the Nevada Supreme Court placed a permanent injunction on the program. The court's 4-2 decision ruled that the ESA program did not violate the state constitution; however, the legislature-approved source of funding was only designated for public schools. Since the legislature did not fund ESAs through a separate appropriation, the program remains the law, but it cannot proceed without new legislation appropriating funds to it.

2. For a history of MPCP and politics and reform in Milwaukee, see Howard Fuller, *No Struggle, No Progress: A Warrior's Life from Black Power to Education Reform* (Milwaukee: Marquette University Press, 2014); Frederick Hess, *Revolution at the Margins: The Impact of Competition on Urban School Systems* (Washington, D.C.: Brookings Institution Press, 2002); Mikel Holt, *Not Yet "Free At Last": The Unfinished Business of the Civil Rights Movement* (Oakland, CA: Institute for Contemporary Studies, 2000); and Joe Williams, *Cheating Our Kids: How Politics and Greed Ruin Education* (New York, N.Y.: MacMillian, 2005).

3. Wisconsin Department of Education, "Private School Choice Programs," http://dpi.wi.gov/sms/choice-programs.

4. Milwaukee Parental Choice Program, "Membership and Payment History, in Total, 1990 to 2015," http://dpi.wi.gov/sites/default/files/imce/sms/pdf/MPCP%20 Payment%20History.pdf.

5. Davis v. Grover, 480 N.W.2d 460, 462 (Wis. 1992).

6. Wis. Stat. Ann. Const. art. 1, § 18.

7. Milwaukee Parental Choice Program (MPCP), "Facts and Figures for 2015–2016 as of November 2015," http://dpi.wi.gov/sites/default/files/imce/sms/pdf/MPCP%20Sept%20Facts%20and%20Figures%202015-16.pdf; and MPCP, "Milwaukee Parental Choice Program Headcount and FTE—2015–16 School Year," http://dpi.wi.gov/sites/default/files/imce/sms/pdf/MPCP%202015-16%20Sept%20 Numbers%20by%20School%20with%20all%20Pupils.pdf.

8. For Patrick J. Wolf's research about MPCP, see University of Arkansas Department of Education Reform, "Milwaukee Parental Choice Program (MPCP) Evaluation," http://www.uaedreform.org/milwaukee-parental-choice-program-evaluation/; and Patrick J. Wolf, "The Comprehensive Longitudinal Evaluation of the Milwaukee Parental Choice Program: Summary of Final Reports. SCDP Milwaukee Evaluation Report# 36," *School Choice Demonstration Project* (2012).

9. George Mitchell, "The Milwaukee Parental Choice Program," *The Wisconsin Policy Research Institute* (1992), accessed May 5, 2016, http://www.wpri.org/WPRI-Files/Special-Reports/Reports-Documents/Vol5no5.pdf.

10. Education Action Group Foundation and Wisconsin Institute for Law & Liberty, "DPI's War on Wisconsin's School Choice Program," Fall 2013, http://www.will-law.org/wp-content/uploads/2015/07/EAG-WILL-DPI-Report.pdf.

11. Kern Alexander & M. David Alexander, *American Public School Law* (Belmont, CA: West/Thomson Learning, 2001), 93–95.

12. Tennessee Department of Education, "Individualized Education Account Program," https://www.tn.gov/education/section/iea.

13. Mississippi Department of Education, "Equal Opportunity for Students With Special Needs Program," http://www.mde.k12.ms.us/TD/news/2015/04/16/mde-begins-work-on-establishing-process-for-special-needs-voucher-program; and "Frequently Asked Questions," http://www.mde.k12.ms.us/docs/special-education-library/esa-faq_20150729154901_105375.pdf?sfvrsn=2.

14. Nevada State Treasurer, "Education Savings Account," http://www.nevadatreasurer.gov/SchoolChoice/Home/.

15. Nevada ESA, "FAQs about Nevada ESA," http://nevadaesa.com/frequently-asked-questions/.

16. Nevada's 100-day public school residency rule has unintended consequences. For instance, it creates an incentive for homeschoolers and private school students to participate in a drive-through public school experience. This is disruptive to public schools. A DOE creates its statewide school budget allocations based upon fall and spring student enrollment figures. These enrollment figures allow a DOE to estimate how many public school students will need federal services—which include Title I, English Language Learners, and special education—in addition to how many teachers and principals are needed in schools.

17. Friedman Foundation for Educational Choice, "Illinois-Tax Credits for Educational Expenses," http://www.edchoice.org/school-choice/programs/illinois-tax-credits-for-educational-expenses/.

18. Arizona Department of Education, "ESA," http://www.azed.gov/esa/, and Arizona Revised Statute, 14-2402.

19. Arizona State Legislature, Arizona Revised Statute, 15-2403, http://www.azleg.gov/FormatDocument.asp?inDoc=/ars/15/02403.htm&Title=15&DocType=ARS.

20. Georgia Department of Education, "Georgia Tax Credit Program," https://www.gadoe.org/External-Affairs-and-Policy/Policy/Pages/Tax-Credit-Program.aspx.

21. The G.O.A.L. Scholarship Program, http://www.goalscholarship.org.

22. The Florida Tax Credit Scholarship Program, 1002.395, http://www.leg.state.fl.us/statutes/index.cfm?mode=View%20Statutes&SubMenu=1&App_mode=Display_Statute&Search_String=1002.395&URL=1000-1099/1002/Sections/1002.395.html.

23. Florida Department of Education, "Tax Credit FAQS," http://www.fldoe.org/schools/school-choice/k-12-scholarship-programs/ftc/ftc-faqs.stml.

24. Florida Revised Statute, Chapter 1002.385 (1), http://www.fldoe.org/schools/school-choice/k-12-scholarship-programs/plsa/.

25. Virginia Department of Education, "The Virginia Education Improvement Scholarships Tax Credits Program," http://www.doe.virginia.gov/school_finance/scholarships_tax_credits/.

26. Jonathan Butcher & Lindsey M. Burke, "The Education Debit Card II: What Arizona Parents Purchase with Education Savings Accounts," Friedman Foundation for Educational Choice (2016), http://www.edchoice.org/wp-content/uploads/2016/02/2016-2-The-Education-Debit-Card-II-WEB-1.pdf.

27. Arizona Department of Education, *A Guide to Utilizing Your Empowerment Scholarship Account*, http://www.azed.gov/esa/files/2013/08/esa-parent-handbook.pdf.

28. Tenn. Code Ann., § 49-10-1403 (a)(1).

29. Andrew D. Catt "Public Rules on Private Schools: Measuring the Regulatory Impact of State Statutes and School Choice Programs," Friedman Foundation for Educational Choice (2014).

30. *Id.* at 3, 1718, 20.

Chapter Seven

Parents and Providers Speak Up

Allysia Finley

Parents play an important role in the education of their children—especially parents of children with special needs, who require more attention and personalized instruction. Since 2011, five states have enacted an education savings account (ESA) program. Specifically, Arizona, Florida, and Mississippi have pioneered ESAs to assist parents of children with cognitive disabilities. Nevada has established a universal ESA available to all public school students, but its future—and that of parents and students who were hoping to utilize it—is in limbo because of a legal challenge. In September 2016, Nevada's Supreme Court upheld the program on the merits, but found its funding source violated the state constitution.

Parents of special needs children are especially suited to benefit from ESAs as public policy tools. For one, these parents are often very involved in their children's education from an early age and, thus, may be more familiar with their aptitudes and problem points. Furthermore, parents of children with special needs are used to playing the role of an advocate. Even more so than vouchers, ESAs require proactive parenting. What's more, special needs children often require a customized education with maximum flexibility.

Yet since the time each of the five existing ESA programs have been enacted, discussions surrounding ESAs have often overlooked the very individuals who seek to benefit from them—special needs students and their parents. Each ESA program is different, but it is useful to examine the stories, successes, and frustrations of ESA policies across state contexts to gain a better understanding of what ESAs can offer students and how they can better serve families moving forward.

ESAs have a huge potential to improve the lives of families, parents and kids. Copious research demonstrates the importance of parental involvement in a child's education. For instance, a meta-analysis by the Harvard Family

121

Research Project in 2005, which covered seventy-seven studies and three hundred thousand students, concluded that parental engagement was associated with higher student achievement including grades and standardized test scores.[1] Data from a 2012 National Education Longitudinal Study showed that engaged parents can help compensate for learning deficiencies due to school failings.[2] Other research shows that parents who are involved in their children's education can improve their family interaction.[3]

This chapter explores how nine parents in Arizona, Florida, and Mississippi discovered and utilized ESAs for their children, and the role service providers have played in the programs. The first section of this chapter focuses on the personal trials and triumphs parents and children experience as they navigate the programs. The next section highlights eight education service providers. The final section contains closing thoughts about what state lawmakers can do to better serve families and service providers in the five states with ESA programs today, and even other states considering ESA legislation.

ARIZONA PARENTS

In ten years, he may not be on the autism spectrum and might be able to attend college and live on his own.

—Amanda Howard, Arizona mom[4]

Six years ago, ten-year-old Nathan Howard was functionally mute. He couldn't answer questions or express original thoughts. He repeated verbatim what he heard on TV. He was floundering in kindergarten at the local public school where, according to his mom Amanda Howard, "he was overstimulated by a lot of people and noise and was bullied."

At one of Nathan's therapy sessions, Howard learned about Arizona's nascent Empowerment Scholarship Accounts, fortuitously just days before the application deadline. Arizona's ESAs, which cover special needs and foster children as well as students from failing schools, military families, Native American reservations and their siblings, are in their fifth year with roughly 2,500 students and 135 participating schools. The average account value last year was $11,400.[5]

After Nathan's application was approved, the Howards finally had the financial means to enroll their son at the Lauren's Institute for Education (LIFE), a private school for autistic children that offers small class sizes, community outings, and electives including karate, yoga, cooking, and social skills. With the remaining funds in their scholarship account, the Howards hired a private tutor to help Nathan in reading and writing.

Now Nathan asks questions, starts conversations, and loves reading. "Potentially, in five years, he could get integrated back into public schools," Howard says. "In ten years, he may not be on the autism spectrum and might be able to attend college and live on his own." Many special needs children like Nathan struggle with the one-size-fits-all public school model. Kids demonstrate a wide range of aptitudes, and the variation is even greater among those with disabilities. Special education classrooms can include students with autism, dyslexia, attention deficit disorder, and Down syndrome. Unfortunately, many public schools are not equipped with the teachers, technology, or specialized services to provide individualized instruction to special needs students. ESAs make it possible for families to obtain services that schools are unable to provide.

We have moved on ... to crafting our own completely individualized education.

—Katherine Visser, Arizona mom[6]

Eleven-year-old Jordan Visser suffers from a host of congenital problems including cerebral palsy, motor processing disorder, hypotonia, dysgraphia, and sensory processing disorder, all of which limit his mobility and ability to interact.

Initially, Jordan's local public school in Scottsdale, Arizona, resisted enrolling him in kindergarten because he had not learned how to use the toilet on his own. The situation deteriorated after Jordan's mom Katherine Visser succeeded in forcing the public school to admit Jordan. He began experiencing anxiety attacks in the mornings before school, a new occurrence, and rapidly regressed in reading, writing, and math. As his medical problems mounted, the Vissers discovered that Jordan was visually impaired with 20/70 vision.

A lawyer whom Visser had consulted in her battle with the local public school to get Jordan the accommodations he needed charged $2,000 merely to review his paperwork and an additional $15,000 for a legal retainer agreement. The lawyer suggested the Vissers apply for Arizona's Empowerment Scholarship Accounts. The Vissers were among the first seventy-five families whose applications were approved. Within four weeks of applying, the family was able to use an ESA to enroll Jordan at Sierra Academy, a K–12 school for special needs students.

Although Visser "loved the school and staff," she withdrew Jordan after a year because she found that she could better meet his needs in a home–school environment. Now the Vissers use Jordan's ESA for physical therapy, private tutoring, piano lessons, swimming, and therapeutic horse riding. Jordan also takes classes at a local science center and social thinking skills camp. "We have moved on from private school to crafting our own completely individualized education," says Visser.

The ESA provides the family with the flexibility and means for Jordan to participate in activities at which he excels, something Visser notes has helped build his self-confidence. His temper tantrums have also abated while his balance and coordination have improved as a result of his positive learning environment and individualized instruction.

> So shocked that I went right into researching [ESAs] to see if it was for real or a joke.
>
> —Holland Hines, Arizona mom[7]

Holland Hines struggled to obtain the help her autistic son Elias needed in public school. Elias, now eleven-years-old, attended public school in Arizona's East Valley until the age of six. As Hines explains, like most kids, his aptitude varies by subject. Though he struggles to express himself, Elias is hyperlexic, meaning he has a precocious reading ability. He is also gifted in music and has even taught himself how to play piano including advanced compositions like Tchaikovsky's *The Nutcracker*.

While Elias spent most of kindergarten in a typical classroom, he was placed with all autistic students during the first grade. The school assured Hines that he would be integrated into a normal classroom later that year. However, the all-autistic class negatively influenced Elias's behavior. Hines noticed his anxiety levels soared at home while his academics slipped. During a visit on Halloween, she discovered the classroom in chaos with kids screaming and throwing tantrums.

Soon afterwards, Hines withdrew Elias from public school and began educating him at home. Upon learning about the state's newly minted ESA program from social media, she was "so shocked that I went right into researching the bill number on the Arizona state legislature website to see if it was for real or a joke."

At an ESA information meeting hosted by the Arizona Department of Education in December 2011, she connected with other parents of special-needs kids. Afterwards, she urged parents to join a Yahoo message board to exchange information. Between 2011 and 2015, the Yahoo parent group expanded from eleven families to about 270. After Elias's ESA application was approved in the spring of 2012, Hines began exploring private school options. The first private school Elias attended moved mid-year because the facility, which had formerly served as a therapeutic agency. Since Hines didn't have time to research new schools, she home-schooled Elias for the remainder of the year.

Hines used the ESA to hire a tutor who could work with Elias three to seven hours a week in logic, math, and test-taking skills—areas that Hines felt she wasn't strong at teaching. She also taught him language arts, classic literature, history, writing, keyboarding, health, and art history and used her ESA debit card to buy curriculum that had been preapproved by the state education department.

In 2014, Hines enrolled Elias in Kimber Academy, a private school which focused on academic courses in the morning and electives such as robotics, theater, dance, karate, piano, and voice in the afternoon. Parents could enroll their children in either or both sessions. "It was a great model for a la carte education," Hines says. However, the school changed its name and relocated, forcing Hines to explore new education options.

Last year, Elias began fifth grade at AZ Aspire Academy in Tempe, which specializes in educating students with ADHD, autism spectrum disorders, anxiety, and dyslexia. Hines explains that the school founder Sonia Gonzales "noticed the need for a new kind of school that would accept students of varying abilities, intellect and functioning levels" and would incorporate one-on-one instruction with "communal classes that would allow the children to expand social skills and community experiences such as PE, art, social skills classes, and the like."

"For the first time in 10 years, and after months of stops and starts and adjustments and readjustments, Elias is finally able to complete an entire week at school, without me being called to pick him up, without any meltdowns—and with more academic and behavioral progress than we have seen in his entire life," she says.

Additionally, Hines can use the ESA to pay for piano lessons, gymnastics, and other activities that would qualify as fine arts or physical education with approval from the state education department.

As the program has expanded to cover more kids including those from foster homes and failing schools, "private schools have been popping up all over the place," she says. "The money follows the child, and the good administrators and professionals follow." Rather than sucking public schools dry, ESAs have shifted "jobs to schools that could better educate kids based on needs rather than one-size-fits-all education."

Within the first six months of her being home, it was night and day.

—Lynn McMurray, Arizona mom[8]

Tim and Lynn McMurray have adopted eight children, including three of Native American heritage who are developmentally delayed due to their biological parents' substance abuse. Their oldest daughter Alicia, who is sixteen years old, suffers from fetal alcohol syndrome and a rare genetic disorder that affects various cognitive and physical functions. "She needs life skills," says Lynn McMurray. "Her needs weren't being met in public school."

Meantime, their thirteen-year-old son Uriah and daughter Valerie were being bullied in public school. Valerie has cerebral palsy while Uriah suffers from a post-traumatic brain injury. McMurray worried their self-esteem was being damaged. Yet despite their disabilities, they were too advanced for "back-to-basics" classes. Uriah "walks, talks, and acts normally," says McMurray.

In 2013, the McMurrays applied for ESAs for all three children. Uriah and Valerie qualified because they were adopted from foster homes as did Alicia who had a significant disability.

In the last few years, Alicia has made huge strides. "Within the first six months of her being home, it was night and day," says McMurray. Alicia can now segregate items by color (she's color-blind) and ask store employees for directions. Friends have noticed that she's more congenial. Valerie can now read and has memorized her multiplication facts, which she wasn't able to do in public schools.

Uriah is acing spelling tests and has become an avid reader. McMurray doubts that her children would have made as much progress were they not home-schooled. Home-schooling also allows the family to take field trips to learn geography. ESAs provide parents scheduling flexibility, which can have a salutary impact on the whole family. McMurray's one complaint is that ESA values aren't clearly explained by the state, which allocates different levels of funding for diagnoses. For instance, Alicia receives $18,835, which is about four times as much as Uriah receives.

FLORIDA PARENTS

She is now in second grade and excelling because of the one-on-one therapy.

—Julie Kleffel, Florida mom[9]

Julie Kleffel, a widowed mom in Longwood, Florida, recalls her nine-year-old daughter Faith's tumultuous early education in public schools. When Faith was born with Down syndrome, her doctor issued a grave prognosis: at best, she might someday be able to sit up on her own. However, Kleffel refused to believe that her daughter would live a sedentary life.

Initially, Kleffel enrolled Faith in a public special education pre-school. Kleffel says Faith excelled there until her class doubled in size, which appeared to strain the teacher's resources and attention. Faith received only five minutes of individualized speech therapy per week. One day, Kleffel recalls picking up Faith from school soaked in her own urine. The teacher, who claimed Faith was purposefully wetting herself, had further embarrassed Faith by forcing her to clean up after herself. But as Kleffel notes, Faith struggles with fine motor skills such as pulling down her zipper. "I mean no disrespect to the teacher," says Kleffel, "but she was just overwhelmed and Faith was regressing."

After the incident, Kleffel withdrew Faith from the school. The advent of Florida's Personal Learning Savings Accounts (PLSA) in 2014 allowed Kleffel to pay for a private tutor, speech and occupational therapy, special shoe inserts, and educational curriculum. Faith's various therapies cost about $1 per minute.

Unlike Florida's McKay Scholarship which is accessible to all special needs public school students, the PLSA is limited to children with autism spectrum disorders, muscular dystrophy, cerebral palsy, Down syndrome, Prader-Willi syndrome, Spina Bifida, Williams syndrome or severe cognitive impairment.[10] However, PLSA students aren't required to have spent the prior year in public schools.

Kleffel describes the PLSA as a life saver and changer. Faith, now in second grade, is "excelling because of the one-on-one therapy." She can now walk three miles, speak in full sentences, and interact with groups.

> Prior to the program, we didn't have any other options than to continue burying ourselves financially.
>
> —Lydia Burton, Florida mom[11]

Four-year-old Kellen Burton was diagnosed with autism in November 2014. One early sign was that he never made eye contact or played with his peers. He also couldn't express original thoughts. Instead, he repeated whatever he heard on TV. He often ate lunch under the table.

After his diagnosis, Florida's embryonic PLSA program enabled the Burtons, who live in Gainesville, to seek early intervention, which has been critical to his development. The Burtons use Kellen's PLSA to purchase therapies, curriculum, and special instructional materials such as handwriting tools, a "Cat in the Hat" board game, and a trampoline. The state doesn't restrict the types of instruction materials that parents may purchase with their PLSA. However, non-traditional items may require additional documentation to show how they meet the student's needs.

Kellen's progress in just the last year has amazed his family. Lydia Burton notes that he can now articulate his likes/dislikes and count past 30. While Burton once doubted whether he'd ever learn to read or write, she now says she "has no doubt that he could live life up to the degree he wants to." What's more, she says, the "ESAs help our family function better" since Burton can stay at home to assist her other toddler who suffers from congenital health problems. "Prior to the program, we didn't have any other options than to continue burying ourselves financially."

It's important to take the kid out of the cookie cutter model.

—John Kurnick, Florida dad[12]

John and Mary Kurnick were among the earliest and most vocal proponents of Florida's PLSA program. "It's important to take the kid out of the cookie cutter model," says John Kurnick. "There are limited time and resources in the public school system, and speech evaluations for therapists can be delayed." Early intervention and flexibility are often crucial for assisting children with cognitive disabilities like autism.

The Kurnicks found that their thirteen-year-old son John performed well in less-structured, more comfortable environments since he could learn at his own pace and revisit concepts that didn't initially "catch." He could also take sporadic breaks throughout the day. What's more, it was easier to schedule his therapy appointments in the morning or early afternoon.

During a typical week, Mary Kurnick volunteers on Mondays at a co-op where John takes classes in three core subjects plus an elective. On Tuesdays and Thursdays, John receives math tutoring. Friday is an "enrichment day" with activities like extreme physical education and outdoor adventures. The PLSA has allowed the Kurnicks to augment and enhance John's home-school regimen.

The Kurnicks use the PLSA for therapies, books, handwriting, and keyboard programs and hope to add robotics materials as well as musical instruments. Within the last year and a half, John has demonstrated tremendous growth, which has buoyed psychologists, neighbors, and family members. "You don't have to worry that your child will be a burden on society," says Mary Kurnick, adding that the whole family's morale has improved as a result.

MISSISSIPPI PARENT

She is a totally different child.

—Martha Beard, Mississippi mom[13]

"When you have thirty students who need individualized instruction, it's hard to get the education you need," notes Martha Beard of Pelahatchie, Mississippi, whose adopted seventh grade daughter Lanna was diagnosed with visual perception disorder, severe ADD, and fetal alcohol syndrome. Tasks she learned one day, she'd forget the next. It would take her hours to complete homework assignments, which led to aggravation for both Beard and Lanna.

While Lanna attended private school through the third grade, a psychologist suggested switching to public school in fourth grade. In the second grade, Lanna had been called out for not paying attention. Lanna "was brought to tears in front of her classmates," Beard recalls. "She felt inadequate."[14]

Like many special needs students, Lanna struggled in public school where she was given an IEP. "I was at the end of my rope when I was told by the county that she could not graduate without passing standardized tests," recalls Beard. Mississippi has one of the lowest high school graduation rates for special needs students in the nation; just 28 percent of the state's students with disabilities graduate compared to three quarters of traditional students. The nationwide graduation rate for students with disabilities is 63 percent.[15] These disparities were one reason for enacting the state's Education Scholarship Accounts in 2015.

Beard first heard about ESAs on the news.[16] Fortunately, Lanna's IEP enabled her to qualify for the program even though many students with special needs without IEPs do not. Lanna was one of the first children in the state whose ESA application was approved.

"So many kids I know wanted to do private school but couldn't because they didn't have an IEP," Beard laments. The IEP requirement disqualifies many students who attended private school or were tutored at home prior to the enactment of ESAs.

Lanna's pediatrician recommended a private school in Jackson called New Summit because it offers small class sizes and customized leaning plans for students with special needs. Tuition is roughly $8,300 per year, but the ESA covers three-quarters of the cost. Beard says tuition would have been unaffordable for her family without the ESA.

Within the first six months of starting private school, Beard witnessed remarkable growth in Lanna. "She is a totally different child," Beard observes, adding that Lanna's confidence has soared. She is now more willing to express herself and do homework on her own. She has also made new friends. "Our family, people who have known Lanna for a long-time, our church family, come to us and say Lanna isn't the same person she was a year ago."

"Because the number of students per class is smaller, Lanna is more relaxed and she's not intimidated to say she needs help. She will ask and answer questions. She participates in classroom activities and now enjoys going to school," Beard notes.

ESAs empower parents to act as retail consumers of education services for their children. Parents can use ESAs to send their children to a private school, which may have more resources at their disposal to personalize instruction. The great benefit of ESAs is they allow parents to choose what works best for their own kids.

ESA programs can also have a beneficial impact on a family by reducing financial strain, providing scheduling flexibility, and improving child–parent interaction. Students develop more confidence in themselves and their abilities when they are making progress. A positive learning environment can also bolster their sense of self-worth, which helps promote learning. ESAs thus create a positive feedback loop that drives personal growth. In a short period of time, often in as little as a few months, parents observe that because of an ESA, their children have the potential to become productive members of society. Yet perhaps just as important as parents' experience is how providers respond to ESAs.

Suppliers of Educational Services

While ESAs help parents with special needs children, they can only benefit if quality providers are available. Fortunately, prior school choice programs have encouraged the proliferation of suppliers. Parents in Florida and Arizona benefit from an array of school choice programs that have helped lay the ground for ESAs. For instance, the nonprofit Step Up for Students helps administer both Florida's tax-credit scholarship and Personal Learning Scholarship Account programs.

Private schools can specialize in helping special needs students and therefore boast a comparative advantage over public schools, which aren't designed to educate kids with a broad range of disabilities. While tax-credit scholarships and ESAs can complement one another, the programs have distinct advantages and drawbacks in driving competition and choice.

For instance, Arizona and Florida boast scholarship programs that offer individuals and corporations dollar-for-dollar tax credits for donating to nonprofit private school scholarship organizations. Last year, roughly 78,000 low-income students in Florida were using scholarships to attend 1,594 accredited private schools.[17] In Arizona, nearly 55,000 kids and more than 330 private schools benefit from the state's four tax-credit scholarship programs.[18] In 2012, Mississippi established a state-funded dyslexia scholarship program. About 150 students this year are using a scholarship to attend three private schools.[19]

However, the scholarship application is usually limited to accredited private schools, so parents can't use the funds to purchase educational supplies and extracurricular activities or to hire tutors and therapists. What's more, the scholarships are often inadequate to finance tuition at private schools for special needs kids.

ESAs should strive to encourage a diverse mix of suppliers in a robust consumer-driven marketplace. Many professionals (e.g., therapists, tutors) are still only discovering ESAs, but as news of their availability spreads, it should help expand the universe of options for parents who prefer to home-school their children.

A major goal of ESAs is to encourage more competition and choice in the education marketplace by empowering parents to act as consumers. As Empower Mississippi (an organization that advocates for expanded school choice) president Grant Callen notes, ESAs should aim "to allow students to choose different education options and force public schools to improve."

Lauren's Institute for Education, Gilbert, Arizona[20]

Consider the Lauren's Institute for Education (LIFE) in Gilbert, Arizona, which offers therapy, academics, and enrichment programs for students with special needs. Co-founder and president Carrie Reed launched the institute in 2008 to help her daughter Lauren who suffers from the rare genetic disorder Sanfillippo syndrome. In the last eight years, school enrollment at LIFE has ballooned from eight students to 102. About 35 percent of LIFE students have an ESA while the rest receive a tax-credit scholarship. Reed says she expects enrollment to continue to surge since "every year, the number of ESA students grows."

This enrollment growth spurt in its early years required LIFE to lease more space in a cramped office complex. In 2015, LIFE moved into a new 11,000 square-foot facility on 10 acres of land. The new facility includes outside play areas, twenty-three classrooms and treatment areas, two basketball courts, two large athletic fields and playgrounds—and the school has room to expand further. "We purposefully don't want to grow too quickly," Reed says.

Reed adds that one drawback of ESAs compared to tax-credit scholarships is their limited window for accepting new applications, which runs from January 1 to April 1. "In October, many parents are begging to get into a private school," Reed says. By contrast, scholarships can be pro-rated if a parent decides to apply mid-year. As a result, parents who experience problems in public schools early in the school year have to wait an entire year before they can use an ESA to enroll their child in a private school.

Reed also points out that ESAs save taxpayers money because funding allocations are less than what the government would spend to educate the student in a public school. This helps the public "see the value of the program," which is critical for maintaining support in the legislature.

Lexis Preparatory School, Scottsdale, Arizona[21]

Lexis Preparatory School aims to prepare kids with mild to moderate learning disabilities like ADHD, dyslexia, and anxiety for college. About fourteen of the K–12 school's sixty-four students use an ESA while twenty-four receive a tax-credit scholarship.

The school charges $20,000 in tuition per year plus $600 to $800 for books, which ESAs can also cover. Lexis director Bonnie Dougherty notes that, "Most parents ask, 'How do kids afford to attend?'" She encourages them to apply for a tax-credit scholarship or ESA. Yet for children with low-level disability diagnoses, a tax-credit scholarship can provide more financial assistance than an ESA—one reason why more students have scholarships.

Thanks to Arizona's school choice programs, Lexis's enrollment has tripled since its launch in 2009. While Lexis hosted a fair for parents exploring ESA suppliers in 2013, Dougherty says most parents have learned about Lexis by word of mouth. The community of parents with special needs kids is close-knit, she notes, and Holland Hines's Yahoo message board has facilitated the exchange of information about providers. When parents share their stories on Internet forums—not unlike how customers post reviews of products online—demand will likely grow for higher-quality providers, which will in turn encourage their expansion.

Pieceful Solutions, Mesa, Arizona[22]

In 2008, Kami Cothrun, who has a master's degree in special education, launched Pieceful Solutions in Mesa, Arizona, with just six kids. The school's name derives from the universal symbol of autism—a puzzle piece. About one in sixty kids in Arizona is diagnosed with autism, Cothrun notes. She perceived a growing need for special services that weren't being provided in public schools. At Pieceful, "there's no one-size-fits-all curriculum."

The K–12 school combines academics, extracurricular activities and speech, music, and occupational therapy. Electives include yoga, cooking, choir, karate, computer science, drama, grocery shopping, and vocational skills such as hospitality. Pieceful's goal is to teach kids how to act in social and professional settings so that they can be fully integrated into society upon graduation.

Pieceful operates two private-school campuses in Gilbert and Mesa, as well as a public charter school in Chandler for kids who do not have an IEP. However, Cothrun says that Pieceful's private schools can better serve special needs students because they don't have to adhere to rigid state education regulations. What's more, "many kids who have come from public schools have a bad taste in their mouth. Many don't want to go to any public or charter."

Enrollment has roughly doubled every year since its inception to 150 kids, 140 of whom have ESAs. Most families, Cothrun underscores, couldn't afford Pieceful's $23,000 in annual tuition without an ESA. "We would not be who we are without ESAs and many of these kids and their families wouldn't be where they are without ESAs," she explains. Pieceful continues to accept new applications, and Cothrun hopes to expand into regions where there are fewer options for autistic kids, such as in the rural suburbs of Phoenix.

One drawback of Arizona's ESAs, she adds, is that students only qualify through twelfth grade while children in public schools with IEPs receive government funding until they are twenty-two. "Many kids aren't ready at eighteen and need to be in school longer," she states. Florida's PLSA program allows students to remain until age twenty-two.

Fit Learning, Reno, Nevada and Blossom Park, Phoenix, Arizona[23]

One innovative individualized learning model that can serve as an alternative to private or public schools is the fast-growing provider Fit Learning. Psychologist Donny Newsome launched the education lab with three other researchers at the University of Nevada, Reno, in 1998. The Fit Learning lab, which was privatized in 2004, "applies the standard scientific method to crack the puzzle of how each individual learns," explains Newsome. The goal is to "rapidly accelerate the learning gains of every student who walks through our doors."

Data enables instructors to customize education to each individual student's needs. In a ten-week period, students can advance between one and four years, he says. While Newsome works with all kinds of students, most are "quirky learners." "There's no such thing as the average student," he notes, adding that many Fit Learning students have been diagnosed with a learning disability like dyslexia or ADHD.

Newsome's Fit Learning lab in Reno could also assist ESA students once Nevada's program launches. He says he's unsure how Nevada's embryonic program will affect his center, but believes that the market for private tutors needs to be tightly regulated to prevent fly-by-night operators from exploiting kids and taxpayers. "Any amateur could put up a shingle," he says, since "there's no fixed credential for a 'tutor.'" This raises the question of whether and how states should monitor the effectiveness of ESA providers.

Two of the lab's founding directors have since moved to New York where they've established Fit Learning campuses. To maintain "quality control," Newsome opted not to franchise the learning lab and to instead offer licensing agreements with affiliate centers like Blossom Park in Phoenix, Arizona.

In June 2015, Blossom Park director Nicky Carter, who has an MBA and a master's degree in education, established a tutoring center that utilizes the Fit Learning model and curriculum. Carter says she found it challenging to incorporate "precision learning into a public school, which is not structured for one-on-one instructions."[24]

Blossom Park currently has four staff members who assist five students, most of whom are referred by other professionals. The lab charges a fixed cost of $90 per hour for tutoring. ESAs, she notes, help some families who could not afford her services.

Jacksonville School for Autism, Jacksonville, Florida

In 2005, Michelle Dunham established the Jacksonville School for Autism with her husband and another parent to "provide a safe learning environment" for their children.

"Early intervention is critical for these children," Dunham explains. "Each kid has very unique and different needs." The Jacksonville School for Autism creates an individualized learning plan for each student and provides a "one-to-one clinical environment" coupled with vocational skills training. Students work at six different companies in the community such as a supermarket, pizza shop, and hamburger joint where they learn how to greet and seat customers, fold pizza boxes and roll silverware.

The Jacksonville School for Autism now enrolls forty students and employs nearly as many staff members. About 15 percent of students use a PLSA while the rest have a McKay Scholarship. The school charges between $25,000 and $45,000 annually depending on the particular services a student requires. Some kids need more individualized support and therapy, which health insurers may also help cover.

Interest in the school is growing with twenty students on its wait-list. Some parents drive over an hour so that their kids can attend. Dunham hopes to accommodate more kids as the school grows. "Every inch of building is being utilized," she adds. "We have a measured growth plan to slowly expand." Her goal is to launch a post-secondary program and provide all-inclusive life services.

She anticipates that the PLSA program will expand rapidly since it imposes fewer restrictions on eligibility than Florida's McKay Scholarship. As noted above, PLSAs don't mandate that recipients spend the prior year in a public school, so more students can benefit.

The 3-D School, Petal, Mississippi[25]

Like the Jacksonville School for Autism, the 3-D School, which stands for "Dynamic Dyslexia Design," in Petal, Mississippi, focuses on early intervention for "high potential" students. School officials perform a rigorous admissions process that involves reviewing a student's report cards, test scores, and classroom work in order to ensure that admitted students are motivated to learn.

Director Cena Holifield explains that students with severe learning disabilities may need more intensive instruction and therapy than what is provided at 3-D. The goal of 3-D's intensive three-year program is to prepare students to return to traditional public schools. Tuition costs about $4,900 and covers a full day of academics plus speech therapy.

About 105 of 3-D's 113 students tap Mississippi's special Dyslexia Therapy Scholarship Program, which, unlike the state's ESA program, does not require an IEP to qualify. Just two of the school's students have an ESA. One reason that so few students have ESAs, Holifield notes, is the program is new and relatively unknown.

Enrollment has grown substantially since the school's founding in 2008, thanks to parent groups that have publicized the Dyslexia Therapy Scholarship. The school now has two second grade classes, three third grade classes, three fourth grade classes, one fifth grade class and one sixth grade class. Another building is being constructed to accommodate enrollment growth.

Mississippi's two scholarship programs have been the primary drivers of enrollment growth. "A lot of children come from homes below the poverty line," Holifield attests. "These kids would otherwise not be able to afford the private help they need."

New Summit School, Jackson, Mississippi[26]

In 1997, New Summit School launched in Jackson, Mississippi, with just five children. While New Summit operates like a traditional K–12 school, it offers smaller class sizes and customized education plans for "all types of kids, some who need social growth and others with learning disabilities who need a safe environment," according to the school's executive director Nancy New.

Over the last two decades, enrollment has increased to more than 350 students between its two campuses in Jackson and Greenwood. While just fifty students use ESAs, New says she's open to expanding enrollment. It helps that New Summit's facilities were recently renovated.

In 2014, two aging buildings were demolished to make room for a gym, science labs, and fourteen new classrooms. The school has also hired another reading specialist, teaching assistant, and speech therapist. "We grew fast, but also needed stronger admission policies up front," she says. "We do not want to get students that we cannot educate." Before admitting students, New Summit interviews the child and reviews his or her report cards. While New Summit accepts plenty of students with special needs, it "is not a school for special education services." The goal is to prepare kids for college.

Tuition costs about $8,300 per year, which New notes is a fraction of how much the school spends educating each student. New Summit raises money to cover the differential. While ESAs have helped more students attend, she says the program hasn't significantly impacted the school's operations in part because the ESA program is still new and only benefits roughly 100 students statewide.

Magnolia Speech School, Jackson, Mississippi[27]

Magnolia Speech School is a quasi-magnet school for students with speech-related disabilities. Some parents have even moved into the Jackson area so that their kids could attend, executive director Valerie Linn notes. Six of its eighty-three students have ESAs.

Like New Summit, Magnolia describes itself as a "transitional school" whose goal is to prepare kids to return to public or private schools. Its staff includes a pediatric audiologist, two certified speech pathologists, an occupational therapist, and two dyslexia therapists. The typical enrollment period is between two and five years. Each spring, students take a formal battery of standardized tests to gauge their progress.

Magnolia charges tuition on a sliding income-based scale with a "sticker price" of $30,000, though most students pay much less. However, tuition makes up just 25 percent of Magnolia's revenues. The rest comes from donations from individuals, corporations, and community members. This year, the school had eighteen students on its wait-list. One impediment to expanding enrollment is the school's ability to raise money from donors.

While most Magnolia students don't qualify for an ESA because they don't have an IEP, Linn argues that that they ought to be eligible anyway. There's merely "a semantic difference" between an IEP and the "service plans" that Magnolia provides, she says. "Why does a child have to fail in public school before they come here?"

For example, third-year Magnolia student Max Felder didn't qualify for an ESA because his local public school wouldn't provide an IEP. The school told his parents that he didn't need special education services because he scored highly on tests. While the Felders enrolled Max in Magnolia anyway, the family has had to ration resources to pay for his tuition.

The main reason state lawmakers restrict ESAs to special needs kids with IEPs from public schools is to limit additional costs that the state might incur by funding students who are currently paying out of pocket (or receiving private financial aid) to attend private schools. This way, the state doesn't pay more—it merely alters where the money goes.

However, requiring an IEP enables self-interested public schools to put up roadblocks for parents like the Felders.

Empower Mississippi president Grant Callen, who led the charge for ESAs in the state legislature, adds that his state has done a poor job publicizing the new program. For instance, he says, the Mississippi Department of Education was supposed to notify all eligible students, but hasn't. Thus, information about the program has spread mainly by word of mouth in the special needs community. Some schools with room to enroll more students have been pro-active, but most don't have marketing budgets.

Another problem, he points out, is a dearth of affordable programs. Educating special needs students can cost upward of $20,000, which most families in Mississippi—and other states—can't afford. Mississippi's $6,500 ESA can help parents afford tuition at less expensive private schools, but many families often still require financial aid. Larger ESA allocations could help ease the fund-raising burden on private schools to provide needy students with financial aid. It would also enable parents of children with special needs to tap educational resources beyond private school tuition or tutoring.

Mississippi's ESA program is unique because it allocates a mere $6,500 per student annually, regardless of disability. While this encourages parents to be economical, it can also limit their options. Callen explains that the legislature decided to fund accounts at $6,500 per student because most private schools in Mississippi charge tuition between $4,000 and $6,000. However, schools for special needs children often charge much more, and $6,500 is rarely enough to cover individualized therapies, tutoring, and curriculum.

The diversity and number of ESA suppliers depend both on the pool of eligible recipients as well as funding. Families can utilize a broader range of services when they are given more resources. Conversely, suppliers will expand when demand for their services grows. By expanding the criteria for eligibility or, alternatively, by increasing ESA allocations, states can encourage a more robust education marketplace.

The proliferation of private education providers is most notable in Arizona, which has the longest standing ESA and tax-credit scholarship programs in the country. Arizona's ESA program (outside of Nevada) also has the broadest eligibility standards. While Florida's PLSA program is growing rapidly, most recipients were already utilizing private providers. The PLSA, therefore, has had the effect of easing the financial stress on families while giving them access to more resources. Large and single-parent families also benefit from the increased flexibility.

In Mississippi, ESA recipients may need to reach a critical mass before the programs can achieve a meaningful impact on the education marketplace. However, Mississippi's program is benefiting families on the margins. If the goal is to increase competition and diversify the marketplace, ESAs will likely need to expand to more students.

Closing Thoughts

Although ESAs remain confined to a handful of states, they clearly have the potential to enrich the education marketplace and improve lives. Parents and policymakers are learning by trial and error. For instance, parents often shop around for the school best suited to their child's needs, which may be a frustrating ordeal. However, parents usually find the results of their efforts rewarding. And while this chapter mainly focuses on kids with special needs, ESAs may benefit every student whose abilities, challenges, and learning styles are unique.

Still, many parents struggle to provide their special needs children with all of the individualized therapies and instruction they require. This is particularly true in Mississippi, whose $6,500 ESA does not nearly cover the cost of tuition at most private schools for special needs students. One potential unintended effect of ESAs is that suppliers including private schools may raise their prices in line with ESA allocations, not unlike colleges that are incentivized to capture more federal aid in today's higher education landscape. This could negate the impact of ESAs.

The marketplace evolves through creative destruction, which promotes competition and over time, benefits consumers. Some suppliers may close, often because of financial challenges, but others may grow in their place. The highest quality operators—in economic terms, those that provide the most utility to students and parents—will expand as parents of special needs children share their experiences via online forums and other mediums. Perhaps the biggest limiting factor for growth is private capital since tuition money and ESAs are usually not enough to start or expand a business. This is where philanthropy could play a role. States could also offer tax deductions to businesses and individuals who donate to nonprofit schools.

So while ESAs are helpful to suppliers and parents, the programs alone might not be able to sustain or promote a robust marketplace. Expanding tax-credit scholarship programs and increasing scholarship sizes could bolster the marketplace as well as reduce the number of students who depend on financial aid from private schools, which consequently might be able to increase their enrollment.

Journalists must report, analyze, synthesize, and distill information. Quantitative data provides important insight, but sometimes numbers don't capture the full story. This is particularly true in the case of ESAs, many of whose benefits can't easily be measured. While the programs' impacts on a child's emotional growth and family interaction don't lend themselves to a simple quantitative analysis, a qualitative analysis is able to highlight some of the faces behind ESAs—and what it looks like when the rubber hits the road. This chapter's anecdotes from parents and suppliers seek to fill in the gaps in current debates and discussions surrounding ESA policies. Ultimately, those served by the programs—not lawmakers or researchers—may be the best judges of whether the ESAs are accomplishing their purpose, and how they might do so in the future.

NOTES

1. William Jeynes, "Parental Involvement and Student Achievement: A Meta-Analysis," (Harvard Family Research Project, December 2005), http://www. hfrp.org/publications-resources/browse-our-publications/parental-involvement-and-student-achievement-a-meta-analysis.

2. Mikaela Dufur, Toby Parcel, & Kelly Troutman, "Does Capital at Home Matter More Than Capital at School? Social Capital Effects on Academic Achievement," *Research in Social Stratification and Mobility*, March 31, 2013: doi:10.1016/j.rssm.2012.08.002, http://www.sciencedirect.com/science/article/pii/S027656241200042X.

3. Glenn Olsen & Mary Lou Fuller, *Home-School Relations: Working Successfully with Parents and Families* (New York: Pearson Education Inc, 2008).

4. Amanda Howard, interview by Allysia Finley, December 15, 2015.

5. Friedman Foundation for Educational Choice, "Arizona-Empowerment Scholarship Accounts," accessed April 7, 2016, http://www.edchoice.org/school-choice/programs/arizona-empowerment-scholarship-accounts/.

6. Katherine Visser, interview by Allysia Finley, December 11, 2015.

7. Holland Hines, interview by Allysia Finley, December 10, 2015.

8. Lynn McMurray, interview by Allysia Finley, December 17, 2015.

9. Julie Kleffel, interview by Allysia Finley, December 10, 2015.

10. Friedman Foundation for Educational Choice, "Florida-Gardiner Scholarship Program," accessed April 7, 2016, http://www.edchoice.org/school-choice/programs/gardiner-scholarship-program/.

11. Lydia Burton, interview by Allysia Finley, November 19, 2015.

12. John Kurnick, interview by Allysia Finley, October 27, 2015.

13. Martha Beard, interview by Allysia Finley, January 19, 2016.

14. "Special Needs Mom Talks about ESA," YouTube video, 6.31, posted by Empower Mississippi, February 2016, https://www.youtube.com/watch?v=duFJb5 ZkACs.

15. Tony Pugh, "Low Graduation Rate for Disabled Students Haunts Miss. Educators," *The State*, March 26, 2016.

16. Friedman Foundation for Educational Choice, "Mississippi- Equal Opportunity for Students with Special Needs Program," accessed April 7, 2016, http://www. edchoice.org/school-choice/programs/mississippi-equal-opportunity-for-students-with-special-needs-program/.

17. Friedman Foundation for Educational Choice, "Florida Tax Credit Scholarship Program," accessed April 8, 2016, http://www.edchoice.org/school-choice/programs/florida-tax-credit-scholarship-program/.

18. Friedman Foundation for Educational Choice, "Arizona-School Choice," accessed April 8, 2016, http://www.edchoice.org/school-choice/state/arizona/.

19. Friedman Foundation for Educational Choice, "Mississippi Dyslexia Therapy Scholarship for Students with Dyslexia Program," accessed April 8, 2016, http://www.edchoice.org/school-choice/programs/mississippi-dyslexia-therapy-scholarship-for-students-with-dyslexia-program/.

20. Carrie Reed, interview by Allysia Finley, February 4, 2016.

21. Bonnie Dougherty, interview by Allysia Finley, November 16, 2015.

22. Kami Cothrun, interview by Allysia Finley, November 19, 2015.

23. Donny Newsome, interview by Allysia Finley, November 17, 2015.

24. Nicky Carter, interview by Allysia Finley, November 18, 2015.

25. Cena Holifield, interview by Allysia Finley, January 11, 2016.

26. Nancy New, interview by Allysia Finley, December 17, 2015.

27. Valerie Linn, interview by Allysia Finley, December 15, 2015.

Chapter Eight

Hubs and Spokes

The Supply Side Response to Deregulated Education Funding

Michael Q. McShane

In a story recounted by Supreme Court Justice Stephen Breyer, an East Boston constituent approached Senator Edward "Ted" Kennedy to ask him why he was so keen on holding hearings about airline deregulation. "Why are you holding hearings about airlines? I've never been able to fly." Senator Kennedy replied: "That's why I'm holding the hearings."[1]

Airline deregulation offers a good frame of reference for understanding the world of options that might be made available in an education savings account-financed education system. Perhaps most importantly, it implores us to think beyond our immediate set of options and understanding of what is possible. Before airlines were deregulated, most Americans had no expectation that they would ever be able to travel on an airplane, as the cost was simply prohibitive. Those operating airlines couldn't imagine low-cost carriers making the kinds of decisions that Southwest or Spirit Airlines have made to improve efficiency. A world of possibilities waited just over the horizon, it was simply a matter of getting out of the way and letting its sun rise.

This chapter argues that the same could be true for education. There are myriad possible educational arrangements, many unfathomable today, that could emerge if more providers were allowed to enter the education marketplace and families had greater flexibility over the funding they have to purchase those options. There is also reason to believe that, given the incentives embedded in the system, an education savings account (from here on, ESA) program would drive down the cost of providing an education, like deregulation drove down the cost of airline tickets. But, all of those benefits rest on a robust supply-side response to the program. If policymakers build it, and no one comes, none of the anticipated benefits will materialize. No children's lives will be improved.

A robust supply-side response on the part of educational providers is essential for an education savings account program to work. If providers find it too difficult or onerous to enter the marketplace, they will simply sit out. These difficulties could include insufficient funding, prohibitive regulations, byzantine processes to make coursework eligible for purchase, difficulties in securing capital to start new ventures, an inability to recruit quality educators, or a host of other problems. These are just a few of the problems that plagued start-up and legacy airlines in the years and decades post-deregulation.

It should be noted that there are also unintended consequences of deregulation that we should be clear-eyed in understanding. Deregulation caused massive upheaval in the airline industry and though, over time, as the data clearly demonstrates, it created more opportunities for people to fly that were dramatically less expensive, it initially led to bankruptcies, strikes, cramped seats, hidden (and not-so-hidden) fees, and numerous other unpleasant realities.

In the pages that follow, this chapter will walk through the story of airline deregulation: what happened, why it happened, and its effects. Next, it will connect the issues at play to those in education. After hopefully convincing the reader that there is sufficient enough connection between the two to extract some valuable lessons, it will offer some lessons from deregulation that can apply to education savings account programs. Finally, it will close with a hopeful look toward the future of education.

SOME BACKGROUND ON AIRLINE DEREGULATION

The early days of airline travel carried over the regulatory apparatus of more primitive forms of transportation. In fact, ticket prices were initially set by the government to mirror the price of a first class ticket on a Pullman railroad car.[2] Prices were set to ensure profitability for the airlines and routes were heavily regulated by the Civil Aeronautics Board (CAB). In 1974, for example, it was illegal for an airline to charge less than $1,442 for a flight between New York and Los Angeles (in inflation-adjusted dollars). As a result, airline travel was incredibly expensive, and in 1965, fewer than 20 percent of Americans had ever flown.[3]

The CAB was created by the Civil Aeronautics Act of 1938.[4] That act empowered the CAB to control entry and exit of airlines into the marketplace, to set fares, to award subsidies to carriers, to assign routes, and to control mergers between airlines. Every time an airline wanted to add a new route between two cities, hearings had to be held and new airlines had to argue that their route "served the public interest" and didn't harm an incumbent airline.

As a result, airlines were unable to compete on cost. The "Big Four"—American, Eastern, Trans World Airlines (TWA), and United—were the largest airline carriers, and by the late 1960s and early 1970s, many economists were producing research that showed that the industry was incredibly inefficient.

Not all airline routes were regulated, however. Intrastate routes fell outside of the purview of the Civil Aeronautics Board. This allowed a far less regulated marketplace to develop within states, and in large and populous states like California and Texas, fully articulated air travel systems emerged. Most notably, out of the plains of Texas rose Southwest, an airline dedicated to providing low-cost service. Southwest operated vastly more efficiently than the regulated airlines. It ran two-person, instead of three-person crews and had more favorable labor deals with its employees. It utilized aircraft much more efficiently with higher passenger load ratios. It also streamlined reservations and sales procedures.[5]

Seeing the opportunity to dramatically drive down the cost of airline travel led President Gerald Ford to appoint Stephen Breyer (later a Supreme Court Justice) to investigate airline deregulation, and his findings and others were debated in a series of U.S. Senate hearings led by Ted Kennedy in the mid-1970s. In those hearings, research on inefficiencies in the existing regulated system and the possibilities that the unregulated markets in Texas and California presented for the nation as a whole led to broad bipartisan support for ending CAB and deregulating airlines. President Carter signed the Airline Deregulation Act in October of 1978.

What were the effects? The top line finding is that from 1978 to 2008, airline prices fell 44.9 percent. Even after adjusting for changes in quality over that time period, this means that passengers save $19.4 billion per year as a result of deregulation.[6] What's more, the recent uptick in fees has not changed the overall sharp downward trajectory in the cost to fly.[7] How did airlines do this? There were many ways they went about it, but most importantly, they made their operations much more efficient, as evidenced by the change in load factor (the percentage of occupied seats on a flight), which averaged below 50 percent preregulation and jumped to 74 percent by 2003. All told, the number of flyers annually has doubled since 1978.[8]

But it wasn't all sunshine and roses. In the years immediately following deregulation, a national recession and fuel crisis made life difficult for carriers. Many had built their entire operations to thrive in a highly regulated marketplace. They had legacy costs from buying airplanes, building facilities, and striking labor deals on the belief that they would have a guaranteed market and guaranteed profits. Braniff Airways went bankrupt in 1982 and reemerged as a hollow shell of itself. Continental went bankrupt in 1983, Eastern went bankrupt and ceased operations in 1989, Pan Am closed in

1991, and TWA went belly up in 2001. Other carriers like American and U.S. Airways went through several bankruptcies and reorganizations, particularly in the aftermath of September 11, 2001.

More recently, airlines have moved to charge more fees instead of raise fares. Amenities that were previously included in the price of a ticket, like checked bags or snacks, are now available only for an extra charge. These fees are projected to raise over $59 billion in additional revenue for airlines.[9] Again, these fees have not staunched the steady decline in costs that air travelers have seen postderegulation, but coupled with other cost-saving steps, such as seats that provide less legroom to accommodate more passengers, they have made airline travel uncomfortable or annoying for some flyers.

DOES REGULATED AIR TRAVEL SOUND LIKE THE U.S. EDUCATION SYSTEM TODAY? IT SHOULD

Nationwide, the vast majority of the American education system functions in a way not dissimilar to the regulated "marketplace" that existed in air travel prior to deregulation. Most providers have a geographic monopoly over a given territory. There is also evidence that the cost of education has been increasing for the past several decades, while the productivity of the sector has not.[10] Where multiple providers exist in close proximity, there are limited dimensions on which they can compete with one another. In general, the only places that markets exist are in the individual states or cities that allow charter schooling, school vouchers, or education savings accounts; the Texases and Californias of education, if you will.

There is evidence, however, from these less-regulated places that schooling can be operated better and at a lower expense. Research has shown, for example, that the DC Opportunity Scholarship Program achieved greater results with fewer resources than the traditional public schools of the District of Columbia.[11] Evaluations of public spending on charter schools,[12] coupled with research on their effectiveness, have also demonstrated that they do more (or at worse, about as well) with less than traditional public schools.[13]

But even in these choice-heavy markets, providers do not compete on price. There is no reason for a school to operate at less than a voucher allotment (unless there are nonvoucher students paying tuition who could not afford a higher price) or for a charter school to send money back to the state. ESAs would reward parents for looking not only at the quality of providers, but also their cost. If two Mandarin tutors offer services of roughly equal quality but one is $350 per semester and one is $250 per semester, parents get to keep that difference and put it toward other things that they want. That is a game changer.

A fully realized education savings account program would blow the doors wide open to innovation and alternative arrangements for education. It would, in effect, deregulate the American education system as we know it today. The question becomes, what would happen on the supply side? How would providers respond? It is, of course, very difficult to say. An ESA-funded system is unlike anything that has been done in education and only has a rough analogy in health savings accounts. So while it is hard to say what lies over the horizon, we can learn from airline deregulation about the complicated interplay of existing and new providers that happens when markets are freed from government control.

Deregulated markets do not simply rise up out of the mist. They already have players, many of which have been in operation for decades. Those players are used to operating under a particular set of rules and have crafted their enterprises to try and maximize results under those rules. They have to change when the rules change. At the same time, new organizations are able to spring up when markets deregulate. Are these new organizations at an advantage or are they too far behind to challenge incumbents? The story of airline deregulation can help answer those questions.

LESSONS FROM AIRLINE DEREGULATION

There are several lessons from airline deregulation that can inform our thinking about education savings accounts and the types of changes they could spark.

Schools could move from "point to point" to "hub and spoke"

The primary change that passengers experienced after airline deregulation was the switch from "point to point" to "hub and spoke" flight patterns. While the old, regulated system was built around direct linear routes from city to city, post-deregulation airlines would amass resources in one city and route their flights through there. While it increased flight times and required more frequent layovers, it was much more cost effective for airlines and made travel much less expensive. The types of planes changed, the frequency of flights changed, and all of the assorted logistics changed as well. This became less convenient for some flyers, who were used to taking direct flights from small or midsized cities to other small or midsized cities. In general, these were re-routed through hubs. But, for those who lived in hub cities or lived in large cities that still justified frequent flights, their service was not disrupted by this new model.

To date, we have "point-to-point" schools. Everything is included. There are no transfers. You enter in kindergarten, you leave in fifth grade. So what would a hub and spoke school look like? It might look like a building with small rooms, cubicles, or desks, computers, and videoconference hardware for students. The school would have responsible adults present to ensure students' safety, but students would also be able to go off to their own desk to work away on individualized coursework. For students that need more one-on-one attention, or who aren't the self-starters that can immediately dig into a project, there could be more hands-on instruction. The school might offer meal services or organize field trips or book clubs to encourage socialization amongst students, but would be a far less top-down organization and more of a holding place and convener of services. Students would pay some chunk of their ESA funds for the space or the activities, and would spend the rest on the coursework they access from their desk. The school could even provide guidance counselors for those that need it to help navigate the various options or to choose from prescribes courses of study. The hub and spoke school might even put on a play or field sports teams (supported by ESA contributions).

Like the transition to hubs and spokes in airlines, deregulation might lead to disruptions in education. A virtue of our point-to-point schools is the fact that they are one-stop shops. Children can be put on a bus, taken to one central location, taught (and fed and given structured exercise and play) and then bused back to their homes. It is a clear and organizationally efficient arrangement that is easy to explain. Postderegulation, airlines had to dramatically change the way that they utilized airplanes because load factor became much more important. No longer would airlines fly large, half-full jets from city to city; now they would fly smaller regional jets from smaller cities to hubs, which would then be connected by larger, and fuller, airplanes. This meant shuffling around pilots, flight attendants, maintenance technicians, and all of the infrastructures to support airline travel.

The same would be true for schools. Schools don't have to operate from 8 AM to 3 PM every day for everyone. Students could design their own schedules that meet their needs and the needs of their parents, who increasingly work jobs with nontraditional schedules. The size and utilization of facilities would have to change, staffing would have to change, and procurement procedures would have to change if schools wanted to be competitive in this new marketplace, but all of those issues would be better aligned to actual student needs rather than what it neat, tidy, and convenient for administrators.

Incumbents Have an Initial Advantage Postderegulation, but it Fades Quickly

In the months and years immediately succeeding airline deregulation, established carriers had an advantage over new carriers entering the market. They had the planes, they had the pilots, and they had the infrastructure. It took a long time for upstart airlines to start honing in on their turf. But those legacy carriers also had legacy costs, something that eventually hurt their competitive footing. Pension obligations, debt on huge capital expenses (like airplanes), and set operations in locations that were no longer optimal all made legacy carriers less competitive and gave airlines starting from scratch a leg up.

One would expect to see something similar in education. Established schools and educational providers would have an advantage at the outset of an education savings account program. In fact, data from the Arizona ESA bears this out—two-thirds of students spent their money on tuition at existing private schools as if the ESA was simply a voucher.[14] Existing public schools would have an advantage as well, as they are both the default option for families and an already established sector. But the advantage that those schools and other established providers might have could fade over time. Existing school buildings need maintenance or might not be located in the optimal place to grow or meet student demand. Apps might be developed for technology that becomes obsolete. Pensions, bargaining agreements, and other labor arrangements might hamstring existing schools. There is every reason to believe new operators would be able to work around these.

Schools looking to thrive in this new marketplace could learn from the story of Southwest after airline de-regulation. What Southwest did was not complicated—it was purposeful. It moved to more efficient flight crews and upped the load factor on their airplanes. It streamlined ticketing and reservations. It experimented with fare deals. Southwest wasn't hamstrung with labor agreements built under the premises of the previous pricing regime. New schooling providers looking to succeed should think about optimizing their back office operations. Can they automate processes? Can they find efficiencies that existing schools have not? There is a great deal of work around attendance, bookkeeping, grading, parental communications, and the like that currently are labor-intensive but don't have to be. There are also efficiency gains around staffing that could be achieved by leveraging technology, new roles, specialization, or a different organization of schools.

Existing schools also need to think about disruptions coming down the pipe when they are designing compensation systems for their employees. Many private schools still use "step and lane" pay scales and defined benefit pensions that will put them at a disadvantage if and when more agile competitors emerge. If these private schools were to move to more flexible payment arrangements and contributory retirement systems that can be budgeted on a year-by-year basis, they will put themselves in a much better position to compete.

Intermediary Institutions Can Help Decrease Market Friction

As economics writer Derek Thompson highlights, the emergence of fare searching websites like Orbitz, Priceline, and Kayak drove down airline ticket prices.[15] Now, in one place, passengers can compare dozens of flights between two cities and make decisions based on price and convenience. They can even plan complicated, multi-stop trips on their own, something that used to be the sole purview of travel agents. These tools allow customers to express their preferences on a variety of dimensions—not just price. Perhaps someone will pay more to avoid a layover, or to avoid connecting through a notorious airport. Perhaps they even prefer the offerings of a particular airline or the seat that they will be able to sit in on the plane. They are free to weigh the various pros and cons and make a decision for themselves.

But it is not just fare-searching websites that help airline consumers. Travel bloggers compare and contrast airline offerings and help flyers maximize the use of their frequent flyer miles. Consumers can find out who offers the best inflight snacks or who has the rudest flight attendants. There are whole communities buried deep in message boards sharing how to get free trips or hotel stays. In short, there are lots of opportunity for consumers to share the knowledge that they have gained about air travel with each other and lots of opportunity for them to consult experts about what options to take.

Similar services could be developed to help families navigate education marketplaces. Rating websites that compare course offerings based on price and quality could help inform decisions. Guidance-counselor-type assistants could help families navigate their options (they could be paid out of part of the education savings account). If airline travel is any indicator, such services could both dramatically improve an individual's abilities to pick the services that best meet their needs and improve the transparency around price that schools do not currently offer. Over time, this should drive down the price, allowing families to get more and more for the money that is deposited into their ESA.

There is an emerging research base on parental decision-making that should inform the creation of such resources. How data is presented matters and those looking to inform parents need to realize that seemingly subtle distinctions can magnify what parents think about schools. Rebecca Jacobsen, Andy Saultz, and Jeff Snyder completed a randomized experiment with more than 1,100 participants that presented the exact same data on school performance in different ways and judged how parents reacted.[16] Even though schools rated as an "A," "90 percent proficient" and "advanced" meant the same thing, respondents routinely ranked schools that received an "A" higher than schools whose results were reported in the other ways. The same was true on the other end of the spectrum. Schools given a "C" were seen as much worse as those rated "basic" even though the classifications again meant the same thing.

Who is offering the information matters, and it looks like there is potential for greater influence from third-party organizations disseminating state data than from the state acting as a one-stop shop for both data collection and dissemination. Jon Valant found that parents were more likely to trust school performance data from independent nonprofit organizations than state governments.[17] Of the people he surveyed, 77 percent rated their trust in the school performance data presented by nonprofits as a three or better (on a scale of one to five), whereas only 60 percent gave the same score to state governments.

Even more than nongovernmental organizations, Valant found that parents trust other parents when it comes to gauging the quality of a school. In an experiment where families were given different information about schools and asked to rate them, he found that seeing two positive comments about a school from another parent as opposed to two negative comments led to a jump of two-thirds of one letter grade (from a C+ to a B). Even though the comments were "brief, appeared alongside formal academic ratings, came from unidentified sources on the internet, and described schools that many respondents knew well," they "fundamentally reshaped the way parents and other adults evaluated school policy."

But there is an added level of complexity here. We are not simply asking parents to pick a school, which has proven hard enough, but to *design an entire educational program for their child*. If simply picking schools has a steep learning curve, cobbling together multiple providers into a coherent program of instruction might have a learning cliff.

Again, though, the lessons of the airline marketplace offer some hope. I have to imagine if you told someone in the 1960s that they needed to book a multiple stop trip via airplane from Kansas City to London to Moscow to Shanghai and back that they would have said that they couldn't do it. It is too complicated. It takes too much insider knowledge. However, anyone today can simply punch those destinations in Kayak and in less than thirty seconds, multiple options are before them that can be booked in mere minutes. Ancillary institutions emerge to help people navigate complex marketplaces.

Funding and Safety Regulation Are Not the Same Thing

There is a persistent misunderstanding about the nature and role of regulation in airline travel and the bodies that are responsible for that regulation. Prior to deregulation, there were two separate bodies, the Civil Aeronautics Board and the Federal Aviation Administration (spun off from the CAB in 1958) that regulated air travel. The CAB regulated routes, prices, and services and the FAA regulated safety. The same body did not do both.

While the CAB did not have a great track record for success, the Federal Aviation Administration (FAA) does, though it is not perfect. Many argue that several of today's FAA regulations are outdated and hinder efficiency with no additional safety benefits. One example of this is the glide path that airplanes have to take into most major airports. Traditionally, flights have to descend in a stair step fashion. They drop a few thousand feet, level off, drop a few thousand more, and so on and so forth until they touch down. It is much more efficient if they were simply able to glide in a smooth, continuous descent. As WIRED Magazine described it, "like sliding down a bannister."[18] But regulations based on outdated technology that could only handle the stair-step fashion required planes to continue descending that way, even though they now are able to make safe, smooth descents.

The separation of funding regulation and safety/operational regulation has a perfect analog in education. Today, the same institutions fund, regulate, and operate schools—the traditional public school system. The regulation related to funding is usually state-level and often contains court-ordered funding formulae with numerous rules for distributing those funds as well as operation. But it doesn't have to be this way. School systems could separate out the regulatory apparatuses, and have one entity in charge of funding and accounting for ESA funds and another in charge of ensuring that the offerings in the marketplace are of necessary quality.

But regulators often forget that K–12 educational providers do not have to work in the field of education if they don't want to. Conceivably, their skills and talents have applications to other industries, so if the regulatory burden is too high, they just won't enter the marketplace. We don't know how many airlines might be able to exist if the regulatory structure was easier for them to enter. Flights might even be cheaper, more convenient, or more comfortable. The thin margin that those innovators might be looking for could be eaten up by the fuel costs of stair stepping down into airports or providing seats with certain types of cushions. Regulations have costs and benefits, and those wishing to regulate ESA markets sternly from the beginning might very well thwart some incredible opportunities. In short, they should be sure that the regulations actually protect kids or promote quality, because the juice might not be worth the squeeze.

Access to Capital Is Incredibly Important

Starting a new airline is a capital-intensive enterprise. Planes are not cheap, nor are maintenance facilities, equipment, gate leases, or ticketing and reservation systems. If a startup airline cannot access capital to deal with these expenses, they will never (pardon the pun) get off the ground. There are, however, ways that airlines can save money. Rather than purchasing planes, they can lease them from other airlines. They can share gates or maintenance workers if they need to.

Interestingly though, many financial institutions initially opposed deregulation. As Bailey et al. explain, financial institutions like to get involved in industries where the players cannot go bankrupt. That mitigates a great deal of risk. Competition drives out lower performing firms, and if those firms owe financial institutions money, the financial institutions are left holding the bag. Because of the fears of higher rates of default and bankruptcy, financial institutions (along with labor unions, which feared deregulated airlines hiring nonunion workers) were opponents of deregulation.[19]

Starting a new school is a capital-intensive enterprise. School buildings are not cheap, nor are teachers, computers, desks, or education management systems. If a new school cannot access capital to deal with these expenses, they will never be able to open.

One way to cope with this problem is to try and help decrease the startup costs of new schools. One promising effort on this front are 4.0 Schools' "Tiny Schools" initiative. Tiny schools start in a library or classroom with a small group of volunteer students and no more than one or two teachers, usually for a couple of hours on a weekend. For up to a year, the teachers try new methods and get instant feedback, refine what they're doing and improve. The students attend voluntarily; they and their parents know they are part of the experiment. If all goes well, after a year, the educators are in a much better place to start a full-fledged school than if they had tried to build a whole school from scratch. What's more, if the plan doesn't work, no students are harmed, and very little money is lost.

Part of the reason that charter authorization documents now stretch into the hundreds of pages is because starting a conventional school means launching an organization with a $1 million-plus budget, contracts with ten, twenty, or more staff and teachers, the rental or purchase of a large building, and the lives of hundreds of children—and that is just the start. When we're talking about that much money and that many people, authorizers want as much assurance as possible that the school is going to work. It shouldn't be a surprise. Starting small can lower the risk of loaning money for the school, which can get schools a more favorable interest rate and overall lower borrowing costs.

But, even with some of these cost-saving and risk-decreasing measures, schools will still need access to startup capital. Here, the expansion of educational options needs a concomitant expansion of financial support mechanisms for new providers. One straightforward solution to encourage states to include capital funding in the voucher or tax-credit programs that they administer or to increase the voucher amount so that money could be put toward capital costs. States could also make it easier for schools to access bond financing and could particularly work with schools in school choice programs to get low-cost financing of their debt by allowing schools of choice access to state moral obligation pledges or other debt guarantees. If the state backs up the debt, the school can borrow money for less.

But, the private sector might also be able to help. B Corporations (B-Corps) and Low-Profit LLCs are ways for socially oriented ventures to have leeway from investors' financial expectations and spend time and resources advancing their social mission. They are a step between a nonprofit and a full for-profit venture, and in some ways, they can have the best of both worlds. B-Corps are expected to promote a dual bottom line, both financial and social success. Low-profit limited liability companies (L3Cs) function similarly to B-Corps, and philanthropies can count their contributions to them as part of their required yearly spend-down, even though that investment can eventually be returned to them. For a financing community that has limited resources, the ability to turn around investments and spread dollars wider is an incredible opportunity for supporting schools.

New school options could also benefit from venture financing, both in the traditional and philanthropic sense. Traditional venture capital organizations have already started financing new education providers. In places where public dollars are available, philanthropic support can be stretched much further, as it is only needed for that first jolt to help get the school established, after which public sources can cover the school's operational expenses. Strategic grants and support from organizations such as the New Schools Venture Fund have been able to push an enormous amount of change for the amount spent.

Whither Public Schools?

Traditional public schools would also be a part of the emerging ESA-fueled marketplace. Like private schools, they would have the advantage of incumbency and would also, at least in the short term, possess a serious advantage when it comes to raising capital. In most states around the country, traditional public school districts are the only schooling entities that can levy property taxes to pay operational expenses or to pay off bonded debt. This allows them to very easily pass on the cost of new facilities, or even operating expenses, to the community. If an ESA program did not include some ability to access these revenue streams, or did not alter them even while funding a competing private-school based system, traditional public schools would have a clear advantage in the marketplace.

That said, public schools would be held captive to their own bureaucratic inertia and the changing whims of the political bodies that oversee them. Decisions would have to be made by committee, elections would be regularly held as checks on their strategy, and many of the labor deals that determine much of how schools function today would still be in effect. This would be an incredible disadvantage when competition with nimble, agile, and smaller educational providers enters an ESA marketplace. The ultimate balance between strengths and weaknesses remains to be seen, but it not clear why the entrepreneurial forces that shook up private-but-regulated industries wouldn't also shake up public-but-regulated ones as well.

THE FUTURE OF EDUCATION PROVISION

When your flight has been delayed, or one of your fellow passengers is trying in vain to shove a clearly oversized roller bag into an overhead bin, it is easy to lose sight of just how incredible air travel is today. It has been barely a hundred years since human beings have first slipped the surly bonds of earth in machine-powered airplanes, and now we can travel around the circumference of the earth with only one stop. The Airbus A380, with two decks and four engines, can pack in over 850 people if arranged entirely in coach, or can have multiroom apartments in a configuration that goes beyond the traditional meaning of the words "first class." For a fraction of the median income of an American worker, one can fly to the great cities of Europe or to any corner of the United States.

This was made possible by airline deregulation, plain (again, forgive the pun) and simple.

Unfortunately, if we look at the American school system in that same time period, we cannot show the same meteoric improvement. Yes, the high school graduation rate and college matriculation rates have improved markedly. That is a big deal. But in many ways these things simply emerged by offering the same thing to more people. Schools still (minus the one-room school houses that once dominated much of rural America) look very similar. Students still attend class in age-graded cohorts and are arranged in groups of roughly similar numbers with a single instructor in the front of the room. And so on and so on.

Deregulating the system, while not perfect, could do great things to push for the kinds of innovations that could transform education the way airlines have been transformed in the past four decades. It would not be without tradeoffs. Nothing is. But, if forty years from now, we were able to look back on education the way we look back on air travel of 1976 that would be an incredible thing. It would represent a serious improvement in the quality of life of tens, if not hundreds, of millions of schoolchildren.

NOTES

1. Stephen Breyer, "Airline Deregulation, Revisited," *Bloomberg Businessweek*, January 20, 2011, http://www.bloomberg.com/news/articles/2011-01-20/airline-dereg-ulation-revisitedbusinessweek-business-news-stock-market-and-financial-advice.

2. Elizabeth Bailey, David Graham, & Daniel Kaplan, *Deregulating the Airlines* (Cambridge: MIT Press, 1985).

3. Derek Thompson, "How Airline Ticket Prices Fell 50% in 30 Years (and Why Nobody Noticed)," The *Atlantic*, February 28, 2013, http://www.theatlantic.com/business/archive/2013/02/how-airline-ticket-prices-fell-50-in-30-years-and-why-nobody-noticed/273506/.

4. Bailey, Graham, & Kaplan, 11.

5. Bailey, Graham, & Kaplan, 94–95.

6. Fred Smith & Braden Cox, "Airline Deregulation," *The Concise Encyclopedia of Economics, 2nd ed.* (Library of Economics and Liberty, 2008), http://www.econlib.org/library/Enc/AirlineDeregulation.html.

7. Thompson, "How Airline Ticket Prices Fell."

8. Smith & Cox, "Airline Deregulation."

9. "Airline Ancillary Revenue Projected to Be $59.2 Billion Worldwide in 2015," *Idea Works*, accessed April 12, 2016, http://www.ideaworkscompany.com/wp-content/uploads/2015/11/Press-Release-103-Global-Estimate.pdf.

10. Eric Hanushek, "The Productivity Collapse in Schools," *Developments in School Finance 1996*, ed. William Fowler, Jr. (Washington, DC: National Center for Education Statistics, U.S. Department of Education, 1997), 183–95, http://nces.ed.gov/pubs97/97535k.pdf.

11. Patrick J. Wolf & Michael McShane, "Is the Juice Worth the Squeeze? A Benefit/Cost Analysis of the District of Columbia Opportunity Scholarship Program," *Education Finance and Policy* 8, no. 1 (2013) 74–99.

12. Meagan Batdorff, Larry Maloney, Jay F. May, Sheree T. Speakman, Patrick J. Wolf, & Albert Cheng, "Charter School Funding: Inequity Expands," *University of Arkansas*, April 2014, http://www.uaedreform.org/wp-content/uploads/charter-funding-inequity-expands.pdf.

13. Edward Cremata, Devora Davis, Kathleen Dickey, Kristina Lawyer, Yohannes Negassi, Margaret Raymond, & James Woodworth, "National Charter School Study 2013," *Stanford University*, 2013, http://credo.stanford.edu/documents/NCSS%202013%20Final%20Draft.pdf.

14. Lindsey Burke, "The Education Debit Card: What Arizona Parents Purchase with Education Savings Accounts," Friedman Foundation for Educational Choice, August 2013, http://www.edchoice.org/wp-content/uploads/2013/08/2013-8-Education-Debit-Card-WEB-NEW.pdf.

15. Thompson, "How Airline Ticket Prices Fell."

16. Rebecca Jacobsen, Andrew Saultz, & Jeffrey Synder, "When Accountability Strategies Collide Do Policy Changes That Raise Accountability Standards Also Erode Public Satisfaction?" *Education Policy* 27, no. 2 (March/April 2013) 360–89, doi: 10.1177/0895904813475712.

17. Jon Valant, "Better Data, Better Decisions Improving School Choosers to Improve Education Markets," *American Enterprise Institute*, November 2014, https://www.aei.org/wp-content/uploads/2014/11/Better-Data-Better-Decisions-4.pdf.

18. Alex Davies, "Planes are Finally Making Logical Descents Onto American Runways," *Wired*, June 25, 2014, http://www.wired.com/2014/06/houston-nextgen-plane-descents/.

19. Bailey, Graham, & Kaplan, 32–33.

Chapter Nine

Settling on Education Savings Accounts

Nat Malkus

Education savings accounts (ESAs) have the potential to deliver what other mechanisms of school choice have not: a competitive marketplace for K–12 education at scale. ESAs reroute existing public education funds to parents who can use them for a wide array of educational products and services. They also allow parents to roll over unused funds for future educational uses, potentially even for postsecondary schooling. This ability to save surplus funds creates something absent in our current K–12 funding system: incentives for parents to make the most of their education dollars.

Beyond broadened choices and new incentives to save, ESAs also have the potential to realize unprecedented scale. Since ESA programs reroute a portion of the existing funding that would have gone to public schools, there is no structural reason to limit eligibility for ESAs among public school students. The combination of the ability to fully customize a child's education, the potential to save funds for future uses, and the large scale of eligibility are significant departures from previous mechanisms of school choice.

Ironically enough, school choice is not the desired end result sought by the movement named after it. School choice is only the means to an end, with that end being a competitive marketplace for K–12 education. Milton Friedman, who many consider the father of the modern school choice movement, argued as much: "Vouchers are not an end in themselves; they are a means to make a transition from a government to a market system."[1] School choice programs such as vouchers and charter schools have had more success providing options at the school level than creating a competitive market system Friedman describes. ESAs have the potential to change the equation.

Vouchers, which provide public funding to give families choice among private schools, have been the primary tool for private school choice, successfully expanding educational choices for thousands of students. By offering school choice, voucher programs and other scholarship and tax-credit programs that function similarly have given students private alternatives from the default neighborhood public schools.

Yet despite their promise, they do not offer choices among the full range of education offerings. Vouchers typically pay for private school tuition up to a limit and any unspent funds are retained by the state or local government. Since vouchers are a unitary block of funding, they do not create the cost controls inherent in a competitive market. Further, voucher programs have not reached the scale necessary to mount a serious challenge to the public school monopoly through the creation of functioning education markets.

Charter schools have had more success in growing to scale, providing new public school choices for millions of students, and posing what may be the first structural challenge to the dominant system of residence based public school assignment. However, while charters diversify public school options, they still only offer choices between *schools*. And because charter schools are directly funded by the state, charter school reforms cannot produce a system where education service providers compete on quality and price.

Vouchers and charters have only made modest headway towards a market system because they take price out of the choice equation. The monopoly enjoyed by the government system of public schools endures because the price families pay for tuition is zero. Families are free to pursue other educational opportunities, including private schools, home schooling, or unbundled combinations of education services—if they can pay the price for them. However, while many families might prefer those alternative options, most remain in the monopoly of public schools because of the enormous difference in the prices of their options.

The current education system is analogous to offering all families a coupon that covers the price of tuition, but only for government-run schools. Families may prefer other options, but the coupon makes the price difference so great that few will follow their preferences. Choice through vouchers and charters is akin to allowing parents to use their coupons for more schools, thereby extending their school options, but those coupons fall short of creating a market that creates competitive pressures on both price and quality.

THE IMPORTANCE OF A CHANGE IN PRICE

ESAs offer a viable path towards an educational market at unprecedented scale by reducing the out-of-pocket price families pay, without doing away with the beneficial role prices play in a market. Without an ESA, families have a choice between a free public school or non-public options that usually cost several thousand dollars—a stark contrast in price. ESAs give parents the option to essentially exchange that coupon for a portion of the dollars that would have funded it, which they can then apply to the cost of other options. ESAs thereby greatly reduce the stark contrast in price. In economic terms, they function like a subsidy. Families can choose to use the coupons for the schools that they can be redeemed at, or they can use the subsidy to reduce their out-of-pocket price for private schools or alternative educational services.

ESAs are also a viable path to scale because they don't necessarily require states to generate new revenue or raise taxes. Instead, they allow states to reroute existing funding streams to put a substantial subsidy into the hands of parents. In other words, they take funds that would have gone to the government coupons and use them to effectively subsidize alternatives. No longer confined to public schools, those subsidies create a viable path to creating functioning education markets.

Without an ESA, families' preferences for alternative educational services would have to be quite strong to justify the price they would need to pay out-of-pocket for them. With an ESA account working like a subsidy, those preferences do not need to change for there to be a substantial increase in demand. Families' out-of-pocket prices would drop substantially, meaning families would be much more likely to satisfy their pre-existing preferences for alternative educational options. Of course, families who are satisfied with their public schools would stay in public schools, but the change in price would make more alternatives viable for families facing budget constraints.

It is important to separate price from cost in this context. Costs need not increase to change the price of parents' educational options. In terms of revenue from the state, ESAs are not a new cost. By rerouting existing funding streams to give parents discretion over their use, ESAs change prices for families at no additional cost to the state or to taxpayers. By changing existing funds into a subsidy, parents' educational decisions will no longer be dominated by the massive price difference between public schools and alternative options.

ESAs can theoretically expand access to all public school students, as Nevada's program is designed to do, without raising costs to the state. Even without eligibility restrictions, ESAs can arguably be revenue neutral or even save taxpayer dollars, because in some cases ESAs could be an effective subsidy for less than what the state would spend for a given public school student. At scale, ESAs that include substantial funding and open eligibility for families will dramatically increase demand for educational services outside of public schools.

The increase in parent (or consumer) demand caused by ESAs should spur development on the supply side. Existing education service providers, mainly private schools at the outset, should compete for this new class of consumers. New providers should also enter the market, bringing with them diversity and innovation in educational services. Moreover, since consumers can roll over unspent funds for other uses, providers should have incentives to compete on both price and quality. Competition on price and quality should lower prices, increase pressure to improve quality, or both. As the supply side develops to offer more high quality providers at competitive prices, demand among families who have not yet taken advantage of ESAs should increase until the supply and demand reach an equilibrium. In this way, ESAs can build a sustainable market for the education services they make possible.

WHAT IS THE POTENTIAL FOR ESAs?

ESAs' potential for providing choice to families is more than theoretical. Five states have implemented ESAs thus far, and to date, none have been successfully challenged on constitutional grounds. That is—despite numerous attempts—to date, no ESA program has been overturned by a judicial challenge. ESAs' legal and constitutional foundations are covered in detail in chapter two, "The Constitutional Case for ESAs," by Tim Keller. In fact, the Nevada legislature affirmed the constitutionality of the state's ambitious ESA program, while simultaneously blocking it based on a flawed funding approach.

The significant administrative and regulatory challenges posed by ESAs are not the primary focus of this chapter and can be addressed without substantially impinging on market function. Though they are necessary challenges to negotiate, they are surmountable and reviewed at length in other chapters. Assuming the constitutional and legal foundations of ESAs are sound, and that the administrative and regulatory challenges are surmountable, it makes sense to focus in this chapter on whether ESAs are likely to deliver on their potential.

But what is that potential, and how should one evaluate whether or not ESA programs deliver on it? The logic behind school choice has been grounded in the value of market-based reforms as an antidote to the bloated and non-responsive public school monopoly. Again, Friedman considered vouchers and the choices they provide as a means to a market system, not an end in and of themselves. ESAs can be considered similarly.

In contrast, much of the pro-school choice rhetoric has centered on social justice and empathy for students, who are disproportionately poor and non-white, stuck in failing public schools. Vouchers, scholarship programs and charter schools all have potential to provide some choices for those students. ESAs can be considered in a similar light, but would a new and viable escape route out of failing schools meet the measure of their potential?

Not necessarily. If ESAs only amount to another small-scale choice mechanism, they may provide a benefit to many students and families, but they will not be the "game changer" some supporters are expecting. ESA users will be able to customize their education providers, but unless ESAs are of sufficient size to increase the supply side of the market, or the diversity of educational services families can take advantage of, the options for customization will be limited. In addition, small-scale ESAs would have limited pressure on price and quality and would under deliver on the potential ESAs hold.

The real potential for ESAs is to create a viable competitive marketplace for educational services. Before evaluating the structures of ESAs and the outcomes those different structures might produce, it's useful to consider how we might define outcomes as "successes." Outcomes of ESA programs can be evaluated against the values of liberty, equity, and efficiency. Liberty is achieved when individuals are provided the freedom of individual choice. Equity is achieved when the benefits of a system are equally enjoyed by all groups. Efficiency is achieved when either the productive capacity of a system increases or participants' preferences are better matched to varied outputs of a system, or both.

The values of liberty, efficiency, and equity are not mutually exclusive in education, but they often clash. All three are important for the families involved in ESA programs and for the perceived success of the endeavor as a whole. For instance, an ESA that greatly increases liberty or efficiency at a substantial cost to equity would likely not help many of the families with the greatest need, and it would pose political challenges for ESAs moving forward. Similarly, an ESA that increases equity with little increase in efficiency would not deliver the benefits ESAs promise. Examined with a balanced approach, these three values are useful vantages to evaluating the outcomes of an ESA.

THE POTENTIAL—AND ACTUAL—STRUCTURE OF ESAs

ESAs' potential to create competitive education markets at scale hinges on their capacity to combine two key ingredients: broad eligibility and sufficient funding for consumers.

Broad Eligibility

A large pool of participants is key to generating sufficient demand for producing innovation from new providers on the supply side. Since ESAs reroute existing public education funding from schools to parents, there is no eligibility limit inherent in their structure. Nevada's ESA program is the best example, because, even as it awaits an allocation from the state, the program is still in state law and illustrates the greatest long-term potential for realizing the potential of ESAs. Nevada's ESA program gives eligibility to all public school students in the state, a full 96 percent of the state's school age children, making it a prime example of minimally restricted eligibility.[2]

Sufficient Funding

Since they reroute existing funding streams to parents, ESAs have the potential to deliver sufficient funding for a wide menu of educational choices. Florida's ESA, the Gardiner Scholarship Program, offers scholarships that average over $10,000 per student. Like other states with ESAs, Gardiner Scholarships are indexed according to what the state would spend on the student given their special educational needs, meaning the scholarship can be considerably higher than average.

Unfortunately, there is a substantial gap between theory and practice—between market possibilities and market realities. Existing ESAs have either minimally restricted eligibility, as in Nevada's design, or substantial per-account funding, as in Florida's Gardiner Scholarship Program. No programs have both. Though ESAs have the potential to deliver broad eligibility and adequate funding in tandem, the limits of the five existing ESA programs may undermine their capacity to deliver on their potential.

Fortunately, the economic theory that offers supports for ESAs' potential also provides a basis for anticipating how limited eligibility pools and limited funding might undermine their potential for creating competitive markets. The next two sections consider the challenges posed by limiting each of these factors.

SETTLING ON LIMITED ELIGIBILITY

Of the five states that have passed ESA bills, four originally limited eligibility to students with disabilities. Though the Arizona ESA program has expanded eligibility to some groups of students without special needs—most notably students attending schools or districts graded a "D" or "F" by the state—only 22 percent of Arizona students are eligible for an ESA. In Florida, 12 percent are eligible, and in Mississippi 13 percent are eligible. However, there is a cap of 500 students initially, with another 500 additional each year, which substantially limits actual participation. In Tennessee, a mere 2 percent are eligible to participate. In contrast, Nevada's ESA opens eligibility to all students attending public schools, about 96 percent of the school age population.[3]

There is no inherent reason that an ESA should be limited to students with disabilities. Ostensibly, the reason most ESAs, both those that currently exist and those that are being negotiated in states like Oklahoma and Virginia, are restricted to special education students is because these limited programs are more politically viable than open access ESAs would be. Whether the tradeoff of substantial limits to eligibility for political viability is worthwhile depends on how detrimental those limits are for the plausible development of competitive markets.

Limits to the overall eligibility pool of an ESA program are important because only a portion of eligible families will choose to leave public schools in exchange for an ESA. Limits on ESA eligibility, which most often restrict the program to students with special needs, would increase net participation to that portion of the restricted pool. Arizona, which has the longest-running ESA and generous funding, has one in one hundred eligible students participating. But let's assume even a much larger proportion of students participate—say, one in ten. Again using Arizona as an example, 10 percent of eligible students could result in about 12,500 new ESA participants, a moderately large estimate that assumes there will be substantial growth over current participation rates.

Lackluster Increased Demand

So many new participants would increase demand for alternative educational options, but would they be enough to spur the supply of schools and other education service providers? There are structural reasons why they might not be. Families with eligible students would be spread across the state roughly according to population density. However, most educational offerings are brick and mortar operations, which present a density problem. The increased demand might be helpful for the minority of offerings that are online and not geographically constrained, but most educational services are geographically constrained and would only see marginal increases in demand.

Further, this would be an even more significant issue for ESAs with special education eligibility limits because educational services for that population are more likely to be brick and mortar centers. These constraints may not apply to all education suppliers under ESAs, however, to the degree that education markets are geographically circumscribed or "local"—as has historically been the case—these constraints are bound to dampen supply-side development.

Eligibility constraints coupled with geographic boundaries are likely to result in a broad but thin increase in demand, which will produce only slow responses from the supply side. Expanded school choice in existing private schools will be a real possibility. This has been the case in Arizona, where two in three ESA holders used funds only for private school tuition. Expanded school choice can benefit participating families, but would hardly result in the development of many new service providers.

The lack of a concentrated increase in demand poses two issues for ESAs that limit eligibility to special education students. The first is that the limited capacity of existing private schools to serve the full spectrum of students with disabilities might further dilute demand and result in an insufficient supply-side response. Certainly private schools may serve students with some disabilities, but the typical private school is likely more able to serve students with less severe disabilities, and less so students with more severe challenges. If existing private schools can only serve a portion of students with disabilities, the already limited eligibility might thin the density of new demand further because relatively fewer participants would be located near providers.

A thriving supply side is key to innovation and new specialized providers, but a very thinly distributed eligibility pool could easily be too small of a stimulus for new providers to enter the market. Thus, limited eligibility ESAs will by definition increase choices for participants, but they may not fuel the supply side enough to realize substantial increases in innovation or efficiency.

The second issue with widely but thinly distributed eligible ESA holders is that, if existing private schools are the most likely set of alternatives to public schools, there may be a mismatch between the strengths of those providers and the needs of the special needs student population. Private schools may not have the necessary expertise or capacity to meet the specialized needs of students with disabilities, and the available capacity of private schools would be a poor fit for those students. If the fit between existing providers' strengths and consumers' needs is weak, the supply side will take even longer to develop.

ESAs with substantial eligibility limits may not produce the demand necessary to fuel new competitive markets for K–12 education. If they don't, ESAs will function similarly to the voucher programs that preceded them, offering choice to some students who would otherwise have none, but they would not likely create functional marketplaces. Liberty would increase with such programs, but only for eligible families. Equity would not be directly affected by eligibility. In terms of efficiency, there would be some increases when participants' preferences are better matched without any increases in overall costs. The improved matching of preferences is akin to an increase in the allocative efficiency of the system, but only among eligible students. However, without the competition on price and quality at a large scale, the system as a whole is unlikely to see broad improvements in efficiency.

In total, ESAs with substantial limits to eligibility should be an improvement over the status quo, but they are unlikely to realize the primary potential ESAs offer. Liberty would increase for few, but not for most, families. Likewise, efficiency would be improved for the few, but ESAs' potential for systemic changes and market development would not be realized. Settling for an ESA with limited eligibility could very well be a trade that loses the potential ESAs offer.

Geographically Concentrating ESA Eligibility

Significant limits to the eligibility for ESAs will limit the supply-side response and many of the benefits that stem from it. However, ESAs may start with those limits and expand eligibility to other classes of students. For instance, Arizona's ESA began with eligibility for special education students and then expanded to include students in the foster care system, those living on Native American reservations, and students attending "D" or "F" letter grade schools.

The effect of expanding eligibility on the supply side will vary based on the geography of students gaining eligibility. Expanding by small classes of students is unlikely to spur supply-side development if the classes are spread across the state, as is the case with foster care students. But including classes of students on reservations and those attending "D" or "F" letter grade schools and districts is likely to increase demand sharply in relatively small areas. Students living on reservations are clustered geographically, low-performing schools are often clustered geographically, and entire low-performing districts encompass specific geographical areas.

These geographically centralized increases in eligibility show much more promise for spurring supply-side response because new providers can serve a substantial number of students in a single location. Concentrating increases in demand on geographic terms will pack more of a supply-side stimulus punch and thereby create a deeper foundation for localized competitive markets for educational services.

Similar geographic concentrations may exist for other classes of students who could be made eligible. A key possibility would be low-income families. Low-income families are often clustered in particular geographic areas, and such students are often trapped in low performing schools and districts. As such, it may be beneficial to target ESA eligibility to low-income students as well as students attending low-performing schools.

Low-income families make a particularly appealing means to expand ESAs on multiple levels. Students from low-income families constitute a large enough portion of public school students that if some limit to eligibility were politically necessary, they could still spur meaningful supply-side reaction. Low-income families have some geographical clustering which would sharpen a supply-side stimulus. In addition to these economic arguments, low-income families are a natural fit with the school choice arguments grounded in social justice and empathy.

Settling on Limited Funding

ESAs function like a subsidy given to consumers, increasing the purchasing power of families and lowering the out-of-pocket price of alternative educational services. Families' preferences don't change because of an ESA; prices do, based on the amount of the subsidy. The amount of that subsidy has enormous importance not only for the potential to create a competitive marketplace, but also for who gets to participate.

Consider an ESA with minimally restricted eligibility, but very low funding at $1,000 per student. That $1,000 will not be enough on its own to furnish a sufficient education for most students, either by private schools or through customized packages of educational services. However, for interested families who can almost afford to take advantage of those alternatives, that $1,000 can make the difference. This is often referred to as "topping off" an ESA. Relatively low-income families who cannot contribute much on their own will not find many viable options at a price they can afford. This is the nature of subsidies: they reduce prices for consumers. Those consumers that are within the margin between the current price and the price minus the subsidy will make different choices. Consequently, an ESA with low amounts of funding is quite likely to result in significantly inequitable participation.

Equity and Adequacy in ESAs

How should we think about what the "right" amount of funding is for an ESA? Three traditional concepts from school finance—equality, equity and adequacy—can be helpful approaches to thinking through the right amount of funding for an ESA. Equality is simply treating all students alike, which often may not yield equity. While equality seems like a good thing, it is not always so if students with greater educational needs, like students with disabilities, receive the same funding as those with average educational needs. School finance is generally concerned with equity, not equality.

In school finance, equity is achieved when similar kinds of students receive the same amount of funding. For equity's sake, students with particular legitimate educational needs–such as those with disabilities, limited English proficiency, or those living in poverty–should receive additional funding associated with those needs. All existing ESAs include increased funding for students with certain needs.

Of course, a system can be equitable but still woefully underfunded, which gives rise to the concept of adequacy in school finance. Adequacy requires that students receive sufficient funds to educate them to a given standard. Adequacy is a related but distinct concept from equity. An ideal ESA would be both adequate, in that it provides enough funds to meet a certain standard, and equitable, in that it provides additional funding for students with legitimate educational needs.

Adequacy is a useful starting point for looking at ESA funding levels, as an adequate amount can be supplemented based on equity considerations. An adequate ESA would allow any participant sufficient funds to purchase educational services to reach a reasonable standard. The adequacy of an ESA would have to be evaluated with the assumption that no parental contribution would be necessary. An ESA would not need to give families access to any educational service provider in the market in order to be adequate, but it would need to be enough to provide reasonable access to sufficient options. Adequate funding in an ESA would allow families to participate in the market for educational services without the need for topping off.

An adequately funded ESA could still allow families to top off their ESA amounts to meet their preferences because doing so would not impinge on the participation of poorer families who cannot afford any topping off. Such an ESA would allow everyone to participate in the market, increasing liberty for all. It would maintain equity if it provided reasonable additional funding for students with legitimate educational needs. An adequate ESA would enable all participants to access educational services sufficient to reach a minimum standard.

It is worth noting that the current public school system also allows families to top off their children's educational options through a variety of means such as test preparation classes, tutors, music lessons, camps and other fee-based opportunities. In the same way, an adequate ESA could be equitable without requiring that everyone have equal resources. Such a system would also increase efficiency by improving the match between educational services and families' preferences and by creating a dynamic marketplace.

Nevada's design for its ESA is worth considering in this light. All public school students in the state are eligible for ESAs in amounts between $5,100 and $5,700. In comparison, the average private school tuition in Nevada for 2015 was above $8,000. About one in four Nevada private schools had tuitions below $5,700, the amount that low-income students qualify for in ESAs. At those rates, students limited to their ESA funds would have relatively few private school options. (Nevada's ESA allows for educational options beyond private schools, but the impacts on families based on income would be similar for educational services beyond private schools.) The extra $600 Nevada ESAs added for low-income families will help increase their choices, but may be too little to make up the difference between the base ESA amount and market prices for reasonable educational services.

In addition, poverty relates to the cost of educating students, over and above their ability to participate in the market. In most states, public schools fund low-income students at higher rates because they are legitimately more expensive to educate. Poverty is broadly considered a legitimate reason for increased education funding, but that additional expense works differently with an ESA because it is a subsidy. If the subsidy for low-income students increases their ability to participate in the market because of their lack of wealth, then it should also add funding specifically due to the legitimate educational needs associated with poverty. If the differential for poverty is only sufficient for one of these reasons—increasing low-income families' practical choices or supplementing their legitimately higher costs—there can be an equity issue.

The ultimate equity problem with an inadequately funded ESA is more fundamental. If it works as a partial subsidy, an ESA is much more likely to be used by wealthier families. As illustrated earlier with the fictitious $1,000 ESA, because they can augment it, wealthier families are much more likely than poorer families to take advantage of the subsidy. Poorer families are less likely to afford preferred alternatives to public schools if the ESA accounts are meager, because their options would be limited. For adequately funded ESAs, the likelihood of differential participation by wealth is minimal. If ESAs are not adequately funded, and a few years in the program appears to primarily serve the wealthy, the inequities in their participation could be damning. But equity issues may not be limited to who participates in the ESA overall; some could also develop from the supply side.

Supply-Side Reaction

As discussed in the context of eligibility limits, the potential for competitive marketplaces through ESAs depends on whether new providers enter the market. An ESA with limited eligibility but substantial funding should bring new providers to the market, but there will certainly be a lag between the increased demand and the supply-side response. In addition, as long as ESAs are considered politically unstable, in that they may succumb to legal challenges, new enterprises may be wary to trust that the increased demand will sustain. ESAs have a promising record with judicial challenges, but the uncertainty those challenges introduce could certainly dampen the supply-side response.

Given the lag between the increased demand and the supply-side response, existing educational providers will have substantial leeway to be selective with which students they serve. For instance, schools could screen applicants by entrance exams, athletic prowess, religious beliefs, or other factors that make them more attractive to the school. The same pressures could exist for education service providers. But the most obvious result of increased demand would be price increases, and they could be substantial.

Consider the potential for price increases from the perspective of existing private schools. For ages, they have had to compete with free public schools, meaning they have faced significant pressure to keep prices down. As a result, many private schools have resisted expenditure increases for teacher pay, facilities, technology, and profit. At long last, ESA subsidies increase the desire for seats in those schools and the money families can afford to spend for them. It is not untoward for those schools to increase their price to fund expenditures that have long been sacrificed. Note that the amount that would constitute an adequate ESA would also have to increase to keep pace and maintain equity.

The expected increases in the market price of educational services would also affect families who are ineligible for ESAs. Most ESAs make current private school students ineligible. Under Nevada's open access ESA design, roughly 7 percent of students who attend private schools would not be insulated from increases in tuition.

Over time, the supply-side could catch up and competition on price could bring the amounts for tuition and an adequate ESA to a new equilibrium. While there is no compelling reason to believe an ESA amount that is based on the funding system of public schools will be adequate, there are compelling reasons to expect prices to rise. As a result, what is adequate funding at the beginning of a new market may not stay adequate for long.

The greatest equity failure for any ESA program would be a "dumping ground" effect. A dumping ground effect would result from an ESA that functionally provides choices to wealthier families but not to poorer families. Low-income students are often concentrated in underperforming public schools, and advocates have recognized this in their arguments for allowing an escape from those schools through school choice. If a large ESA is disproportionately less likely to serve those very students, poor students could actually become more trapped in public schools that are forced to take all comers. Schools with concentrations of disadvantaged students will face an array of challenges and the students they serve will likely have poor educational outcomes. The point here is not that high-poverty schools cannot successfully educate students, but that concentrated poverty creates challenges for schools and that a poorly conceived ESA could exacerbate those challenges.

Whether due to inadequate funding, supply-side selectivity, or both, if ESAs fail to benefit the very students at the center of the choice movement, they surely will fall short of realizing their potential overall, and to serve disadvantaged students in particular. Since much of the historic rhetoric on choice has focused on such disadvantaged students, it would be all the more damaging to the long-term prospects for choice if those students were not only systematically underserved by the programs, but further disadvantaged because of them.

POTENTIAL REMEDIES FOR EQUITY ISSUES

Adequate Funding

How might the problem of underfunded ESAs be avoided? The most obvious means is to ensure ESAs are funded at an adequate level. Unfortunately, since ESAs reroute existing funding streams, the funding is dependent on which funding streams can be included. Public schools are primarily funded with state, local, and federal dollars. A state can pass ESA legislation that reroutes the state revenue, but not necessarily the local and federal funds. The relative amounts of the funding streams vary by state and even by district, but state funds generally make up about 45 percent of total educational spending.[4] If states cannot tap into local or federal funding streams, their ability to increase ESA funding is limited.

Regulation

If increasing the funding level of an ESA is impossible due to structural or political impediments, what about regulating participating education service providers? Regulation can help in some ways that minimally interfere with market function. Requirements that ensure quality information about options can go a long way to improving market function. However, substantial regulation in the form of price controls or selection criteria can interfere with market function and undermine the benefits ESAs seek to provide.

State regulators do not have the power to dictate prices to private enterprises, but they can restrict providers that are eligible to receive ESA funding. Heavy-handed regulation can also have substantial effects on which schools and education service providers are willing to participate in the program. Arguably, the providers that are willing to give up autonomy to participate are likely to be lower quality providers.

While not an ESA, the Louisiana Scholarship Program is an example of a program negatively impacted by heavy regulation. The state voucher program capped tuition at the value of the voucher and insisted participating schools have open admissions policies. The well-intentioned criteria for participating schools had a substantial drag on participation, to the point that only one in three Louisiana private schools were willing to accept the vouchers, and evidence suggests that those schools were struggling to retain students.[5]

Increased ESA Amounts for Low-Income Families

Another means of protecting equity and encouraging market function might be to substantially increase the ESA for low-income families. For some

ESAs, this is not a question of whether to do so, but rather a question of to what degree. Consider the Nevada ESA design, which provides an additional 10 percent of state funding—about $600—for low-income students, defined as incomes less than 185 percent of the federal poverty level. Does a 10 percent differential make sense?

As alluded to above, there are two distinct reasons to provide low-income students with larger ESAs. The first is that students living in poverty truly require more resources to educate to the same standard as their wealthy peers. This is an equity argument for increased funding. The second reason is that low-income students have fewer dollars to top off an inadequate ESA and thus fewer market choices. By this logic, an increase is warranted to ensure the competitive marketplace does not primarily serve the wealthy. Given that there are two reasons low income-students should receive additional funding, the $600 increment seems paltry; would a $300 increment for either reason seem reasonable when considered in isolation?

In addition, there is no clear defense for having a single increment for poverty, as those below the poverty line would ostensibly require additional funds to participate in the market than those with 85 percent higher incomes would. This is reflected in policies governing free and reduced-price meal eligibility in Nevada and other states, which offer free meals to students whose family incomes are below 130 percent of the federal poverty line and reduced-price meals to those between 130 and 185 percent.

The poverty differential also plays into the expected price increases that might result from ESAs. If the base ESA amount were lowered somewhat to enable a substantial increase for students in poverty, the subsidy would create a lower average ability to pay but an arguably more equitable distribution of ability to pay. That lower average ability to pay would blunt increased prices to some degree. It is not clear whether the increase in demand would be lowered on net by giving an increased share to lower-income families, because reductions in demand by wealthier families would be offset to some degree by increased demand by lower-income families. Structuring ESAs to ensure the participation of low-income students may be difficult, and the specifics of the tradeoffs on ESA amounts are not black and white issues. However, it would be prudent to consider the long run effects of the increment on equity.

If a substantial increment cannot be built in, philanthropy could play a critical role in reducing equity problems. Philanthropic support for low-income students is not new, but can be especially powerful in the context of an ESA. On their own, philanthropists may help low-income students by footing the full bill for their private educational services. On top of an ESA, those philanthropic dollars go much further because they only need to fill the gap between the ESA amount and the cost of services. Those dollars could be easily targeted directly to students in poverty. Beyond that, those targeted dollars could increase access to the competitive market for services, which produces benefits for the market as a whole. Philanthropic funds that increase an inadequate ESA enough to form an equitable, sustainable, and competitive market would create benefits across the board.

THE DANGERS OF SETTLING ON ESAs

Families that choose to participate in ESA programs stand to benefit from choice. The immediate benefits for individual participants will vary, but they will certainly include increased liberty of choice, which is a good in its own right. On average, participants will also enjoy a better match between their preferences and their chosen educational services, and since families that choose not to leave public schools should not suffer substantial adverse impacts, there will be some increase in the efficiency of the educational marketplace as a whole.

However, settling on the terms of ESAs introduces substantial risks that the programs will not deliver on their potential. Those risks threaten participants, the sustainability of ESA programs, and the educational choice movement as a whole. For example, to the degree that eligibility limits prohibit participation, the benefits in liberty and efficiency will be enjoyed by a relative few. The limits to the scale of the market also cast doubt on the potential benefits of innovation and customization that come from a thriving competitive market.

The risks are possibly more pointed for ESA programs than for participants. ESA programs that cannot grow into competitive markets may end up being another small-scale choice mechanism. The future of such ESA programs might be like that of many voucher programs, stuck in a political struggle for survival with uncertain evidence backing their existence and a political constituency ready to shut them down. A different form of the same school choice battle would be a sad return on the potential of ESAs.

Equity issues would be an even greater risk for the sustainability of ESAs. ESAs that have inadequate funding levels, but substantial scale, are well suited to deliver the potential benefits of a competitive marketplace to many participants, but the equity issues that may result could easily preclude many participants from seeing those benefits. If substantial inequity results, allowing private educational services to select the most advantaged students, a dumping ground effect could result. If public schools are left to serve the least advantaged, the benefits that ESAs make possible for some could harm families who are left out.

For the choice movement as a whole, ESAs provide opportunity and risk in equal parts. Large-scale ESAs are the moonshot of the school choice movement, the first chance to establish competitive markets to rival the public school monopoly. ESAs could do what vouchers have not been able to: in the words of Friedman, "move from a government to a market system."[6]

The danger for the choice movement is not that large-scale marketplaces might not develop, but that they might develop and fail to deliver on their promises, or worse, produce demonstrable inequities. The risks that threaten ESA programs' sustainability can also threaten the perceived viability of choice reforms writ large. If the successful establishment of a choice-based education marketplace fails the students and families it is designed to serve, it could deal a mortal blow to the choice movement.

Despite the abundance of caution in this chapter, there is significant reason for optimism about ESAs. Small programs can grow and realize their potential over time. Nimble legislatures can identify issues such as insufficient funding and restructure or invest more resources into ESAs accordingly. Philanthropic funds could also go a long way towards making marginal ESA programs effective. This chapter applies the economic concepts that underlie the logic of ESAs to probe for choke points and risks that could undermine them. But the point of highlighting them is to improve the likelihood that they will deliver as promised.

Finally, ESAs offer an unprecedented opportunity to develop large-scale education marketplaces. The potential benefits are enormous, and the future that ESA advocates only once planned is now becoming reality. While some may doubt that large-scale changes to the nation's school system are possible, charter schools have proven that the fabric of the education system can be radically altered in a relatively short time span. Promising even more fundamental changes and a practical path forward, ESAs may prove that to be true again.

NOTES

1. Milton Friedman, "Public Schools: Make Them Private," *Washington Post*, February 19, 1995, (republished at www.cato.org/pubs/briefs/bp-023.html).

2. Friedman Foundation for Educational Choice, "School Choice: Nevada— Education Savings Accounts," 2016, www.edchoice.org/school-choice/programs/nevada-education-savings-accounts/.

3. All estimates of eligibility for ESAs are drawn from EdChoice: "School Choice: School Choice in America," 2016, www.edchoice.org/school-choice/school-choice-in-america/.

4. National Center for Education Statistics, "Table 235.20. Revenues for public elementary and secondary schools, by source of funds and state or jurisdiction: 2012–13," August 2015, https://nces.ed.gov/programs/digest/d15/tables/dt15_235.20.asp?current=yes.

5. Atila Abdulkadiroglu, Parag Pathak, & Christopher Walters, "School Vouchers and Student Achievement: First-Year Evidence from the Louisiana Scholarship Program," (working paper, School Effectiveness & Inequality Initiative, December 2015), http://seii.mit.edu/research/study/school-vouchers-and-student-achievement-first-year-evidence-from-the-louisiana-scholarship-program/.

6. Friedman, "Public Schools: Make Them Private."

Conclusion

Nat Malkus

Education savings accounts (ESAs) have the potential to do what previous approaches to school choice have not: disrupt the primary delivery model of education in the United States. By altering several of the basic building blocks of our school system—including how funding is distributed, how competition on price and quality functions, and even whether or not schools are a necessary institution in the education of many students—ESAs could be a new frontier in school choice that fundamentally changes the landscape of American education.

Of course, by their very nature, new frontiers are uncertain at the outset. As Adam Peshek and Gerard Robinson mentioned in this volume's introduction, Uber upended the taxi industry by challenging the basics of the industry—but in 2009, no one could have guessed just *how much* change Uber would bring in eight years. Health Savings Accounts (HSAs) were introduced in 2003 to change how consumers paid for their health care in ways that would make them more cost conscious. Today, HSAs continue to grow in popularity, but whether or not they have successfully changed the way consumers interact with the health care system is an open question. Massive open online courses (MOOCs) emerged around the same time as Uber and some have hailed them as the next frontier in postsecondary education. But today, MOOCs may have already passed their peak, generally considered tangential to the university system rather than a serious challenge to it.

In the same way, ESAs might have the capability to be the Uber of the education landscape, or they could prove to be the equivalent of MOOCs. Today, ESAs' popularity is growing rapidly. In the five years since the first ESA program began in 2011, ESAs have grown faster than either charter schools or voucher programs did in their first five years. State legislators are quickly catching on to the idea, and as of 2016, five states have passed ESA legislation and another twenty-two have offered it. Existing programs are also expanding the scope of ESAs. This is most apparent in the Nevada program, which though currently awaiting an appropriation, is designed to provide eligibility to nearly every student in the state.

Despite their potential and rapid growth, ESAs are not well understood. This volume gathers experts on the legal, political, regulatory, and economic issues surrounding ESAs to provide a comprehensive, fair-minded treatment of them and to consider their rationale, the political and legal dynamics at play, the challenges they pose, and what it might take for them to work.

While brimming with possibility, the reality is that today, ESAs remain a very new and relatively small-scale education reform. Whether or not ESAs prove to be small-scale choice programs in a few states or grow into a wide-open frontier of educational possibilities will depend in large part on how these young programs are implemented and managed.

BIG IDEAS

Throughout the chapters in this volume, a few clear themes emerged. One is the new opportunities that ESAs can create for students, families, and the education system. A second is that ESAs will require a number of new structures, inside and outside of government, that must be created with care so ESAs can be successfully supported and regulated. A third is that ESAs' audacious goal—to create functioning marketplaces for educational services—will present unprecedented challenges that may require states to actively monitor and adjust ESA programs as they develop.

ESAs Offer New Opportunities

School choice advocates have argued that school choice has always been available to parents who have the means to pay tuition on their own, but that most families cannot afford this luxury. ESAs are one way that parents can be afforded that "luxury," and the benefits for students can be extraordinary, as the stories Allysia Finley highlights in chapter 7 demonstrate. With state funds under parents' control, the children with special needs Finley describes are thriving in ways that schools they attended in the past could not provide.

But apart from special education status, ESAs allow personalized approaches to education that can benefit all kinds of students. However, for students to reap those benefits, the supply side—or potential education service providers—must respond to demand for ESAs. Michael McShane of the Show-Me Institute uses lessons from airline deregulation to argue that ESAs could be the kind of sweeping deregulation that allows existing schools and education service providers, as well as new organizations, to compete to better meet students' needs. He argues that a light regulatory environment is key to maximizing a robust supply side of education service providers.

Several contributors in this volume noted that ESAs will amount to a disruption in how education is delivered, but in chapter 1, Matthew Ladner, senior advisor for policy and research at the Foundation for Excellence in Education, suggests that disruption is a positive feature of a new system of education, not a bug. He argues that ESAs have the potential to improve educational offerings by inviting innovation, allowing for competition on quality and price, and incentivizing efficiency. He notes that these are three aspects absent from many states' public education systems that could spur sustained improvement instead of continuing in current frameworks that produce lackluster results.

It's impossible to predict how valuable the new options, providers and innovations that ESAs might produce will be, but all three are made possible by the departure from the traditional system of education through public schools. Since they are a departure from one system, ESAs must have new systems of regulation and support to sustain the new opportunities they produce.

ESAs Require New Structures

ESAs can open the door for parents to customize their student's education, for suppliers to innovate and compete, and for educational marketplaces to develop. But as Gerard Robinson and other authors point out, there is much more to a functional program that simply passing a law. Numerous structures and systems must be constructed so that ESAs can function as intended. In various chapters, authors noted that not only legislation, but also accountability mechanisms, accounting systems, information platforms, and regulatory frameworks have to be carefully designed to create successful ESA programs.

And for ESA programs to have any chance at success, they must be created through legislation that both families and new education service providers can be confident will last. As Tim Keller describes in chapter 2, ESA laws must meet specific state requirements so they might survive the inevitable judicial challenges. As of this writing, no ESA programs have suffered a defeat at trial, and by combining common ideal elements of an ESA using appropriate language tailored to the constitutional requirements of each state, legislators can establish programs that are likely to withstand judicial challenges. In the most recent challenge, Nevada's Supreme Court explicitly ruled that the state's ESA program is constitutional. The constitutional viability of ESAs is key for the development of education marketplaces because both participation by parents and education service providers will depend on the confidence they have that the programs will last. An important additional hurdle beyond constitutional challenges is securing stable funding sources. The contest over Nevada's ESA program has moved from a legal challenge to a political one, because the only way around the permanent injunction barring its operation is securing a sufficient and reliable funding source through the state legislature.

Once constitutional and stably funded programs are passed, ESAs will need appropriate government oversight and regulation, well-designed accounting systems, sensible approaches to accountability, and supports for parents who undertake the responsibilities involved in the program. In chapter 6, Gerard Robinson, former commissioner of education for the state of Florida and former secretary of education for the Commonwealth of Virginia, describes the multiple ways to distribute regulatory and oversight responsibilities across state agencies. While there is no "right" way for states to designate those responsibilities, Robinson argues persuasively that the success of ESAs will depend on how state agencies shape the regulation and oversight of programs that allow for their success. Given the different agencies states can use to implement ESA programs and the various regulatory models they can take, creating a stable administrative foundation for ESAs will be an important, if not easy, task.

A key task for the supervising government agency of any ESA program will be establishing a system that delivers funding to parents and minimizes the likelihood for mistakes, fraud, and abuse. Several authors discussed the different funding mechanisms states use, be they through reimbursements, restricted use debit cards, e-commerce portals, or one-stop websites. All stressed that the appropriate use of technology could simultaneously serve as an application portal, provide families with a convenient and unrestricted purchasing experience, limit purchases to qualified products and services, and even identify fraudulent providers.

Though such consolidated systems are complex, minimizing the friction parents experience using an ESA, as well as the potential for fraud, might certainly be worth the investment. In chapter 3, Adam Peshek, director of educational choice the Foundation for Excellence in Education, describes a number of private companies that offer these kinds of technologies so states don't have to reinvent the wheel.

Several contributors also discussed the vital role information systems will need to play in a functioning ESA program. John Bailey, former vice president of policy at the Foundation for Excellence in Education, discusses how well intended regulation in the traditional education system often restricts new ideas, fails to keep up with the pace of innovation, and accumulates into knots of red tape. These regulatory challenges for the traditional K–12 public school system would be even more counterproductive in the kinds of choice-based educational markets ESAs might develop. Bailey argues that ESAs can use market forces to hold providers accountable, and that the best forms of regulation are those that do not stifle innovation, but encourage it, by improving the information available to parents. Platforms that leverage user feedback to help parents make better decisions, like those used by Uber, Yelp, or Healthgrades, can tremendously improve market function. Far from suggesting zero regulation, several authors suggest that reducing the friction and increasing the efficiency of the market mechanisms ESAs allow is the best path forward.

Building the various structures that will support an ESA program and encourage a vibrant educational marketplace to thrive is no simple task. The contributors in this volume discuss these varied aspects precisely because they will require new approaches and novel thinking to create programs that encourage innovation, protect families and taxpayers, and help students. Matthew Ladner reminds us that ESA programs won't function perfectly from the start, and that for all the possibilities they offer, the oldest ESA program is only five years old. As such, those who implement ESA programs should expect to learn from the successes and the failures that have already played out, and they must be ready to adjust programs according to these lessons.

ESAs Present New Tensions in Creating Functioning Education Marketplaces

As is the case with any new frontier, with new opportunities come new challenges, and the authors in this volume identify several uncertain terrains that ESAs will have to carefully navigate. Chief among these are developing a strong supply side response, expanding participation, helping parents navigate their new responsibilities, and ensuring programs provide sufficient funding for equitable participation.

Regulating Providers While Keeping Barriers to Entry Low

In chapter 8, Michael McShane explores the possibilities that can result from the expansion of educational service providers under an ESA. The tension for any regulatory structure is minimizing barriers to entry to encourage a strong supply of providers, while minimizing low-quality services and outright fraud. Finley describes several schools that have grown to ably serve many more students under the ESA programs in Arizona and Florida. ESAs will certainly expand operations for existing private schools, but the entrance of new providers will require access to capital and a dependable ESA program.

If potential service providers are uncertain about the long-term stability or the constitutional viability of ESA legislation, the supply side response could be underwhelming. As McShane argues, ESAs can certainly be a disruptor to the current system of education as airline deregulation was for the aviation industry. However, for a robust set of educational service providers to emerge, new entrants will have to view that disruption as a permanent rewriting of the rules that will allow them to jump in and thrive.

Eligibility Debates and Political Challenges

Another tension for ESAs lies in the need for scale. I argue in chapter 9 that for ESAs to reach their full potential to create functional marketplaces for educational services, ESAs will have to reach a scale sufficient to support competition. However, the politics of passing ESA legislation often require that programs begin with limited eligibility. That tension raises the question of whether limited scale ESA programs that can pass political muster might be too small to achieve the full potential ESAs could create.

The near universal design of the Nevada ESA program holds out high hopes that small scale ESAs mustn't always be the case. Provided the legislature allocates funds for it, Nevada's program should grow much more rapidly than other programs that have substantial eligibility limits. However, even then, there are no guarantees that participation will be sufficient to garner widespread innovation, competition on price and quality, and other market benefits. Even if they never reach a critical mass for functioning educational marketplaces, small-scale ESA programs could still remain beneficial for families who can access services that would otherwise be out of their reach. As Finley catalogues in chapter 7, those success stories alone could warrant the programs. However, to achieve the grand potential that many authors discuss in this volume, states will have to expand eligibility to realize the benefits of robust education marketplaces.

Trusting Parents to Make ESAs Work

Multiple contributors mentioned how ESAs give parents new freedoms and responsibilities. The tension for state officials lies in how to balance the freedom and guidance parents are given to navigate customizing their children's education. In order for students to benefit from unbundled education services, parents of students with ESAs must learn to navigate numerous, and somewhat complex, decisions. Parents can use ESAs for private school tuition or a variety of educational services, and may need assistance in making distinct choices.

Several authors suggested that provided parents are armed with substantial information from feedback and rating systems, they should be able to make the same informed decisions they make in other areas in life, ranging from restaurant choices to healthcare. However, parents who elect to construct a unique education program from unbundled services that can, in aggregate, prepare students for further education or career options, may need additional supports. Gerard Robinson outlines that though the state requires parents to assume responsibility for their child's educational program when they participate in an ESA, the state has a role to play in specifying what those responsibilities entail.

Some assistance, in the form of a parent handbook or perhaps direct counseling, may be beneficial both for parents individually, and for the long term success of ESA programs. Robinson also describes how intermediary organizations, such as Step up for Students, can be another important source of such assistance. Whether support comes from the state or intermediary institutions, ESAs might prove more successful in states that support parents to make wise decisions in the context of sustainable long-term education plans.

Determining Funding

One of the most important unanswered questions is how much money an effective and equitable ESA must contain. Again, political and fiscal realities could constrain the amount of funding that might go into each ESA, raising the question of what level of funding is sufficient for a functional program. As Finley describes, Mississippi's ESA helps some parents take advantage of private school programs, but the $6,500 included is not enough to cover many private schools that serve students with disabilities (which the state's ESA is restricted to). Several school leaders she spoke with mentioned the need to raise additional money to cover the costs for some ESA students.

In chapter 9, I explain how limited funding of ESAs can be a substantial threat to their long-term viability, both for low-income families who would like to use them, but cannot afford to top them off with their own funds, and for the programs themselves. If in the end ESA programs are underfunded, they will certainly be disproportionately used by more affluent families, resulting in equity issues that could prove politically disastrous.

Several authors mentioned the potential to give substantially more ESA funding to low-income families to head off potential equity issues, but whether, and by how much, ESAs are differentiated by income level depends on the state. Part of the challenge lies in the fact that ESAs are state programs, and generally cannot tap local or federal education funds, which in many states constitute half of education spending. Some ESAs are much more generous, like Florida and Arizona's programs, and are therefore less likely to face challenges. Ultimately, it will come down to how each state institutes their ESA program and whether the funds are sufficient to give a broad swath of families practical choices.

UNANSWERED QUESTIONS

Over the next five to ten years, the editors expect that existing ESA programs will mature and, as recent state legislative activity suggests, more programs will be established. However, what form and function ESAs ultimately take is an open question. The overall shape of these programs will depend on a few key questions, including what size ESA programs grow into, how parents will use them, how they will affect public schools, how equitably they will be accessed, and how regulation and flexibility will be balanced.

Scale of ESA Programs

Perhaps the single most important question for the future of ESAs is how large they might become. Today, there are reasons to suspect that ESAs might remain small and other reasons to suspect they could grow to considerable size. Many authors noted that Nevada's ambitious program design is the first choice program of any kind to offer eligibility to so many students in a state. Indeed, a funded Nevada program would break precedent by providing a foundation for an educational marketplace across an entire state.

In contrast, other states started ESA programs in order to provide for students with disabilities, and have thus had a relatively small number of total participants. Those limits, and the limited participation they engender, are not set in stone for all ESAs, as illustrated by the steady expansion of Arizona's ESA. Originally restricted to students with disabilities, Arizona's ESA expanded to include students in foster care, those living on a Native American reservation, or those attending low-performing schools or districts—in total, 22 percent of students statewide. In other states, however, limits are set in legislation that has included enrollment or funding caps.

Certainly, the size of ESA programs is not an either or proposition. ESAs may take different forms in different states. Relatively small scale ESAs that benefit a few hundred families can be worth the costs of establishing the program. In fact, a well-run small-scale ESA may prove more beneficial than a poorly run large-scale operation. However, several authors in this volume suggest the greatest benefits will come from an ESA that can establish functional educational marketplaces. Such marketplaces depend on a large pool of participants providing sufficient demand to produce a strong supply side response, all of which are unlikely to result from small-scale programs. Whether ESAs can create such marketplaces, and how many will, are questions worth watching as ESAs mature.

School Choice or Unbundled Education Services

Another crucial aspect of the future of ESAs is whether they will be used primarily to attend private schools, or whether they will increasingly be used on unbundled educational services outside of traditional schools. In the short term, existing service providers—primarily private schools—are the most likely to meet the demand created by new ESA participants. As McShane notes, this has been the case in Arizona, where about two thirds of ESA dollars have been spent on existing private schools.

However, Finley's reports from Florida and Arizona suggest that new schools can step in early, and grow rapidly, to meet the needs of families using ESAs. A distinct, and perhaps more fundamental question about what ESAs will eventually become, is how rapidly unbundled educational providers will enter the market. The important question is how many families will look beyond schools to seek out unbundled educational services, and that measure will depend both on the eligibility of the ESA programs and the portion of those eligible that choose to go the unbundled route.

If the two-thirds of Arizona ESA dollars that have gone to private schools is any indication of how often parents will use ESAs for a customized education—one that uses multiple providers instead of a single school, the unbundled services glass might seem half empty. That may not always be the case because, as McShane suggests, incumbents' advantages may very well be short lived.

Even the oldest ESA program is only five years old, so it is quite possible that unbundled education services will build in popularity. Such services may well increase as information feedback systems can provide parents with a sense of quality assurance and as more early adopters prove this novel approach to education is viable for more risk averse parents. As with all things, the prospects for unbundled services is a matter of perspective, and many could see the fact that a full third of parents used ESAs for services outside of traditional schools as a glass half full.

Balancing Regulation and Flexibility

A separate but related question is how states will circumscribe what services will be eligible for ESA expenditures. States certainly have some responsibility to limit and identify fraudulent uses of ESA funds and one of the principal preventative means of doing so would be to redline acceptable service providers. How states decide on who should and should not be allowed to provide services for ESA funds can have substantial implications for what the programs look like. This is a balancing act. States that are more restrictive are bound to more thoroughly prevent fraudulent or foolish uses of ESA funds, but they do so at the risk of omitting providers that provide services that may seem "outside of the box" but that parents want to use for good reason.

The degree to which states regulate appropriate use of ESAs will be shaped by the approach of the state agency governing them, but it will also be influenced by the technology used to administer them. Reimbursement based systems will require administrative resources and at the same time, give agencies a more direct means of regulating use and risk sticking parents with the cost of inadmissible claims. The use of restricted debit cards offers more ease for states and families but is dependent on a system of merchant codes that requires the state to make influential decisions about the kinds of suppliers that will be eligible, again affecting the balance of regulation and flexibility.

As Adam Peshek suggests, one-stop websites might be the best solution to these issues, giving agencies substantial control over providers, protecting parents while at the same time allowing them clear methods of what providers they might choose from. An additional benefit of such a website is that it can serve as an information feedback system to parents, by parents, allowing the community to regulate the market efficiently, instead of the agency doing so inefficiently. These structures are, like ESAs, still developing, and will be worth watching to gauge their influence moving forward.

Ensuring Equity in ESAs

ESAs are almost unprecedented in that they introduce pressures to increase quality and keep costs down, and they do this because they allow parents to use unspent ESA funds on other valuable educational services. The possibility, novel in education but common in most other service economies, is complicated by the fact that ESAs that are underfunded may make it difficult for low-income families to participate in the programs. ESAs are intended to offer a sufficient basis for providing students an education.

As I argue in chapter 9, if ESAs are either underfunded or do not provide a significant enough increment for participating low-income families, those families would face a choice of remaining in public schools or choosing low-cost alternatives. Such an ESA could create very significant equity problems, inviting judicial challenges and eroding popular support for the programs. The profile of these equity issues would be commensurate with the scope of the program, making them particularly acute for large-scale designs like Nevada's.

ON THE EDGE OF A NEW FRONTIER

The future of ESAs is uncertain. With their rapid growth, potential scale and unprecedented flexibility, there should be no doubt that ESAs are a new frontier in public education, but there is no telling whether that frontier will yield another small-scale program for educational choice or a new world for American education.

To a significant degree, the future of ESAs will be dependent on a variety of stakeholders and participants. State governments have to do the heavy lifting initially. Not only must they craft and pass reliable legislation, they must also develop hospitable regulatory and administrative systems that will give parents and educators the freedom to build a vibrant education marketplace. States will also have to be nimble and adaptive to learn lessons from experience and make necessary changes to cultivate ESAs' development. In some cases, state leaders may have to press the case to increase funding, expand eligibility, or make other difficult and substantive changes for ESAs to succeed over the long term.

Of course, the success of ESAs will rest primarily on the shoulders of parents. For ESAs to succeed on the whole, parents will have to take on new responsibilities, invest substantial effort, participate in new feedback systems, and take risks. Though they stand to gain substantial new freedoms and opportunities, parents who are early adopters of ESA programs must venture from the prevailing system to make them a success.

To realize the full potential ESAs offer, entrepreneurs will have to step into the marketplace as well. As with parents, new and existing service providers will face risks and obstacles to realize the rewards a new marketplace offers. They also have new opportunities to develop new products, services, and platforms that are unimaginable in the current landscape of American schooling.

Those may seem like long odds for ESAs to realize their full potential. But the benefits of ESAs that bring unprecedented choice, dynamism, innovation, and opportunities to a constrained system of education may well be worth the effort. Indeed, the sense of possibility and enthusiasm that ESAs provide educators and families make them worth exploring, watching and working on to see what lies on the other side of the new frontier.

About the Editors

Nat Malkus is a research fellow in education policy studies at AEI. His work has appeared in publications including the *Elementary School Journal, ZDM: The International Journal on Mathematics Education*, and *Theory and Research in Social Education*, as well as popular outlets such as *U.S. News & World Report*. He began his career in education as a public middle school teacher and holds a Ph.D. from the University of Maryland, College Park.

Adam Peshek is the director of the educational choice at the Foundation for Excellence in Education, where he provides strategic support to state leaders interested in developing, adopting, and implementing policies that increase educational options for students. Since 2014, he has focused on ESAs and has worked in each state with an ESA program from policy formation through implementation. He has provided testimony in more than a dozen state legislatures and is a frequent commentator on ESAs, school choice, and education policy across the country.

Gerard Robinson is a resident fellow in education policy studies at AEI. He previously served as Florida's commissioner of education and as the secretary of education in Virginia. Mr. Robinson also served as president of the Black Alliance for Educational Options. He began his career teaching fifth grade in a private, inner-city school. His work has appeared in publications including *Education Next, Education Week*, and *U.S. News & World Report*. He has a master's of education from Harvard University, a bachelor of arts from Howard University, and an associate of arts degree from El Camino College.

About the Contributors

John Bailey served as the vice president of policy at the Foundation for Excellence in Education. He worked at the White House and at the U.S. Department of Commerce. He served as the second director of educational technology at the U.S. Department of Education, cofounded Whiteboard Advisors, and served as a senior program officer at the Gates Foundation.

Michael Chartier serves as a state programs and government relations director for EdChoice. Previously, he served as the director of intergovernmental affairs for Indiana governor Mitch Daniels. He graduated from The George Washington University with a bachelor's degree in political science.

Robert C. Enlow is the president and CEO of EdChoice. He is the coeditor of *Liberty and Learning: Milton Friedman's Voucher Idea at Fifty* (Cato Institute, 2006). His opinions have appeared in publication, including the *Wall Street Journal*, *New York Times*, *National Review*, and *USA Today*.

Allysia Finley is an editorial writer for the *Wall Street Journal*, where she reports on education reform, local and state government, politics, and business. She graduated from Stanford University with a major in American studies and minor in creative writing.

Tim Keller serves as managing attorney at the Institute for Justice, where he led the defense of Arizona's individual scholarship tax-credit program in *Arizona Christian School Tuition Organization v. Winn*. He also defended Arizona's ESA program, which he helped design.

Matthew Ladner is the senior advisor of policy and research for the Foundation for Excellence in Education and a fellow with EdChoice and the Goldwater Institute. He has testified before Congress, the United States Commission of Civil Rights, and numerous state legislative committees.

Michael Q. McShane is director of education policy at the Show-Me Institute and an adjunct fellow in education policy studies at AEI. He is the editor of *New and Better Schools* (Rowman and Littlefield, 2015) and the coeditor of *Educational Entrepreneurship Today* (Harvard Education Press, 2016).